Margaret Laurence

Margaret Laurence.
*(Detail from "Patchwork" by Jane Eccles. Permanent collection, University of Guelph)*

REVISED EDITION

# MARGARET LAURENCE
## The Long Journey Home

Patricia Morley

McGill-Queen's University Press
Montreal and Kingston • London • Buffalo

Pages 15–152 have been published in a previous edition
by Twayne Publishers, © 1981, G.K. Hall & Co.

Canadian Cataloguing in Publication Data

Morley, Patricia, 1929–
    Margaret Laurence

Includes bibliographical references.
ISBN 0-7735-0856-2

    1. Laurence, Margaret, 1926–1987 – Criticism and
interpretation. I. Title.

PS8523.A86Z79 1991          C813′.54          C90-090528-X
PR9199.3.L33Z79 1991

# Contents

# About the Author

Patricia Morley is a writer and teacher who has lived in the Ottawa area, in a small town not unlike Laurence's Neepawa, for nearly forty years. Following a pattern that is now common for North American women, Dr. Morley returned to university studies and then began teaching after spending fourteen years at home bringing up four children.

As Professor of English and Canadian Studies at Concordia University in Montreal (1972–89), Morley taught Canadian literature and Women's Studies. Her work at the Simone de Beauvoir Institute of Concordia was acknowledged in 1989 when she was made a Lifetime Honorary Fellow of the Institute.

Her books include *The Mystery of Unity: Theme and Technique in the Novels of Patrick White* (1972), *The Immoral Moralists: Hugh MacLennan and Leonard Cohen* (1972), *The Comedians: Hugh Hood and Rudy Wiebe* (1976), *Robertson Davies* (1977), *Morley Callaghan* (1978), and *Kurelek. A Biography* (1986). She has written scores of articles, and reviews beyond count. She is now a full-time writer and is currently working on fiction, biography, and a study of the lives of Japanese women since 1945.

# Preface

Margaret Laurence's work is easily divided into two parts, according to its setting. Her African work is much less known than her Canadian fiction, which is generally read and studied in isolation from her earlier writing. This study intends to show the links between Laurence's African and Canadian writing, the unity or continuity of her work, and the maturation of her sociopolitical concerns over the last twenty-five years.

Accordingly, her works are examined in chronological order (with the exception of *Jason's Quest*, her novel for children); and a combination of critical methods is employed to analyse aesthetic, textual, and historical problems. The biographical information given is relatively brief, partly because of the series format and partly because a full-scale biography at this date would be premature. A short chapter on the history of the Métis in Canada helps to explain the plight of this dispossessed group whose problems are of major and increasing concern to Laurence.

Africa, Laurence has written, taught her to look at herself. It was catalyst and crucible for much of her work. The analysis, here, of her collection of Somali poetry and prose, with its long introduction by Laurence, and of her study of Nigerian writing, is not concerned with the African literature *per se* but with Laurence's attitudes, as revealed through her critical stance. Her basic vision is seen as religious, and humanistic.

Travel has played a major role in Laurence's life. It has helped to shape her literary vision, and provided her with a central metaphor: the psychic journey towards inner freedom and spiritual maturity. Because journeying and strangerhood have played an intimate part in Laurence's life, it has been given to her to see their meaning in human experience and to penetrate (in her phrase) "the pain and interconnectedness of mankind." The themes that shape her Manawaka fiction–roots, ancestors, human complexity, acceptance of the Other, and the search for inner freedom and growth—these concerns first emerge in her African writing. The way home for Laurence lay through Ghana and the searching desert sun of Somaliland.

The last chapter focuses on the value of Laurence's work and its relevance to contemporary literature and society. The five works set in Canada in Laurence's fictional town of Manawaka are meant to be read together. This cycle of fiction constitutes a remarkable gallery of vital individuals, a composite portrait of women's experience in the late nineteenth and twentieth centuries, and the imaginative recreation of an entire society.

Laurence has turned the Manitoba town of her youth into a metaphor of universal human experience. The epic quality of her fiction, and her ability to give symbolic form to social or collective life, has earned for Laurence a justified comparison with Tolstoy, while her literary vision of the two-way flow of time places her among philosophical novelists like Proust. Laurence's art builds upon the fiction of Canadian writers such as Sinclair Ross, and greatly advances that tradition.

PATRICIA MORLEY
*Concordia University*
*1980*

# Preface (1990)

The personal portrait of Margaret Laurence in the Epilogue, and the analysis of her life and the entire body of her work found in the main text, emerge from two distinct periods of time. Much of the research was done in the late 1970s and included extensive talks with Laurence herself. I am indebted to Concordia University for Sabbatical Leave, to the Social Science and Humanities Research Council of Canada for funding, and to the National Film Board of Canada for transcripts of documentary films on Laurence.

After 1987, in the absence of any formal biography, I felt the need to explore her last years, the dozen years that fell between the publication of *The Diviners* and her untimely death at the age of sixty. I am grateful to Jocelyn Laurence for permission to work on the Laurence papers in the Archives of York University; to Project Ploughshares; and to many individuals, including some of the writer's closest friends: Neil Einarson, Timothy Findley, Joan Johnston, Helen Lucas, Almuth Lutkenhaus Lackey, Phyllis Platnick, Enid Delgatty Rutland, Clara Thomas, Alice Olsen Williams, Budge Wilson, and Lois Wilson. The memories and insights which they shared are invaluable.

PATRICIA MORLEY
*Manotick, Ontario*
*1990*

# Abbreviations

| | |
|---|---|
| *T* | *A Tree for Poverty: Somali Poetry and Prose* |
| *TSJ* | *This Side Jordan* |
| *TT* | *The Tomorrow-Tamer* |
| *PCB* | *The Prophet's Camel Bell,* and *New Wind in a Dry Land* |
| *SA* | *The Stone Angel* |
| *JG* | *A Jest of God* |
| *LD* | *Long Drums and Cannons: Nigerian Dramatists and Novelists 1952–1966* |
| *FD* | *The Fire-Dwellers* |
| *BH* | *A Bird in the House* |
| *JQ* | *Jason's Quest* |
| *D* | *The Diviners* |
| *HS* | *Heart of a Stranger* |

# Chronology

1926   Jean Margaret Wemyss born July 18 in Neepawa, Manitoba, to Robert Wemyss and Verna Simpson Wemyss. Paternal grandfather Robert Wemyss dies.

1930   Verna Simpson Wemyss dies suddenly. Her older sister Margaret comes to Neepawa to care for her niece.

1931   Margaret Campbell Simpson marries Robert Wemyss.

1935   Robert Wemyss dies.

1936   Jane Bailey Simpson (maternal grandmother) dies.

1938   Margaret Simpson Wemyss, with children Margaret and Robert, move to home of her father, John Simpson.

1939   Margaret (Laurence)'s first story, "Pillars of the Nation," written for a *Winnipeg Free Press* Contest, wins honorable mention: marks beginning of fictional name Manawaka.

1940–   Attends Neepawa Collegiate, edits school newspaper, wins
1944   Governor General's Medal.

1944–   Studies English at United College, Winnipeg. Publishes
1947   poetry and two stories in college paper, *Vox*.

1947–   Works as a reporter for *The Winnipeg Citizen*, 1947–48.
1949   Marries Jack Laurence, returned veteran and civil engineering student, September, 1947. Jack graduates from the University of Manitoba, 1949, and the Laurences go to England.

1950–   Jack Laurence's work takes the couple to the British
1952   Protectorate of Somaliland. Daughter Jocelyn born during leave in England, 1952.

1952–   The Laurences live in Ghana. Son David born there in
1957   1955. *A Tree For Poverty. Somali Poetry and Prose* published, Nairobi, 1954. Begins first novel, *This Side Jordan*. First African story, "The Drummer of All the World," published in *Queen's Quarterly* (Winter, 1956).

1957    Ghana achieves independence. The Laurences return to
        Canada. Laurence's stepmother, Margaret Simpson
        Wemyss, dies.

1957–   Laurence is in Vancouver, writing the African stories. *This*
1962    *Side Jordan* published, 1960. Separates from husband,
        moves to England with her children, to a flat in Hemp-
        stead.

1963    Moves to Elm Cottage, Buckinghamshire. McClelland and
        Stewart, Toronto, publish *The Tomorrow-Tamer* and *The
        Prophet's Camel Bell*. The latter is published in England
        under the same title, but in New York as *New Wind in
        a Dry Land* (Knopf, 1964).

1964    Simultaneous publication in New York of three books by
        Knopf (*The Tomorrow-Tamer, New Wind in a Dry Land*,
        and *The Stone Angel*) brings wide international recogni-
        tion.

1966    *A Jest of God* published in Toronto, London, and New
        York. Work proceeds on *The Fire-Dwellers* and on *Long
        Drums and Cannons. Nigerian Dramatists and Novelists
        1952–1966.*

1967    Becomes Honorary Fellow of United College, University
        of Winnipeg: first woman, and youngest person, to be so
        honored.

1968    *Long Drums and Cannons* published, London and New
        York.

1969    *The Fire-Dwellers* published simultaneously in Toronto,
        London, and New York. The Laurences divorce. Margaret
        purchases a cottage on Otonabee River near Peterborough,
        in fall, 1969, and spends part of summer 1970 there.
        Academic year at University of Toronto as Writer-in-Resi-
        dence, Massey College.

1970    *A Bird in the House* (winter) and *Jason's Quest* (spring)
        published simultaneously in Toronto, London and New
        York.

1971    Is made a Companion of the Order of Canada. Summers
        on the Otonabee, beginning *The Diviners*; winters at Elm
        Cottage.

1972    Receives LL.D. at Trent University, Peterborough, and
        at Dalhousie University, Halifax; and D. Litt., University

of Toronto. Continues to write for *The Vancouver Sun* (begun 1970) and *Maclean's*.

1973    Summers on the Otonabee. Writer-in-Residence at University of Western Ontario, fall term. Sells Elm Cottage and moves back permanently to Canada, August, 1973; buys Lakefield house and rents it until spring, 1974.

1974    Writer-in-Residence at Trent University, spring term. "Margaret Laurence and Friends," organized by a group of Trent faculty as a small tribute, blossoms into an extraordinary weekend of readings and discussion attended by over 1,500 people, including many famous Canadian writers. Moves into Lakefield house, May, 1974. Delivers Convocation address at Carleton University. Continues to write book reviews and articles for magazines. *The Diviners*, published simultaneously in Toronto, London, and New York, is awarded (in 1975) the Governor General's Medal for Fiction, 1974.

1975    Is awarded D. Litt. by the universities of Brandon, Western Ontario, and Mount Allison; and LL.D. by Queen's University, Kingston. Delivers Convocation address at these same universities, with the exception of Western Ontario. Wins Molson Prize for *The Diviners*.

1976    Woman of Year Award from B'nai B'rith Toronto Women's Branch. Controversy over the teaching of *The Diviners* in Ontario high schools. *Heart of a Stranger*, collected essays, published in Toronto only.

1977    D. Litt. awarded by Simon Fraser University. Wins Periodical Distributors' Award for mass paperback edition of *A Jest of God*, October 17.

1978    *Margaret Laurence, First Lady of Manawaka*, a fifty-minute documentary directed by Robert Duncan for the National Film Board, is released. Her major essay "Ivory Tower or Grassroots? The Novelist as Socio-Political Being" summarizes her work and concerns.

1979    Two books for children, *The Olden Days Coat* and *Six Darn Cows*, are published in Toronto.

1980    *The Christmas Birthday Story*, pictures by Helen Lucas, provokes controversy with its innocent suggestion that Mary and Joseph would have welcomed either a boy or a girl. Awarded second prize by Canadian Library Association's Best Children's Books of 1979 for *The Olden Days Coat*. Joins Energy Probe's Board of Directors.

1981   Sells her cottage on the Otonabee River near Lakefield. A film version of *The Olden Days Coat*, directed by Bruce Pittman, is released by Atlantis Films.

1981–  Works with Operation Dismantle, Energy Probe, and Pro-
1983   ject Ploughshares. Bronze portrait bust by sculptress Almuth Lutkenhaus is installed in Trent University's library. (Laurence greatly admired the sculpture *Crucified Woman* by Lutkenhaus.)

1984–  Controversy over her novels being taught in high schools
1985   surfaces once again. Peterborough School Board approves their use, April 1985.

1985   Undergoes surgery for cataract in right eye. Continues peace work. Begins memoirs.

1986   Works on memoirs while suffering generally poor health. Celebrates sixtieth birthday with large party in home and garden of Joan Johnston, beside the Otonabee. Cancer is diagnosed in late August. Continues work on memoirs in September and October, taping for transcription by Joan Johnston. Editing of memoirs begins in late October and November. Living in her own home and navigating with the aid of a walker, Laurence is cared for by her adult children.

1987   Her death, on January 5, sparks a tremendous outpouring of tributes. A memorial service at Bloor Street United Church on January 9 is directed by the Reverend Lois Wilson.

CHAPTER 1

# Laurence's Unbroken Journey

## I  *The Life*

TRAVEL has played a major role in Margaret Laurence's life. It helped to shape her literary vision, and provided her with a central metaphor. In the Foreword to her 1976 collection of essays, Laurence speaks of journeys geographic and psychological, all of which contributed to her maturation. The long, interior journey "back home" involves an increasing awareness of oneself and one's community. This psychic journey, back into roots and forward into change and growth, is at the heart of human experience and hence of literature.

Laurence was born and grew up in a small town in Manitoba. The third decade of her life found her in Africa, where her engineer husband worked from 1950 to 1957. Five years in British Columbia were followed by a decade in England. By the early 1970s, Laurence had finished her expatriate years and was back in Canada, not in the West but in a small Ontario town. Canada, Africa, England, Canada: full circle. Perhaps because journeying and strangerhood have played such an intimate part in Laurence's life, it has been given to her to see their meaning in human experience, and to penetrate "the pain and interconnectedness of manking." Her exposure to other cultures increased her understanding of her own particular culture, and of the social complex in a wider sense.

Laurence develops her central metaphor of the journey in both personal and social terms, to include the ideas of survival with dignity, love, and growth. The metaphor became a living reality for her in the desert of Somaliland, among a nomadic people. In this setting, the elements of the archetypal myth as told in Exodus and celebrated in the liturgy of the Haggadah were realities as well as symbols. Drought, wilderness, sojourning, hospitality to strangers were life and death matters in the Haud.

By some strange stroke of fate or providence, Laurence read for the first time in her life the five books of Moses while en route to the British Protectorate. She had neglected to bring something to read, and found a Gideon Bible in her hotel room in Rotterdam while waiting for the passenger/cargo ship to Somaliland. She was particularly moved by a verse from Exodus which became part of her experience, a verse which recurs in her work and is set as epigraph to her essay collection: "Thou shalt not oppress a stranger, for ye know the heart of a stranger, seeing ye were strangers in the land of Egypt." Laurence's years in Africa provided not only lessons in human nature and self-knowledge, but also a great complex of metaphors on which she has drawn throughout her writing career.[1]

The biographical details of Laurence's life are confusing, since her aunt became her stepmother and so many of her ancestors are called Margaret or Robert. She was born Jean Margaret Wemyss in Neepawa, Manitoba. Her father was of Scottish ancestry; her mother, née Simpson, was Irish. Both branches of the family were Protestant, which meant that the religious and cultural traditions of Puritanism were prominent features of the author's upbringing.

Her father Robert belonged to the Scots family of Wemyss, sept of the clan MacDuff of Burntisland, Fifeshire, in the Lowlands of Scotland. They had their own plaid pin, and the motto, "Je pense."[2] Robert's father John, after graduating from Glasgow Academy, came to join his parents in Canada in 1881. He articled as a lawyer in Winnipeg, and established himself as a barrister in Neepawa. It was John Wemyss, Laurence's grandfather, who incorporated the town in 1883.[3] Her father, Robert, was born in 1896, eldest of three children and first son of John Wemyss and his wife, Margaret Harrison. Robert became a lawyer, and a partner in his father's firm.

On her mother's side the family is traced back to County Tyrone, Ireland.[4] Laurence's maternal grandfather, John Simpson, was born in 1856 in Milton, Ontario. The boy who became the terror of the family clan, and Laurence's *bete noir*, left school at twelve, after his father's death. In 1878 he reached Winnipeg by stern-wheeler, and walked fifty miles to Portage La Prairie, supporting himself as he went by cabinet-making jobs. He married Jane Bailey in 1882, and moved to Neepawa in 1895, where he set up a joint business in cabinet-making and undertaking. He was more admired than loved, though many depended on his strength. This harsh bear of a man and his gentle wife are the models for Vanessa's maternal grandparents in the admittedly autobiographical stories, *A Bird in the House*. John and Jane Simpson had seven children, including four daughters, one of whom, Verna, became Laurence's mother, and another, Margaret, her stepmother.

Verna Simpson Wemyss died suddenly in 1930 of an acute kidney infection. Her older sister Margaret, a Calgary schoolteacher, came to Neepawa to care for her four-year-old niece, Jean Margaret; she married Robert Wemyss the following year. Four years later, in the midst of the Depression, Laurence's father died. Soon after, with twelve-year-old Margaret and five-year-old Robert Wemyss, Lawrence's stepmother moved into her grandfather's house. Until her death in 1957, Margaret Simpson Wemyss shared a very warm relationship with her stepdaughter. Mrs. Wemyss was instrumental in founding Neepawa's Public Library, and became its first librarian. She encouraged her stepdaughter in her early writing with tactful criticism and honest praise.[5] Laurence describes her stepmother as "a magnificent lady, with a great sense of home and responsibility, and she was devoted to English literature."[6]

The town of Neepawa, some one hundred and twenty-five miles northwest of Winnipeg, provided the inspiration for Laurence's fictional Manawaka. Neepawa's Whitemud River, where she skated under Northern Lights (*HS* 214), became the Wachakwa River, while Riding Mountain on Clear Lake where the Laurences had a summer cottage, some hundred miles north of Neepawa, models for Galloping Mountain on Diamond Lake.

Neepawa was already well settled by the time of its incorporation in 1883. With the railway, it became a major grain outlet and the center of a rich agricultural district from Riding Mountain in the north to the Assiniboine land in the south. It was also rich in dairy products, wood, and salt. Neepawa (Cree for *abundance*) was aptly named. The district was originally settled in the 1870s by Scottish pioneers trekking westward from Ontario in search of land. These founding families formed the tightly woven, predominantly Scottish group that Laurence describes with such biting accuracy in *The Stone Angel, A Jest of God,* and *The Diviners.* Sixty years earlier, a shipload of destitute crofters from the north of Scotland had been brought by Alexander Selkirk to found the Red River Colony, in the area of the Red and Assiniboine Rivers where Winnipeg now stands. The Scots thus formed one of the strongest elements in Manitoba settlement.

Critic Clara Thomas notes that Neepawa is not really a prairie town. It is less flat, more wooded; its tree-shaded brick houses made it resemble Ontario towns. Yet it would be equally inaccurate simply to identify it with the latter. Thomas speaks of its identity as a western town, whose inhabitants claim "part of the wide-ranging, uninhibited freedom of spirit" traditional to the West.[7] Because Laurence herself refers to Neepawa as a prairie town, and because its cultural ambiance is clearly Western, as Thomas admits, Neepawa is treated as such in this study.

The Scottish side of Laurence's ancestry has loomed larger in her imagination than the Irish, doubtless because of the Scottish culture of Neepawa. Laurence thinks of herself as a Scots-Canadian, and identifies sympathetically with the Highlanders despite the fact that Fifeshire is in the Lowlands. As a child, she was extremely aware of her Scottish background: "No one could ever tell me whether my family had been Lowlanders or Highlanders . . . but the Highlanders seemed more interesting and more noble to me in every way." Scotland inhabited Laurence's imagination as a bold, dramatic country of high adventure and noble deeds. In a recent preface to "Road from the Isles," the 1966 article quoted above, Laurence writes: "But I always felt my spiritual ancestors were Highlanders, and possibly that is why I gave Morag Gunn, in *The Diviners,* ancestors who came from Sutherland and who were turned out during the Highland Clearances" (*HS* 145).

The article goes on to detail the Scottish influences on her as a child, her adult reading of the atrocities of the Clearances after the Battle of Culloden, and her realization (during a visit to Scotland in the 1960s) that her true ancestors and cultural heritage were Canadian: ". . . gradually I began to perceive that I was no more Scots than I was Siamese."

Laurence's discussion of what Scotland meant to her reveals the twofold temper of her imagination, its social realism, and its romanticism. It also reveals her capacity for sympathetic identification with people whose experience, at least superficially, has been strikingly different from her own. The Clearances devastated the Highlanders because they were betrayed by their chieftains, the symbolic king/father figure with almost mystical powers in a tribal culture:

> To be betrayed by one of these must have been like knowing, really knowing, that one's own father intended, if he could, to murder you. The outcast Highlanders must have arrived in Canada as a people bereft, a people who had been wounded psychically in ways they could not possibly have comprehended. . . . They had been in the deepest possible ways forsaken; in the truest sense their hearts had been broken. . . . I had known, of course, as every person schooled in Canada knows, of the external difficulties of the early Scottish settlers, the people of Glengarry and Red River. What I had never seen before was a glimpse of their inner terrors, a sense of the bereavement they must have carried with them like a weight of lead in the soul. What appeared to be their greatest trouble in a new land—the grappling with an unyielding environment—was in fact probably their salvation. I believe they survived not in spite of the physical hardships but *because* of them, for all their attention and thought *had* to be focused outward. They could not brood. If they had been able to do so, it might have killed them. (*HS* 148)

In the preface to "Road from the Isles," Laurence notes that learning about the tribal systems in Africa added to her understanding of the Scots' clan system. In other articles she has identified the Somalis, the Highlanders, and the Canadian Métis as victims of similar types of imperialist aggression. Once again we see the continuity of Laurence's career and her developing literary vision.

From Neepawa, Laurence went to United College, Winnipeg, to study English on a scholarship. This Arts and Theology college, with a student body in the 1940s of approximately seven

hundred and fifty, was affiliated with the University of Manitoba.
Thomas describes its founding institutions, Methodist and Presbyterian, and its tradition of liberal thought, a tradition "particularly sympathetic to her positive, affirming temperament."[8]

During her three college years, Laurence began what was to
be a lasting friendship with writer Adele Wiseman, and became
involved with "the Winnipeg Old Left," a group dedicated to
social reform. In *Vox,* the college paper, she published poetry
and two stories ("Calliope" and "Tal des Waldes"); and was
assistant editor in her final year. She remembers Arthur Phelps
and Robert Hallstead as teachers who influenced her at college.[9]

Laurence worked as a reporter for the *Winnipeg Citizen* in
the year following her graduation, writing book reviews and a
daily radio column, and covering labor news. In September
1947 she married Jack Laurence, a native of Alberta, a veteran,
and a civil engineering student at the University of Manitoba.
He graduated in 1949. They spent the latter months of 1949 in
England, and left for Africa early in 1950.

Jack Laurence was engaged to create a chain of artificial
lakes or earth dams in the deserts of the British Protectorate of
Somaliland, now Somalia. The British Colonial Service felt that
Somaliland was no place for a woman, but Jack described his
wife as a hardy Canadian girl, "a kind of female Daniel Boone,"
and Laurence was permitted to go.[10] For the next two years
she lived in isolated desert camps, sometimes in a tent or Land
Rover, and came to know and admire the nomadic tribesmen
whose lives depended on courage, endurance, and religious faith.
Out of this sojourn came her first published work, a translation
of Somali poetry and folk tales.

During the latter months of Laurence's time in Somaliland,
while she was pregnant with her first baby and could not live
on the dam sites, she worked in Hargeisa as confidential secretary, doing typing and shorthand for the Chief Secretary of the
Protectorate. Laurence refers to this as her last paid job other
than writing. It was Philip Shirley, the Chief Secretary, who
was convinced that the manuscript of *A Tree for Poverty* must be
published, "for the Introduction alone," and who helped to
secure a grant from the British government for its publication
in Nairobi in 1954.[11]

The next five years were spent in the Gold Coast, now Ghana, in Accra and Tema Harbour, where Jack Laurence worked. Their children, Jocelyn and David, were born in 1952 and 1955 respectively, the first in England and the second in Ghana. Laurence drafted *This Side Jordan* in Ghana, beginning it in August, 1955, just after the birth of her son, but the African stories were written in Vancouver. Ghana achieved its independence in 1957, within months of the Laurences' departure. Obviously, the political atmosphere in the years immediately preceding independence must have been extremely highly charged.

These years were also marked by the deaths of John Simpson, Laurence's maternal grandfather (in 1953, at the age of ninety-seven), and of her beloved stepmother, Margaret Simpson Wemyss (in 1957, of cancer). Laurence told Donald Cameron, a Canadian writer and critic, that the theme of death in her writing reflects not simply the frequency of deaths in the family but a coming to terms with the knowledge of one's own eventual death. To Clara Thomas, in 1972, she spoke of the profound effect on her of her maternal grandfather, a stern man who seemed incapable of expressing any emotion but anger yet who had admirable qualities of strength and pride. *A Bird in the House*, with its moving last lines, acknowledges the major place of this man in Laurence's life.

Laurence speaks of her years in Africa as "a seven years' love affair with a continent." Out of it came the translations of Somali literature, a first novel, a collection of stories set in Ghana, and a remarkable travel memoir which is also a spiritual autobiography. And out of Africa, as we will see, came Laurence's maturity and a deep understanding of her own roots: "I learned so much from that experience."[12]

Nineteen fifty-seven to 1962 found Laurence in Vancouver looking after her small children, marking essays for the University of British Columbia, undergoing a gall bladder operation, working on the African material, and beginning to repatriate her imagination. She remembers starting *The Stone Angel* in 1961 on the day she received a phone call informing her that *This Side Jordan* had been awarded the Beta Sigma Phi First Novel Award.

She read O. Mannoni's study of the psychology of colonization early in 1960, just before *This Side Jordan* was published. The

Congo Crisis had taken place shortly before. In hospital, recuperating from her operation, Laurence got the idea for "The Voices of Adamo," a story which owes its genesis to Mannoni's study and the events in the Belgian Congo. Laurence acknowledges the former as the only theoretical influence on her work. It illumined both the colonial and the tribal mentality. She read *Prospero and Caliban. A Study of the Psychology of Colonisation* with "the shock of recognition one sometimes feels when another's words have a specific significance in terms of one's own experiences" (*NW* 229), and corresponded briefly with the French ethnographer in 1960.

In 1962 the Laurences separated. Margaret went to England with the children, took up residence in a Hampstead flat, and moved, the following year, to a rambling old house on Beacon Hill, Penn, Buckinghamshire. During the following decade in England she wrote numerous book reviews for journals and newspapers, rewrote *The Stone Angel,* and completed the body of fiction that composes her Manawaka cycle, with the exception of *The Diviners.* These years in England were interrupted by a trip to East Pakistan in 1963 to see her husband and attempt a reconciliation; to Egypt in 1966, having been commissioned to write some travel articles on that country; and to Canada, in the later 1960s and early 1970s, for several terms of Writer-in-Residence at various Canadian universities.

In December, 1963, Laurence moved to Elm Cottage in Buckinghamshire. Its place in her affections is confirmed by the dedication to *The Diviners:* "For the Elmcot people/ past present and future/and for the house itself/ with love and gratitude." She rented at first, until money from *Rachel, Rachel,* the film version of *A Jest of God,* enabled her to buy Elmcot in 1966. Her children attended local schools in High Wycombe. "Elmcot people" includes Ian and Sandy Cameron, who cared for Laurence's house and teen-aged children during her term of residence in Massey College, University of Toronto (1969–70), and the stream of Canadian writers and musicians who passed through the old house during Laurence's tenure. It was Ian Cameron who wrote the music for Laurence's ballads in *The Diviners.*

Local villagers and British culture do not appear to have played much part in Laurence's life. The latter is perhaps surprising, considering the number of years spent in England. Many of her Beacon Hill neighbors remained ignorant of the fact that Laurence was a writer. Seven years in Africa led to five books, but contemporary British life is reflected only in *Jason's Quest*, the novel for children which Laurence wrote near the end of her decade in England.

Laurence seems to have always worked retrospectively, drawing from the deep wells of remembered experience. The African years took literary shape in Canada during the five years that followed; the Manawakan portraits of Laurence's grandparents and parents and of herself were created in England in the sixties; and material from her years in Vancouver goes into Stacey's experience, half a decade later. Only with *The Diviners* does Laurence confront Canadian life that is contemporary with the time of writing.

The 1970s have been marked by Laurence's return to Canada, the writing and publication of her epic novel, *The Diviners*, and her increased involvement in Canadian life—literary, social, and political. She now lives in the Peterborough area of Ontario, northeast of Toronto, in a nineteenth-century brick house in the village of Lakefield, as well as in a cottage on the nearby Otonabee River. Both homes were purchased in the early years of the decade.

From this base, Laurence has influenced and advised the coming generation of Canadian writers, through several years as Writer-in-Residence at Ontario universities, by numerous personal contacts, and active cooperation with The Writers' Union of Canada. The latter association, known as TWUC, was formed by two meetings in 1973; Laurence served as Interim Chairman from June to November, 1973. The development of her political consciousness during the 1970s may be seen in her joining, on several occasions, in TWUC street demonstrations protesting unfair conditions for Canadian writers; and in the large portraits of Louis Riel, Gabriel Dumont, and Norman Bethune that hang on the walls of her cottage, "The Shack."

Honors and awards continue to come to the woman who has turned the prairie town of her youth into a metaphor of universal human experience. After the publication of *The Diviners* Laurence seemed to feel a sense of completion in her literary career, and was widely reported as saying that she did not plan to write another novel. She is, however, currently at work on a new book. The river of her life continues its two-way flow.

## II  *Laurence on Laurence*

One way in which we may examine Laurence's life, work, and literary aims is through her own statements. These are extensive. Laurence has been widely interviewed, and has written numerous essays of a highly personal nature. We are not, of course, blind to the fact that an author may not be his or her own best critic or may be convinced that he or she has accomplished something other than is the case. Nevertheless, an author's comments retain a peculiar interest if not a peculiar authority. Familiarity with Laurence's work reveals that she is a highly self-conscious writer, and that the emphasis in her clearly articulated goals has altered over the last twenty-five years.

She spoke with Donald Cameron, *circa* 1970, of her thematic concerns, her fictional characters, and her religious beliefs. Here, as elsewhere, she describes her primary theme as freedom, a complex concept which has psychological, political, and spiritual ramifications:

This is the theme that my life has made me, and I don't know why. It's an accumulation of every single thing that's ever happened to me, probably. It may also be a cultural thing. Having grown up in the Prairies, in a fairly stultifying community in some ways, and yet having come from, on the one hand, Scots ancestors who certainly were extremely independent if not bloody-minded, and equally bloody-minded Irish ancestors . . . —it seems to me that these two things probably have worked in kind of juxtaposition in my life: on the one hand a repressed community, on the other a community in which the values of the individual were extraordinarily strongly recognized, if only sometimes by implication.[13]

She goes on to acknowledge that freedom, for human beings, is always partial, imperfect, and that another major theme in her work, or an aspect of the first theme, is human communication and isolation. Human beings, she is convinced, *can* reach one another, yet "*ought* to be able to communicate and touch each other far more than they do, and this human loneliness and isolation, which occurs everywhere, seems to me to be part of man's tragedy. I'm sure one of the main themes in all my writing is this sense of man's isolation from his fellows and how almost unbearably tragic this is."

With regard to her method of writing fiction, Laurence stresses that characters come first, and the work takes shape around them. Characters are usually in her head for years before she begins to write about them. Their development is partly at a subconscious level. She links this process to "Method" acting: "I take on, for the time I'm writing, the *persona* of the character, and I am trying to make a kind of direct connection with this person, not to manipulate them but to listen to them. . . . They exist in their own right." Her goal in the novel is to "present the living individual on the printed page, in all his paradox and all his craziness."

To Cameron, Laurence describes her religious beliefs as a kind of religious agnosticism. She is no longer sure of what the word *God* means, but is convinced that the universe is not "empty." The Bible contains symbolic truths about human experience, and reflects our search for a consciousness greater than our own. This Christian heritage is described as having enormous emotional power. Laurence mourns her areas of religious disbelief as "Eden lost." Puritan attitudes were absorbed "through the pores," including the tendency to feel guilty and the compulsion to work. Laurence has transmuted the latter into her dedicated approach to writing, the only activity she now dignifies by the term *work*.

During her Vancouver years, after the time spent in Africa, Laurence taught Sunday School, first for the United Church and then for the Unitarians. She attended Unitarian services in Vancouver for some time, and wrote a Christmas nativity story for this church. Her interest in the Unitarians did not last, since "ancestors" meant nothing to them and a great deal to Laurence. She offers a wry definition of a Unitarian as one who believes in "one God at most." After many years of absence from church services, Laurence began in the late 1970s to attend the United Church, "the church of my ancestors."[14]

At about the same time as the Cameron interview, Laurence talked with Graeme Gibson for a CBC broadcast. Many of her comments to Gibson were concerned with individual works in the Manawaka cycle, and will be discussed later. Gibson's queries about the writer's role in society, and about form in the novel, solicited interesting responses. Laurence feared that direct social involvement might turn fiction into propaganda.[15] She saw the writer's responsibility *to tell the truth*, to express what many know but few say. This is very difficult. For Laurence, one basic truth is that human beings "are capable of great communication and love and very often fall very far short of this."

Questions about form in the novel usually bring Laurence back to some discussion of the fictional characters, since "the material itself" decides the form. A novel is a voyage of discovery which begins with the main characters: "Usually there are a number of people who have been inhabiting my head for a number of years before I begin on a novel, and their dilemmas grow out of what they are, where they come from. . . . I would hope that the thing that comes across the most strongly is the creation of individual characters." Form is inseparable from content, and content means characters and their problems: ". . . hopefully out of this grows some kind of form."

To both these interviewers Laurence spoke of time and place as the basic shaping forces on any writer. Her gift, and task, is to express the idiom of her time and place. She possesses an intimate genealogical knowledge of four generations in her fictional town of Manawaka: the generations of her grandparents, parents, self, and children. The work of Chinua Achebe, a Nigerian novelist with whom Laurence feels strong affinities, covers the same historical span. Beyond great-grandparents, the ancestors become everyone's ancestors: "It all becomes myth at that point." To Graeme Gibson, she remarked that real liberation stems from coming to terms with the past, not from rejecting it. This point is made repeatedly in her fiction and nonfiction alike.

The clearest statements of what her own place and time have meant to Laurence are found in "A Place to Stand on" (1970, originally entitled "Sources") and "Where the World Began" (1971), both collected in *Heart of a Stranger*. Here, as in "Road from the Isles," she states that Neepawa and its Scots-Presbyterian pioneers, not Scotland, represent her real past: "My true roots were here" (*HS* 219). Neepawa provides "elements" of Manawaka, but this town of the mind, her own private world, is "not so much any one prairie town as an amalgam of many prairie towns" (*HS* 15).

Place means land and people. Laurence writes of the ambiguity she felt towards both. To Cameron, she spoke of the stultifying aspects of local culture which, along with respect for individuality and independence, helped to nurture her love of freedom. Here she acknowledges the welcome security of that admittedly repressive atmosphere. The land was lonely, isolated, yet very beautiful. Its inhabitants evoked similarly complex emotions: "how difficult they were to live with, how authoritarian, how unbending, how afraid to show love, many of them, and how willing to sow anger. And yet, they had inherited a wilderness and made it fruitful. They were, in the end, great survivors, and for that I love and value them" (*HS* 16). The theme of survival with human dignity and warmth is termed an almost inevitable theme for a writer "who came from a Scots-Irish background of stern values and hard work and puritanism, and who grew up during the drought and depression of the thirties and then the war." Laurence notes that her characters, in the first three Manawaka books, are each threatened, and each finds the ability to survive and grow.

Laurence agrees with Graham Greene that the creative writer perceives his world once and for all in childhood and adolescence. Hence she considers it natural and inevitable that so much of her work should relate to the prairie town of her youth and first self-consciousness: "Manawaka will probably always be there, simply because whatever I am was shaped and formed in that sort of place, and my way of seeing, however much it may have changed over the years, remains in some enduring way that of a small-town prairie person" (*HS* 18).

The latter essay echoes these sentiments: "My eyes were formed there" (*HS* 213). Neepawa is described as a place of incredible happenings, "horrible and beautiful." It was bizarre, never dull: stultifying to the mind, but not to the imagination. Laurence was young during the 1930s, when drought and de-

pression loomed "like evil deities which had been there always."
She writes of the oddities of the place, its social snobbery, its
cruelties. The latter included a solitary old man in a shack
beyond town whom boys delighted to bait: "Everything is to be
found in a town like mine. Belsen, writ small but with the same
ink" (*HS* 216). It offered a microcosm, and a lifework.

Psychic survival is linked with one's ability to come to terms
with the past. For Laurence, this has been accomplished partly
through the act of writing, a point she makes in almost all these
essays. Her research into contemporary Nigerian writing opened
her eyes to the parallels with her own work. The pattern involved "the attempt to assimilate the past, partly in order to
be freed from it, partly in order to try to understand myself
and perhaps those of my generation through seeing where we had
come from" (*HS* 14). She considers that she was fortunate in
going to Africa in her early twenties because this prevented her
from writing an autobiographical first novel. But she was always
mindful of the necessity of making, sooner or later, the journey
home in terms of her writing.

Another important essay from roughly the same period is
further evidence that the late 1960s were for Laurence a time
of self-assessment and summation. Four of the five Manawaka
works had been written in the previous decade (*The Stone Angel,
A Jest of God, The Fire-Dwellers,* and *A Bird in the House*),
along with the collection of African stories and the study of
Nigerian writing. "Ten Years' Sentences," written in 1968 and
published in 1969, is elegiac in tone, with a sense of new directions. Laurence calls the 1958–68 period the most difficult and
most interesting decade of her life.

She points to two basically different moods or philosophic
stances reflected in her work to this date. Her three books of
the 1950s and early 1960s (*This Side Jordan, The Prophet's Camel
Bell,* and *The Tomorrow-Tamer*) reflect the predominantly optimistic outlook of many Africans and western liberals of the time.
These works are also the product of a young writer, with "the
unmistakable mark of someone who is young and full of faith."[16]

The Nigerian war altered that initial stance. Laurence was
researching Nigerian literature at the time, had met Nigerian
writers such as Christopher Okigbo and Wole Soyinka in Eng-

land, and had spent seven years in Africa in the 1950s. She was deeply moved by the massacres of Ibo tribesmen. In "Ten Years' Sentences," she writes of "the appalling grip on the human heart of tribalism in its hate aspect." She is careful not to isolate herself and her people from these horrifying passions. Tribalism is a universal human phenomenon, with a good, bonding side, and a destructive, frightening side, where the in-group (be it Hausa, Ibo, or Scots Presbyterian) sees its members as human, and the nontribe as subhuman. Although she denies that *disillusioned* is an apt word to describe the effects of the Nigerian war on her attitudes, it obviously sobered her youthful optimism. Her 1969 divorce, which followed seven years of separation, may also have affected her view of life in the late sixties.

Laurence describes her viewpoint at this time as having altered from "modified optimism to modified pessimism." One thinks, in this connection, of the dark stories of alienation and pain in *A Bird in the House,* stories such as "The Loons," "The Half-Husky," and "Horses of the Night." She contrasts her African work, where her theme is freedom, with her later fiction. In *The Stone Angel,* which is midway in the time period under discussion, the altering emphasis may be seen:

The world had changed; I had grown older. Perhaps I no longer believed so much in the promised land, even the promised land of one's own inner freedom. Perhaps an obsession with freedom is the persistent (thank God) dance of the young. With *The Stone Angel,* without my recognizing it at the time, the theme had changed to that of survival, the attempt of the personality to survive with some dignity, toting the load of excess mental baggage that everyone carries, until the moment of death.

The two themes come together in her 1972 statement to Clara Thomas, where freedom is reinstated: "When I first began writing, the theme to me then seemed to be human freedom and in a profound sense it still is human freedom. But this is linked with survival, which, as you say, has to be linked with some kind of growth and I would express this in terms of an inner freedom."[17]

A few years later, by the mid-1970s and the completion of
*The Diviners*, Laurence's self-definition is both more affirmative
and more political. The idea of fiction as propaganda is still
stoutly rejected. But Laurence's sense of her country as an ex-
colonial one which has come of age gives a militant edge to her
nationalism, an edge which was lacking a decade earlier. Meanwhile, her lifelong concern for social justice may be seen taking
more political forms. One indication of these changes is her
refusal to contribute a television script on early Canadian settlers
to a series funded by Imperial Oil, a company she felt was
"doing dire things" to Canada.[18]

In the same 1975 interview, Laurence told Bernice Lever
that there is no sense of nationalism "in a political sense" in
her fiction, because that is not the place for it; and that Canadian
literature now has its own models, forged from its own culture,
which serve to give Canadians a strong sense of identity: "Our
writers can affect this whole struggle simply, by forging our
myths and giving voice to our history, to our legends, to our
cultural being. . . . What I'm dealing with in my work in fiction
is that whole cultural background and characters which start
in my case with a small prairie town. *This may be political in
a different sense*" (italics added).

Earlier, when *The Diviners* was published, Laurence talked
with Valerie Miner in Lakefield and in the context of a student
seminar at Trent University. The mood is clearly optimistic.
Laurence's return to Canada, and her steady contact with Canadian students in her capacity as resident writer, helped to
dispel the "modified pessimism" engendered by the Nigerian
Civil War and other events of the 1960s.

Queried as to the difference between her survival and Sylvia
Plath's suicide (both women were living in Hampstead in the
early 1960s, just separated from their husbands, with two children
and literary ambitions), Laurence said it went back to one's
childhood: " 'mine was obviously much easier than hers.' "[19]
Was it not difficult to look after two children alone? No, they
were "extremely supportive." Laurence sees "a mystery at the
core of life" (her Nigerian study has a similar phrase), and
describes *The Diviners* as a reflection of the strong sense of
hope she now feels in her own life.[20] She quotes, without refut-

ing, her son's description of her as "the classic Yiddishe Mamma";
her strong sense of family is extended to the tribe of Canadian
writers: "'who influenced your style?' 'Sinclair Ross, W. O.
Mitchell, Ethel Wilson.' 'Who are your friends?' 'Peggy Atwood,
Harold Horwood, Don Cameron, John Metcalf, Marian Engel.' "[21]
Laurence has returned to the basic optimism of her 1950s
stance. Her sense of herself as a woman who knows her own
strengths and her newly vocal political views are closely connected: "'There is a place for social statement in literature in
an indirect way.'" The Black Celt balances despair with survival-
humor: "'I think each of the novels—especially *The Diviners*—
ends on a profound sense of hope. The Black Celt gives you a
feeling of ambiguity, a knowledge that life in many ways is
sombre.' "[22] Life may be tragic in that it moves towards death:
"'But all the same, life is alive.'"

Laurence's political commitment is even more overt in an
article contributed to a 1978 *festeschrifte* in honor of George
Woodcock. She calls a novelist, by definition, a sociopolitical
being; the writer of serious fiction is inevitably a social historian,
because "our perceptions and therefore our interpretations are
formed by the communities in which we grew up."[23] She describes history and fiction as twin disciplines: implicit here is
the corollary that the interpretation of history is a political act.
She defines human beings as "social and spiritual animals," both
religious and political, and in need of gods and ancestors. The
latter emphasis is familiar, but the bold appropriation of words
like *religious* and *political* belong to her post-1972 phase.

Laurence illustrates her sociopolitical thesis by the work of
Chinua Achebe and herself, describing both as "Third World
novelists." Peter Such is quoted with approval: "'International
art' ... means the cultural forms of the dominant imperial cultures of the times." Laurence compares the struggle of Nigerian
writers to overcome the psychic damage inflicted by British
imperialists with the subtler but similar problems of Canadians.
She speaks of mid-twentieth-century Canadian writers such as
Hugh MacLennan, Sinclair Ross, Ernest Buckler, and Ethel
Wilson as "sod-busters," neglected heroes who were the first
generation of noncolonial Canadian writers and who prepared
the way for the current generation of novelists like herself.

The denial of "international" standards of excellence does not mean a denial of the tradition of language and literature, a tradition affirmed by Laurence. It is, rather, a refusal to bow to foreign idols: read irrelevant comparisons, and criticism that ignores the conditions and traditions that have helped to create a particular national or regional literature. Laurence describes the colonial atmosphere of Canada in the late 1950s, when she returned from Africa, as follows: "My people's standards of correctness and validity and excellence were still at that time largely derived from external and imposed values; our view of ourselves was still struggling against two other cultures' definitions of us." This remark is reinforced by a joke remembered from college days (the late 1940s), whose point was that Canadians lacked confidence and a realistic appreciation of self-worth.

She goes on to compare these colonial attitudes with the situation in which women find themselves today, and to credit the women's movement in the 1960s with giving her "a much-needed sense of community." Finally, Laurence sums up the development of her fictional themes, which are now defined as political in the broadest sense, in relation to her own experience of growth:

My sense of social awareness, my feelings of anti-imperialism, anti-colonialism, anti-authoritarianism, had begun, probably in embryo form in my own childhood; they had been nurtured during my college years and immediately afterwards, in the North Winnipeg of the Old Left; they had developed considerably through my African experience. It was not very difficult to relate this experience to my own land, which had been under the colonial sway of Britain once and now under the colonial sway of America. But these developing feelings also related very importantly to my growing awareness of the dilemma and powerlessness of women, the tendency of women to accept male definition of ourselves, to be self-depreciating and uncertain, and to rage inwardly. The quest for physical and spiritual freedom, the quest for relationships of equality and communication—these themes run through my fiction and are connected with the theme of survival, not mere physical survival, but a survival of the spirit, with human dignity and the ability to give and receive love.

Laurence fits female heroines from the Manawaka cycle into
this pattern, and reemphasizes that freedom and survival are
simultaneously social and spiritual states, hence both political
and religious themes. She notes, further, that dispossession is
another of her central themes, developed through the Highland
Scots and the Métis. Actually, this theme is found in Laurence's
work from the beginning, but her self-conscious emphasis of it
is new.

Laurence is that relatively rare creature, a good judge of her
own work. The critic thoroughly acquainted with the Laurentian canon comes to this 1978 article with a sense of *déja vu,*
having already arrived at similar conclusions. Her political development, towards a greater self-consciousness of the rights
of individuals, nations, and groups to possess their heritage and
work out their own destiny, seems inevitable.

## III   *The Work*

Five books are the product of Laurence's seven years in Africa
and her continuing interest in that continent. Her Manawaka
books also number five. A book for children and a collection
of essays bring the total to twelve. Laurence's African writing
and her Canadian-based fiction are closely related. Together
they represent a seamless fabric, a steady growth and maturation of a way of seeing which was first formed in Neepawa,
Manitoba. The Canadian prairie where her world began is both
harsh and beautiful: a land of extremes, of testing, of dignity
in the face of defeat. This environment, together with the fact
that Canadians have never been an imperial power and have
emerged relatively recently from their own experience of being
colonized, helped to prepare for Laurence's sympathetic understanding of Somaliland and Ghana in the 1950s. At the
same time, the prevailing liberalism of Canadian culture bred
a naiveté in the young Laurence which the African experience
cauterized.

Laurence's first published work was a labor of love. Her
translations, *A Tree for Poverty: Somali Poetry and Prose,* are
the first written expression of this ancient oral literature. Laurence had never experienced a foreign culture before Somaliland.

Her Preface to the 1970 Canadian reprint apologizes for "un-
witting condescending, in the manner of white liberals, out
of pure ignorance." Both the 1952 Introduction and the later
Preface stress the significance of human differences, cultural
and individual. In commenting on the folk tales, Laurence
writes of the pride, courage, and humor of the ordinary Somali
herdsman, in a land where independence is necessary to survival.

The rigors of desert survival evoked a deep response in the
woman from the Canadian prairie who had been raised amid
drought and depression. Laurence describes her grandparents'
generation as people who had inhabited a wilderness and made
it fruitful, people whom she loved and valued because they
were great survivors. She also admired the Somalis for their
toughness, their ability to eke out life, their refusal to die
easily. The desert sun, she writes in *The Prophet's Camel Bell*
(1963), exposed the heart as well as the land. Her descriptions
of the harsh and exotic beauty of the desert are often moving,
but the most interesting portions of the travel narrative deal
with her encounters with people—the Somalis, the expatriates,
and, most of all, herself. The travel narrative uses fictional
techniques and is essential to our understanding of its author.
It is one of her major works.

Laurence's African fiction, a novel and a collection of ten
short stories, dramatizes fear and hope, but the resolutions
are clearly optimistic. The themes are Laurence's typical ones
of freedom and communication. *This Side Jordan* portrays two
social groups (white colonial administrators and Africans) co-
existing in Ghana in the 1950s as the country moved towards
political independence. The British expatriates, managers of a
well-established textile company, are threatened by the planned
changeover to African management. The difficulty for Laurence
was to be fair to the colonial managers and their families. In
rewriting the novel, she attempted to make this group more
sympathetic, and in retrospect she feels that she has been more
successful in probing their mentality than that of the Africans.
Most reviewers, including Africans, disagree. Like the stories
in *The Tomorrow-Tamer*, the novel is a sensitive portrait of
social change in West Africa and the pressures it exerts on
individuals and groups.

There is nothing sentimental in the handling of her themes. Man is rarely free, and no one knows this better than Laurence. The other side of the coin is bondage, entrapment, alienation. Some of the bonds are forged by her characters for themselves; some are imposed from without, through various ironies of circumstances beyond their control. Alienation and exile are seen as forms of bondage or psychic slavery. In African and Canadian stories alike, Laurence depicts an often agonizing struggle to break these bonds, to overcome alienation, to achieve an integration both personal and social which is imaged as a freedom to love and accept love, to share, to meet, to touch. Such a state, Laurence implies, is our spiritual home, the human goal, the grail. In stories where the mode is primarily ironic and tragic, the focus is upon the forces that block movement towards this goal. In stories where the structure is comic, the characters are engaged, difficulties notwithstanding, in the long trek home.

*Long Drums and Cannons: Nigerian Dramatists and Novelists 1952–1966* (1968) is a pioneering study of Nigerian literature written in English. It was published in the middle of the twelve-year period during which Laurence wrote her Manawaka books. Because she feels a sympathetic identification with many Africans, her comments on their work reveal many of her own attitudes towards writing. In the Preface she speaks of the social and political engagement of Nigerian writers who are concerned with generational conflict and other disturbances during a period of transition. She writes of "the slow dying of the destructive aspects of tribalism, the anguish and inadequacy of uncompromising individualism as an alternative"; of the necessity of planting universal themes in some specific geographic and cultural soil; and of the need for self-knowledge. People, she notes, are both creative and destructive; free, yet dependent upon gods and ancestors. The past must be acknowledged in the present, and must be taken into account in any ongoing process.

Change and growth, rather than tradition and the past, are emphasized in Laurence's novel for children, *Jason's Quest*, which was written just after the Nigerian study in the summer of 1967. (The word *novel* is used advisedly: *Jason's Quest* is unusually long for a children's book, and the animal protagonists have something of the inner vitality that marks all Laurence's characters.) Devotion to the past is all very well, but it can stifle a society: "surely new things have to happen, too, don't they?"[24] Life depends on change, growth, and the wisdom of experience.

Laurence calls the story "a gift" given to her during a period of difficulty with *The Fire-Dwellers*.[25] *Jason's Quest* is a delightfully witty, whimsical story which reveals the romantic and optimistic bias of Laurence's imagination, and her capacity to ground fantasy in specific geographic and cultural soil. It is discussed in detail here (and only here) since its setting and technique make it anomalous in Laurence's canon, yet its themes and the quest structure are typical.

*Jason's Quest*, as the title indicates, is a modern version of the archetypal romance. It is the story of four animal friends who venture together on a bold quest. The Grail, or Golden Fleece, varies with the individual. The two cats, annoyed by the popular cartoon image of cats as villainous and stupid, are in search of noble deeds. The young owl, Oliver, seeks the wisdom proper to his species. Jason, the smallest member of the expedition, has the greatest purpose. His goal is nothing less than the cure for his mole people, who are suffering from an invisible plague which makes them tired and lackadaisical. This illness is gradually destroying Molanium, their underground city and civilization, whose traditions date back to the Roman conquest of Britain. The four friends set out from rural England for the metropolis of London. They undergo a series of adventures, defeat the Great Rat and his followers, and return to Molanium with a bride for Jason and an inspired diagnosis of the plague: *boredom.*

A quest is the pure form of the romance genre. Laurence's version for children is both idealistic and satiric. She draws on clichéd, melodramatic phrases (such as "Boot, saddle, to horse and away!" or "Half-a-league, half-a-league, half-a-league onward!") to parody the romance form, and sets formal or archaic phrases in comic juxtaposition with contemporary slang: "A state of general amnesty shall be declared. That means no bashing, anyone." At the same time, her tale follows the traditional pattern of the quest, with its simplified conflict between basically good protagonists and obviously evil antagonists, with perils survived, heroic rescues accomplished, and the grail achieved at last. At stake is the very survival of "the great and noble city." The narrative structure is both comic and romantic, as it drives towards an apocalyptic battle between the forces of good and evil, a marriage, and the restoration of the Good Society.

In *Long Drums and Cannons*, Laurence writes of the need to anchor universal themes in a specific cultural soil. That soil, in *Jason's Quest*, is the England of the 1960s, both rural and urban. The four friends move from a rural atmosphere of flint-and-brick cottages, small, well-kept gardens, and pubs with open fireplaces, into the vast, threatening city: a tourist's London of fashionable boutiques, Trafalgar Square, Portobello Road, the Hippodrome, Covent Garden marketplace, colorful immigrants from Australia and the Caribbean, and the underground world of London's subway system.

Along with the city's gaiety and vitality, Laurence captures something of its postwar problems, under the guise of the adolescent thugs who serve the Great Rat, and the three dim-witted owls in Trafalgar Square. "Ugh," "Brr," and "Phew" are hilarious versions of pampered, racially prejudiced, disaffected youth who cannot be bothered to learn to read and who hate pigeons for no better reason than that they are not owls. It is interesting that fantasy frees Laurence to draw upon England's culture, since her relationship to that culture must surely have been affected by her strong, anti-imperial bias.

Another theme from *Long Drums* is echoed here. The Nigerian study, written during that country's bloody civil war, calls for "an alternative to tribalism." In *Jason's Quest*, the villainous rat-pack, in true romance fashion, remains unredeemably evil; its sneering, sadistic, black-booted members are scattered or imprisoned. But the other creatures, who are closer to the realism of comedy, are seen to be morally mixed. The cats, the owl, and the mole discover that there are good and bad versions of their species. They also find (in the growth of self-knowledge which belongs to comic form) that they are themselves mixtures, brave and cowardly, loving and selfish, generous and tactless: "there's good and bad in all tribes" (*JQ* 133, 203). The four friends belong, significantly, to species that are traditional enemies.

Much of the tale's success depends upon its characters. The two cats, frivolous Topaz and her rather glum Aunt Calico, are comic portraits of youth and maturity: the first vain, but capable of strength in a crisis; the second sensible, responsible, occasionally quick-tempered. Oliver's diffidence allows the shy child to identify with him. Jason's fear that he is inadequate for his task serves a similar purpose. Jason discovers that one can act more bravely than one feels, and that the will *to try* is all-important. The vivid minor characters, such as the retired queen of music hall theater or the wise old owl in Trafalgar Square, are comic yet sympathetic.

The swaggering Blades, with knives in their belts, are psychologically accurate portraits of bullies everywhere. They are manipulated by their leader, The Great Rat, through fear and intimidation: a parody of the allegiance that a questing knight freely offers to his Lord. The "G.R." usurps their power of independent thought, like C.S. Lewis's cannibalistic devil in *The Screwtape Letters,* and deserts them in an attempt to save his own skin. The rats are dedicated to disunity, and thrive on hate. Their business is fear. The Blades offer "protection" to the smaller animals, for a price, and hate the four friends for being "full of hope and the joys of spring, questing for cures and suchlike" (*JQ* 183). Laurence's use of the quaternity, here, may be an example of the influence of the Australian Patrick White, a novelist with whom she feels an affinity.[26] Together, the four friends comprise the characteristics of one well-rounded individual.

Laurence's sense of humor, which has been given less critical attention than it deserves, may be seen in top form in *Jason's Quest.* The underground mole city is a witty symbol for the human psyche, and "Thither," the moles' name for the outer world, a parody of human concepts of other planets. The title for Molanium's leader, the Venerable Mole, plays on the Venerable Bede, an eighth-century monk who wrote a history of Christianity in England. The moles' veneration of history and tradition parodies British culture and also Laurence's own emphasis on the importance of roots. Obviously, she is capable of poking fun at herself. Graffiti in the moles' Council Hall includes "Horatio erat sic," the learned language and the simplistic comment comically incongruous. Travel guides have their animal counterparts, as in The Smaller Edition of the London A to Z, offered to the four friends by a newsstand mouse. Well-known Christian hymns are parodied, not irreverently, in hymn titles such as "Molanium the Mighty, With Twenty Tunnels Blest" (a favorite with Jason's sisters, Grace, Beauty, and Faith). Here, as in her adult fiction, Laurence makes effective comic use of alliteration, onomatopoeia, hyperbole, incongruity, and puns.

With the exception of *Jason's Quest* English culture had little effect on Laurence's work. But Africa's impact on her literary vision was profound. In her Introduction to Adele Wiseman's novel, *Crackpot*, Laurence speaks of "the pain and interconnectedness of mankind, with our burden and necessity of ancestors and gods."[27] Foreign cultures revealed that interconnection. Laurence has emphasized that she began to write out of her Canadian experience only after living in and writing about Africa. In an unpublished article of 1969, she writes of her desire to reveal the long, gradual, and unending process of self-knowledge which for her began in Africa, "for it was really Africa which taught me to look at myself."[28] The themes that shape her Manawaka fiction—roots, ancestors, human complexity, acceptance of the Other, and the search for inner freedom and growth—these concerns first emerge in the less well known writing about Africa. The way to Manawaka lay through Ghana, Nigeria, and the searching desert sun.

The increasing politicization of that vision, given Laurence's antipathy to imperialism, was inevitable. The Nigerian study emphasizes that the artist is necessarily *engagé*. The concern for the Canadian Indian and Métis that forms part of Laurence's Canadian-based fiction may be seen in her reaction to Somaliland and Ghana, and to Nigerian literature. Individualism and anti-imperialism came naturally to a Scots-Canadian bred in the West. Laurence's remote ancestors had suffered Culloden; she herself had experienced the effrontery of remittance men, and the insidious dominance of a Central Canadian mentality which, from the nineteenth century well into the present one,

saw the West as a means of advancing the interests of the older
metropolitan centers.[29]

Laurence's youthful dislike of the political situation and
attitudes represented by imperialism was refined during her
years in Africa, with lasting consequences for her writing. Her
exposure to the psychology of colonization led her (as it had
led Mannoni) to far-reaching human insights. In Somaliland
she found pompous and whining sahibs who aroused her indignation as she had anticipated (*NW* 252, *HS* 37). She also found
courageous, altruistic whites whom she greatly admired. More
important, she found in imperialists and colonials alike that
*mixture* of characteristics that was to give depth and complexity
to her fictional characters.

It is difficult to know whether Laurence had been attracted
to African writers and countries because she suspected parallels
with her own writing, or whether her study of Nigerian literature affected her developing vision. The links appear to run both
ways. There are startling similarities between her views and
those of many Africans, including her views of time as a vital
continuum, of the physical world as penetrated by spirit, of
human life as a quest or journey, and of life's goodness despite
its tragic aspects. Writing of Nigerian drama and the African
world view it contains, Wole Soyinka contrasts its spirituality
with the Manichean nature of European traditions: "It merges
into the larger universe of wind, rain and ocean, growth and
regeneration, a humanistic faith and affirmation which is the
other face of tragic loss"; "life, present life, contains within it
manifestations of the ancestral, the living and the unborn....
Continuity for the Yoruba operates both through the cyclic
concept of time and the animist interfusion of all matter and
consciousness."[30] Perhaps Africa helped Laurence to separate
the Christian sense of a divine immanence in the natural world
from various dogmas she was unable to accept.

Laurence's main body of work, for which her African experience had prepared her, consists of five Canadian-set novels: *The
Stone Angel, A Jest of God, The Fire-Dwellers, A Bird in the
House,* and *The Diviners.* The case for calling her collection
of linked stories a novel will be argued later. These fictions
either take place in her fictional town of Manawaka, or else

this prairie town is present in the psyches of the characters who grew up there and who have moved to other parts of the country. Laurence's handling of *place*, a vitally important factor in the tradition of Canadian prairie fiction, is subsumed in her handling of *time*, since human consciousness of environment is inevitably linked to the personal experience of it in time. And both are inseparable from the formal problems of narrative *voice*, as Laurence emphasized in an article published in 1972. Time, in fiction, is not clock time but historical time, existential time. Laurence speaks of the heritage of memory from one generation to the next as the time-span of any fiction:

The time which is present in any story, therefore, must—by implication at least—include not only the totality of the characters' lives but also the inherited time of perhaps two or even three past generations, in terms of parents' and grandparents' recollections, and the much much longer past which has become legend, the past of a collective cultural memory. Obviously, not all of this can be conveyed in a single piece of prose. . . . Nevertheless, it is *there* because it exists in the minds of the characters.[31]

She proceeds to link fictional time, as defined above, to fictional character, emphasizing once again the independent life of the latter:

Once the narrative voice is truly established—that is, once the writer has listened, really listened, to the speech and idiom and outlook of the character—it is then not the writer but the character who, by some process of transferal, bears the responsibility for the treatment of time within the work. It is the character who chooses which parts of the personal past, the family past and the ancestral past have to be revealed in order for the present to be realized and the future to happen. This is . . . an expression of the feeling which I strongly hold about time—that the past and the future are both always present, *present* in both senses of the word, always now and always here with us.[32]

In an article that develops these statements, Sherrill Grace points to parallels between Laurence's understanding of human perception of the past and the theories of Henri Bergson and

Samuel Coleridge. Both Laurence and Bergson use the metaphor of psychic baggage. Laurence never mentions Bergson or Coleridge. Grace argues, not that they have influenced her, but that these critical comparisons are useful.[33] Like Bergson and Coleridge, Laurence sees the memory as organic and creative. Her protagonist Morag, refuting the popular misconception of a fixed past, observes that "everyone is constantly changing their own past."

Laurence may well be familiar with the theories of Bergson and Coleridge, but her work suggests that more direct influences have been literature, myth, and personal experience. Nigerian writers, with their emphasis on ancestors and roots, woke a deep fellow feeling in the Canadian woman. Her experience of spending the first two decades of her life in a town where her grandparents had been pioneers, and with relatives of several different generations, was very unlike the experience of someone growing up in a "nuclear" family. Authors who attract Laurence's critical attention frequently have similar preoccupations. The hero of Percy Janes's *House of Hate*, for example, is described as carrying "his entire family with him in his mind."[34]

Many critics have commented on the similarity between the concerns of Laurence's fiction and the theories of Carl Jung. Again, the parallels are implicit, unlike the openly acknowledged debt to Mannoni. Certainly, Jung's ideas of the collective unconscious and of archetypes have become part of our modern interpretation of literature; Laurence uses them, as we see in the foregoing quotation on time and on legend, as "the past of a collective cultural memory." Jung's system is vast and varied. However, Laurence is obviously concerned with the growth of the individual psyche towards wholeness, a process which Jung called individuation and which is central to his theoretical system.

The search for inner freedom, Laurence's primary theme, implies a quest structure. Her strong personal interest in this ancient literary form, and in myth, is indicated in her review of Margaret Atwood's novel, *Surfacing*. Laurence observes that the qualified hope of the novel's ending will surprise no one "who knows the meaning of *rites de passage* or who has read even fragments of *The Golden Bough, Beowulf* or, somewhat more recently, Amos Tutuola's *The Palmwine Drinkard."* Laurence continues:

> For it is the ancient Quest which is the journey here, the descent into the dark regions, where some special knowledge is gained, some revelation, before the return to the world of known creatures. The Woman does return, and will go back to the world of humans, but she has been given a knowledge of her own power, a power which had frightened her and which she had therefore denied, and a knowledge of her previous willingness to be a victim, a willingness which had of course also victimized others.[35]

The Quester also achieves the knowledge that "the ancient gods of forest and lake are by no means dead." "Rites of Passage" becomes the title of the fourth chapter of *The Diviners,* a section where Morag descends into dark regions and returns with knowledge of her own power. This chthonic experience underlies Nigerian drama and its world view.[36] All Laurence's protagonists make this journey, and descent; and all return successfully.

Laurence concludes that this theme, "humankind's quest for the archetypal parents, for our gods, for our own meanings in the face of our knowledge of the inevitability of death," is central to mythology, religion, and history.[37] Certainly, it is central to Laurence's fiction. Her protagonists struggle to achieve inner freedom, and all (not simply Morag) undergo rites of passage. Hagar wrestles with pride; Rachel, with fear; Stacey, with frustration; Vanessa, with her refusal to acknowledge her grandfather as part of herself; and Morag, with the fearful gift of creativity. The spiritual and psychological truth in Laurence's dramatization of these universal human experiences underlies the strength and beauty of her work.

CHAPTER 2

# Africa: Catalyst and Crucible

## I The World of Others

WE have already noted the close links between Laurence's African writing and her Manawaka cycle of Canadian-based fiction. In Africa, exposed to puzzlingly different peoples and cultures, Laurence's understanding of herself and her own culture took a great leap forward. In the introduction to her travel memoir, *The Prophet's Camel Bell*, she comments that the strangest glimpses in foreign lands may well be those you catch of yourself. In Africa she was a stranger, subject to the alienation that she depicts as central to human experience everywhere. In Africa her recurring themes of strangerhood, exile, bondage, freedom, and human dignity took shape and were first expressed, as Laurence herself notes, in nonfiction: "I began to write out of my own background only after I had lived some years away" (*HS* 11). Above all, Africa deepened her appreciation of human differences and of shared universals in a world of people whom she describes as being both different and similar to themselves. Africa was catalyst and crucible for much of Laurence's work.

*The Prophet's Camel Bell* (1963) is probably the most important work to come from Laurence's seven years in Africa. Her African writing includes her translations of Somali poetry and prose, a respectable first novel, a magnificent collection of short stories, and a study of Nigerian literature written later in the 1960s. But the travel memoir, record of Laurence's two years in the Somali desert, is central because it spans more than a decade in the writer's development. It is based on diaries from the early fifties, but is written out of a later maturity which

judges and frequently scorns the initial reactions.[1] It is thus
both a spiritual autobiography of a critical decade in Laurence's
life, and a portrait of a people valued for their ability to endure
incredible hardships with dignity and courage. It was written
at approximately the same time as the African fiction, and its
characters are sketched with a novelist's skill.

Africa cauterized Laurence's youthful naiveté and liberal
optimism. This is clear from her essays, the travel memoir, and
her Nigerian study. Soyinka, she declares, is no liberal humanist,
no naive idealist ignorant of human evil: "He is dealing with
the violence which is the other side of the coin of every personality, even the gentlest" (*LD* 32–33). Her conclusion to the
Nigerian study reiterates that neither Elechi Amadi nor Wole
Soyinka are liberal humanists, that these writers never suggest
that man improves with the passing of time "and will ultimately
be able to direct wisely and knowingly every facet of his life."
By implication, Laurence shares in the world view she ascribes
to these African writers who see mankind as vulnerable, paradoxical, struggling, growing, with "mystery at the centre of
being" (*LD* 184).

Africa also developed Laurence's interest in and sympathy
for the Canadian Indian. His degraded situation had been observed in her youth. It is treated peripherally in *The Stone Angel*
and *The Fire-Dwellers,* and becomes a significant theme in "The
Loons" and *The Diviners.* Finally, the phenomenon of imperialism, along with exposure to different cultures in Africa, bred
in Laurence that sensitivity to human difference, that compassion
for alienation and misunderstandings of a social as well as a
personal type, that mark all her writing. Africa confirmed Laurence in her intuition that "it was not a matter of intelligence
but of viewing the whole of life through different eyes" (*NW* 99).

Two essays, written in 1964 and 1975, reveal the links between the victims of imperialist policies and attitudes in Africa
and Canada, in Laurence's view. Her brief introductions to these
articles, for *Heart of a Stranger,* make the parallels very explicit.
Laurence describes "The Poem and the Spear" as more than an
essay on an early nationalist leader in Somaliland. It is also an
attempt to understand a tribal people's plight, "faced with imperialist opponents who do not possess superior values, but who

have greater material resources and more efficient weapons of killing. A long time later, this same theme came into my novel, *The Diviners,* in the portions which deal with the Highland clans and with the prairie Métis" (*HS* 44).

Elsewhere, she writes that exposure to the African tribal systems had given her an understanding of the Scottish clans. Similarly, the introduction to "Man of Our People," on George Woodcock's biography of Gabriel Dumont, stresses the relevance of the tragic struggles of the prairie Indian and Métis people in the nineteenth century to her life view and her writing, especially *The Diviners* (*HS* 204). Laurence's emotions are obviously warmly engaged in these autobiographical essays, which include very little of her usual ability to see both sides of a controversy.

Mahammed 'Abdille Hasan, the man the British called the Mad Mullah and against whom they campaigned for twenty years, is described by Laurence as a man fighting for his land and his religion, aided by "the strangest of all military weapons— poetry" (*HS* 45). A devout Muslim, the Sayyid (Noble Lord) objected to his people being governed by outsiders and infidels, indeed he believed that the ultimate aim of British colonization was the Christianizing of the Somalis. Inspired by the fiery epic poetry of this charismatic leader, the Somalis fought with spears and rifles against a foe with Maxim guns and, eventually, airborne bombers: "the British believed him mad because they had to believe him mad and had to believe themselves and their own policies impeccably sane" (*HS* 71).

The parallels with the nineteenth century Métis leader Riel hover unstated here but are emphasized at the end of the essay, where Laurence expands the point made in her preface: "There are many common threads: both were the leaders of communities of basically tribal and nomadic people (the camel herders of Somaliland; the Métis buffalo hunters of the Canadian prairies) faced with imperialist and colonialist powers which possessed *only one superior quality,* namely superior means of slaughter, and which intended to take over the people's land and the administration thereof" (*HS* 74, emphasis added). With her interest in oral cultures and in supra-rational qualities such as courage, endurance, and religious faith, Laurence refuses to grant preeminence to the culture with written records, rationalist traditions, and a superior technology.

Laurence read O. Mannoni's *Prospero and Caliban. A Study of the Psychology of Colonisation* in Canada in 1960. It clarified and confirmed her own experience in Africa. Moved by his book and by events in the Belgian Congo at this time, Laurence wrote "The Voices of Adamo," a story of an African youth who is cut adrift from family and village, taken into an African regiment as a drummer, and suddenly discharged. Adamo's murderous reaction to the "freedom" he sees as abandonment and betrayal helps to explain, as does Mannoni's study, the tragic violence that has often accompanied the passage of former colonies to independence.

Like *The Prophet's Camel Bell*, Mannoni's study stems from self-searching. Race relations in Madagascar in the 1940s provided the French ethnographer with parallels between the structure of society and the structure of individual personality. Using two complementary character types, Mannoni explains the "ingratitude" and hostility of native peoples towards their former masters. Mannoni sees the dependence complex and the inferiority complex as present in everyone in rudimentary form, but most Europeans repress one and most colonized people the other.[2] The colonial administrator acts paternally, thereby invoking the subconscious hostility that Freud associated with the father figure. When a native is detached from tribal life, secured to a new master, then abandoned, his oedipal instincts issue in hostility and violence.

Mannoni portrays the colonial European as someone secretly convinced of his own inferiority, needing the homage of dependents as ego reassurance, and projecting on those dependents his inner guilts and fears. This fits Laurence's portrait of expatriates in *This Side Jordan* and her African stories, despite the fact that the novel and many of the stories were written before 1960.

Mannoni strikes another chord which is basic to Laurence's work: the validity of the Other, the difficulty yet the importance of understanding other individuals and cultures. Mannoni writes: "I saw that the problem for human beings, however much they differed from one another, was to acquire, not the ability but

the *will* to understand each other. It is as difficult to see something of oneself in all men as it is to accept oneself completely
as one is."[3] In Laurence's travel narrative she quotes Mannoni's
reference to the colonial's lack of awareness of "the world of
Others, a world in which Others have to be respected" (*NW* 277).
Her African writing in general reveals her advances in self-
acceptance and understanding, advances fostered by being a
stranger in another continent.

## II   Somaliland: Strange Glimpses of the Self

Laurence takes the title for her translations of Somali poetry
and prose from two lines in a Somali *gabei* which seem to
suggest this literature in its entirety. For a nomadic people with
few possessions and no written language, Laurence writes, oral
literature is both refuge and riches, truly "a tree / For poverty
to shelter under." She has worked from literal translations, para-
phrase, and dramatic renditions where facial expressions and
gestures helped to convey the original meaning. *A Tree for
Poverty* is the first collection of Somali literature to be translated
into English. Her travel narrative, and the preface to a 1965
essay on Somali poetry, acknowledges the help of friends Musa
Galaal and B.W. Andrezejewski (*HS* 77).

In the Preface to the second edition, in 1970, Laurence calls
her translations "amateurish." Be that as it may, the collection
tells us something of Laurence as well as of Somali literature.
The autobiographical aspect of fiction is a commonplace, but
little has been written about the autobiographical element in
literary criticism, perhaps because critics are reluctant to admit
the subjectivity of their profession. As with physical travel, the
journey into literature is an interior one. Laurence's first criticism
reveals some of her literary values, her sensitivity to other people
and cultures, and her interest in the sociopsychological conditioning of women as a group. The latter factors culminate dra-
matically in *The Diviners*.

Laurence's Introduction sketches the conditions in which this
literature has been produced and its national characteristics.
She describes the Somalis as a complex, imaginative, sensitive,
and emotional people, "a nation of poets." Literature is inevi-

tably predominant in a country devoid of almost all the materials needed for the other arts, and in a culture with religious taboos against the making of idolatrous images. Somaliland attracted Laurence's interest and admiration for many reasons, but especially for the courage of its hard-pressed people, many of whom can never defeat the killing environment of heat, drought, and poverty.

She goes on to summarize the two chief types of Somali poetry, and its characteristics of rhythm, alliteration, and compression. The short *belwo* (literally, "a trifle") is a love poem, simple and lyrical, sung to a few well-known tunes. The long lines of the more complex *gabei* are chanted. *Gabei* are narrative and intellectual poems dealing with love, philosophy, politics, and war: it would have been *gabei*, "the strangest of all military weapons," that the Sayyid wrote to inspire his followers. The *gabei* poet must be, in Somali terms, a learned man, well versed in Muslim theology and religious history as well as in the lore of the land. Laurence praises the richness of Somali language, its ability to compress a great deal of information into a simple word, and its closeness to everyday speech and life.

Women's poetry, in Somaliland, is written by women for women, since they are not present in the tea shops or around campfires where male poets recite. The language barrier prevented Laurence from obtaining any women's poetry. Another difficulty was a certain puritan reticence on the part of her Somali friends who paraphrased the literature for her. Laurence concludes that two distinct literary cultures, male and female, exist side by side. She notes that women's status, in tribal and religious traditions, is infinitely inferior to that of men: "The double standard is extremely strong."[4] The drudgery of life after marriage quickly destroys a young woman's beauty. Subsequent power, which is no less real for being indirect, is purchased with shrewdness, wit, and malice: "The change, in a few years, from the graceful lovely girl to the withered, shrill-voiced matron is terrible to see."

Laurence's attraction to other cultures, and her respect for them, are clear from her first published work. Somaliland, as she notes in the 1970 Preface, was her first contact with another culture, and taught her a great deal about "the validity of human differences." In the Introduction to the translations, she observes that basic differences between cultures should not be underestimated. She applies this general principle to the place of camels in Somali poetry. Camels play a major role in Somali life, and thus very naturally supply images for poetry. She recognizes, with wry humor, that the image of a lover as a sick camel translates poorly across cultures.

Somali prose, divided into stories translated directly or freely paraphrased, occupy two-thirds of the collection. Some are Arabic in origin. The stories are likely to strike European or North American readers as curious, grotesque, even pointless. But Laurence links their literary techniques and character types to local conditions. She notes that the type of unfortunate little man occurs in the stories of people who live uncertain, poverty-stricken lives (cf. the *schliemiel* in Yiddish tales): "laughing at him, we laugh at ourselves, and weeping for him, we weep for all the tragedy we know exists."

Paradoxical contrasts in behavior are termed Eastern, proper to a locale where absolute power and wealth coexist with extreme poverty; where cleverness is envied, cruelty accepted, and independence necessary to survival. Laurence praises Somali literature for its realism, "a realism that recognizes the presence of both good and evil in the world and in the individual." We find, later, a similar perspective in her book on Nigerian literature, where Nigerian writers are praised for having this kind of realism. Neepawa had already exposed Laurence to the vagaries and passions of human nature.

Jacob's wrestling with the angel of God, a favorite and recurring metaphor in Laurence's work, appears first in her comments on Somali literature. The folktales feature ethical paradoxes, characters who have both guile and genuine piety. This is ascribed to the rigors of desert life, and linked to biblical stories, particularly Old Testament ones. The same Jacob who was beloved of God and who wrested a blessing from His angel increased his flocks by means of magic and by cheating Laban (*T* 27, 72). Hagar Shipley, as she wrestles with her son, her conscience, and her God, is in strange and moving company when we remember this Old Testament story, and the ways in which it becomes image and analogue in Laurence's work.

Many of the portraits in *The Prophet's Camel Bell*, such as the venerable Somali who extended hospitality to the Laurences after they had been lost for several days, resemble characters in the folktales. After being disappointed by the generous old man's sanctimonious pride, Laurence recognized the folly of her expectations: "He was not perfectly designed and lifeless like a cardboard cut-out figure" (*NW* 92).

The travel narrative cautions that "the strangest glimpses" of creatures in distant lands will be sudden revelations of the self. The quest for self-knowledge provides a subtext for the book. The verse from Exodus, which enjoins that strangers be treated as oneself and which is later set as epigraph to Laurence's essays, occupies a prominent place in the first chapter of a book filled with metaphors of travel, exile, and the search for the Promised Land of inner freedom. En route to Somaliland, where she would be a stranger in a strange land, Laurence read for the first time the five books of Moses. The themes and metaphors of the Pentateuch, which belong to desert experience, stayed with her in Somaliland, and thereafter.

The timeless desert with its sand and thorn trees taught Laurence quietness, and caution. With that note of self-mockery that often belongs to her fictional narrators, she describes her efforts to arrange their new home, and contrasts her buzzing with the desert calm: "I might enter its quietness or not, just as I chose. Hesitantly at first, because it had been my pride to be as perpetually busy as an escalator, I entered" (*NW* 34). Local wildlife concealed unsuspected dangers. She began to see that the quiet hills required a person to tread carefully. Especially with people. Her initial brashness, a verdict Laurence applies to her behavior when she was new to Africa, often failed to elicit the desired information. Two Somali teachers politely declined to answer questions on Somali sex life: "All at once the brash tone of my voice was conveyed to my own ears, and I was appalled" (*NW* 46).

Gradually, Laurence perceived her mistake: "People are not oyster shells, to be pried at"; "I no longer questioned people in this glib fashion" (*NW* 50, 78). Somali medical problems provided other glimpses of the chimera, self. Did Laurence *need* their gratitude? Repulsed by seeing herself "playing doc-

tor," she decided she would do nothing in this connection, then
recognized this was over-reacting: "Would I do nothing simply
because I could not do everything? The searching sun of the
Jilal exposed not only the land but the heart as well" (*NW* 77).

Over and over, in analyzing incident and character, the travel
book illustrates Laurence's sensitivity to other ways of seeing
and feeling. The lack of such sensitivity is part of the colonial
mentality. To illustrate: why should Africans resent someone
who feels friendly towards them? "But they looked at me from
their own eyes, not mine" (*NW* 32). What does it feel like to
offer a cup of water to a woman whose child may be dead the
next day from thirst? "What I felt, as I looked into her face,
was undeniable and it was not pity. It was something entirely
different, some sense of knowing in myself what her anguish
had been and would be, as she watched her child's life seep
away for lack of water to keep it alive" (*NW* 81). In a recent
essay on Laurence's travel writing, George Woodcock calls this
incident "an admirable example of the traveller's perceptiveness
and narrative skill," one which takes us into the center of
Laurence's mind.[5] Her ability to write great fiction is due in
part to her imaginative comprehension of the Other, an ability
nurtured by her African experience.

Woodcock's title, "Many Solitudes," points to the novelist's
sense of human differences, and to her determination to respect
the varied attitudes and points of view which reflect them.
Woodcock calls *The Prophet's Camel Bell* one of the finest and
most evocative travel books ever written by a Canadian. He sees
it as an intermediate genre between the novel and the ordinary
travel narrative, and links it to her fiction by theme and structure:
"her novels are all in a sense travel books, vividly descriptive
in terms of environment, involving a great deal of journeying,
both inner and outer, and coming at the end to those self-
transforming realizations that are the destinations of all internal
voyaging."[6]

The character sketches in the travel memoir do indeed read
like stories. The latter half is devoted largely to individual
portraits drawn from three cultural groups: Italians, British,
and Somali. Each is shaped so as to reveal the person's essential
loneliness or psychic exile, the many solitudes of Woodcock's

apt phrase. This shaping reflects a novelist's skill. And like the characters in *This Side Jordan* and *The Tomorrow-Tamer*, they are caught between their old world and a new one only partially understood.

Many of the Italians had come to the Protectorate from Ethiopia, where they had gone as settlers in the 1930s after the Italian takeover. They were largely mechanics and road builders, living without wives in a settlement of men. They were socially nonexistent to the British (as in the story, "The Perfume Sea"), but were dependent on them for jobs. Personally, they were deeply committed to Africa, and out of touch with the country of their birth. In an independent Somali, where would they go? Laurence reflects:

> It is unlikely that most of them would stay on—the Somalis would not have the money to employ them, and they probably would not want to stay anyway, for the bitterness between themselves and the Somalis will not easily be eradicated. . . . Some may have gone back to Italy, to the families who are now strangers to them. And this may be the worst of all—after so many years, to find they are once again exiles, this time in their own land. (*NW* 184)

Individual chapters are devoted to the four Somalis who served the Laurences as translator, cook, mechanic, and driver. Hersi, whom Laurence calls their quick-thinking and stutter-tongued interpreter, was nicknamed Half-tongue by his own people. Hersi was initially reluctant to speak of Somali literature ("Stories? What on earth were those? 'We are not having such things presently times,' he would murmur evasively") until he discovered that a respected Somali poet had revealed some of the folktales and poetry to his employer. From then on Hersi became one of Laurence's chief sources, a teller of tales. Not content with telling, he would act them out, "taking on the characters like cloaks."

Hersi's "exile" evolved from his limited education, which meant that his prospects of employment were always insecure. Reading and writing were his chief accomplishments, yet his imagination remained largely tribal: "He needed an established status in both worlds, but he achieved it in neither" (*NW* 191).

He lives for us through the grotesque lyricism of his English, his dramatic rendering of the folktales, his humor, tolerance, and courage.

Hersi's initial reluctance stemmed in part from his conviction, common among the Somalis, that the British were devoid of emotions and (there being very few British children in the Protectorate) uninterested in sex. They would therefore, Hersi concluded, be incapable of appreciating Somali literature. Ironically, the British held a similar view of the Somalis.

The Laurences' cook was the first person with whom they spoke in Somaliland and the last they saw when they left. Son of a sailor, Mohamed had supported himself as a servant since the age of ten. In one of those vignettes which continue to haunt the mind, Laurence debunks the facile belief that people do not miss what they have never known. The uneducated Mohamed had a war-orphan friend whose schooling was being paid for by the government: "Mohamed brought Abdillahi over one day to meet us. Abdillahi, whose English was excellent, began to discuss the Gezira Scheme in the Sudan, a project about which he had been reading. Mohamed, who could not follow the conversation at all, and who had never heard of the Gezira Scheme, stood very much apart, his face vacant as sand. He never brought Abdillahi to see us again" (NW 197).

Mohamed is the center of several tragicomic episodes which Laurence found sobering. Her attempt to teach him reading and writing, at his request, was a dismal failure. Both had grossly underestimated the difficulties: "What else had I underestimated?" A feud between Mohamed and his assistant left the Laurences angry and confused: "We felt ourselves to be misunderstood, and we knew that we had misunderstood both of them." They fired the assistant knowing that justice had not been done.

Mohamed's marital difficulties tempt Laurence to assume that the problems are similar to those in the lovelorn columns of North American newspapers. But the cook has married without the consent of his tribe, or his bride's tribe. In a harsh environment the tribe is the nomad's protection. Mohamed has been away from his tribe for years, but it remains the only community with any real meaning for him. His marital dispute is settled by tribal elders, while the Laurences suppress their uneasy knowledge that Mohamed wishes to substitute them for his tribe and family. After they have left Somaliland, they hear that Mohamed has become a union organizer for domestic servants. He had been compelled to seek the elders' blessing, but could not return to their ways: another exile.

Arabetto, half Arab half Somali, had more "feeling" for machinery than the other drivers and mechanics, perhaps because he had grown up in a town. Earlier, Laurence has developed the idea that familiarity with machinery in general constitutes a kind of subculture; Jack Laurence recalls his childhood experiences with the insides of cars and clocks. Machinery has always been part of his life. Transforming desert tribesmen into mechanics is like "trying to construct a bridge that would cross centuries and oceans in a single span" (*NW* 24), a metaphor relevant to "The Tomorrow-Tamer" story.

To the Somalis, Arabetto is an outsider. He has no tribe, a vital difference. He prefers Arab to Somali culture, and modern Egyptian films to the folktales of either group. Laurence recounts without comment the melodramatic plots of the former, and Arabetto's enthusiastic response. There is humor and pathos in these fantasies. Two scenes fix Arabetto in our minds. The first shows the youth alone at the camp's edge, cranking his beloved Gramophone and humming lines from his favorite tune: "Hurry, hurry/Fly like a bird—." The second is Arabetto's one-room, mud-floor house, with embroidered spreads and pillows done by his wife: "In the midst of the traditional designs were two streamlined cars. Whenever I think of Arabetto, I recall those embroidered cars, and the quick and syncopated song he so often played on the tinny old gramophone out in the desert" (*NW* 217).

One relationship proved tragic. Abdi, a survivor of the now-legendary Somaliland Camel Corps, was assigned by the government to drive their Land-Rover. His family lived with his tribe, and he regularly lost children and kinsmen during the terrible droughts. Laurence saw two men in the old warrior: one humble, one proud; one gentle and compassionate, one fierce and violent. The anger which his religion forbade him to express when his tribesmen died for lack of water might be vented on beating a snake or a trapped hyena to a bloody pulp. After his angry departure, she wrote: "He is courage and pride and anger writ large. Perhaps his is the face of Africa—inscrutable to the last" (*NW* 229).

When a flash flood left the Laurences stranded in the desert, Abdi got help from hostile tribesmen and found the way out, thus saving their lives. This meant different things in different cultures. Henceforth, Abdi's demands on the Laurences grew. He reacted to acts that Jack found necessary and fair (such as the firing of a relative of Abdi who had proved to be a poor worker) as if he had been personally betrayed. Laurence attempts to cope with her own feelings of rejection by her usual therapy, writing. She recorded that perhaps Abdi had always hated them, because the hardships of his people's lives made it impossible for them to see Europeans as people, and because reliance on the traditional hatred of the imperialists made him feel secure.

Later, Laurence applies Mannoni's theories to Abdi's behavior. In his eyes, their brush with death established a bond, a tacit agreement of mutual loyalty which Abdi felt had been repudiated by the firing of his relative:

His later and increased demands, which seemed so outrageous then, seem in retrospect to have been a frantic effort to prove that the bond still existed. . . . Even the words which we at first took as compliments and then as unscrupulous flattery, now seem to have been neither, to have been in fact almost totally unrelated to us as individuals. *You are a king. You are a queen.* If a man must seek a power at court, must he not also seek to reassure himself that the chosen official is indeed a strong one, capable of giving protection? (*NW* 230)

She concludes, ruefully, that neither party understood the other, and that the actions of each were inevitable. Abdi will never know her benediction on an old warrior whose "truest and most terrible battle, like all men's, was with himself" (*NW* 231).

Towards the end of "The Imperialists" chapter, Laurence expands the brief comments on Mannoni prompted by Abdi's behavior. Both Laurence and Mannoni see in the refusal to extend mutual respect an infantile escapism combined with an urge to dominate. This psychological pattern explains the facile superiority of the racist *and* the sentimental idealizing of native cultures, the latter stemming from the child's dream of a world uniquely his. In her view, the imperialists failed to understand either others or themselves, and the two failures were interconnected. What Mannoni terms "primitive" projections, and Laurence, "the need for a fine and private place this side of the grave," distort the real world and block human communication. Both writers broaden the concept of imperialism, which includes racism, into a universal human tendency: *we are all imperialists* until forced to confront these fantasies.

The realities of thirst, famine, and desert hardships forced Laurence to abandon what she calls "the game of healer," or the notion of Abdi as faithful retainer. Abdi the man had outlooks very different from those of the Laurences, but outlooks "valid for him" (*NW* 279).

Despite the generosity of Laurence's views at the conclusion of the chapters on Abdi and the imperialists, her admitted bias makes for certain patterns in this connection. In *This Side Jordan* there are no admirable imperialists, but there are British characters with whom we can sympathize. The stories collected in *The Tomorrow-Tamer,* however, offer a much more varied cast of European characters. Matthew, in "The Drummer of All the World," is naive, but not domineering nor secretly convinced of his own inferiority. Will Kittredge, the architect in "The Merchant of Heaven," is a sensible and likable man whose first-person narrative voice seems close to that of his creator's. Violet Nedden, the schoolteacher in "The Rain Child," is a less naive version of Matthew. And the apolitical Italian hairdresser in "The Perfume Sea" is certainly no imperialist.

When colonials are seen as a group, as they are in the novel set in Accra, or in the Hargeisa Club in Somaliland, Laurence reacts negatively. She freely admits her bias near the beginning of the Somali narrative: "my feeling about imperialism was very simple—I was against it. I had been born and had grown up in a country that once was a colony, a country which many people believed still to be suffering from a colonial outlook, and like most Canadians I took umbrage swiftly at a certain type of English who felt they had a divinely bestowed superiority over the lesser breeds without the law" (*NW* 21).

Confronted with individuals, however, Laurence readily acknowledges that many of them do not fit the stereotype: "It is easy enough to label someone from a distance, but how could you possibly think of a man as an imperialist when he told you, sorrowfully and in perplexity, that he tried to start a football team but the Somalis didn't seem to take to the game?" (*NW* 24). Alf, the first Englishman they met there, was dedicated to teaching the Somalis to drive and maintain trucks. He was oblivious of the cultural chasms. Laurence came to believe that his ignorance mitigated his discouragements, and that there was a heroic quality about the man.

Similarly, the chapter on imperialists is largely devoted to portraits of individuals who do not fit the type. It opens with a scene resembling musical comedy. "Medals sprouting like corsages," the British are gathered to celebrate with due ceremony the English monarch's official birthday. After the comedy of their pretensions, Laurence cuts sharply to a biting attack on sahib-type behavior. She concludes that this type of person is as dead as the dinosaur: "R.I.P."

Very much alive, however, are the Baron, the Padre, the Administrator, and a host of colorful characters who live for us in Laurence's descriptions. She accepted the elderly Church of England clergyman because he neither patronized nor condescended to the Somalis. Both he and the tribesmen lived by faith, and understood one another. The British feared that this frail man in cast-off clothing would be found dead of thirst or sunstroke, but the Somalis regarded him as a holy man and fed him in their encampments.

Matthew was an unusual District Commissioner who spoke fluent Somali and understood the complexities of tribal law and organization. He frequently acted as conciliator. Laurence tells an incredible story of Matthew's encounter with angry tribesmen who feared that the poison bait set for locusts would kill their grazing camels. To persuade them it would not, Matthew ate a handful of the poisoned bran. The tribesmen, who had attempted to murder him, dispersed, and later offered him the full blood-compensation of a hundred camels: " 'I like them,' he said quite frankly, 'because they are so bloody-minded.' He valued in them the very qualities which many Englishmen abhorred—their argumentativeness, their passionate dramatization of events, the indestructible pride of these desert people" (*NW* 270).

The Administrator, second to the Governor, appeared to Laurence initially as a cold, restrained man, simply doing his job. She discovered her error when the Administrator reacted with unexpected intensity to the manuscript of her translations. The passage that he felt must be published was a description of the tribesmen's harsh and uncertain existence during the drought. Laurence began to realize his deep attachment to the land, and her own ignorance. He and his wife, who had served in government desert camps for destitute tribesmen, would be exiles when they returned to England from a land that had become their home.

Leaving Somaliland, Laurence shared their feeling of regret, the product of "unwisely loving" a land where she would always remain a stranger. This ambivalence, and her general treatment of imperialists, may be placed beside the idealistic attitudes that originally took the Laurences to Somaliland, and that may well have been shared by other Europeans in colonial situations. These motives included an attraction to a pioneer style of living and the desire (Laurence speaks of a *need*) to do a job "that plainly needed doing . . . a job in which the results of the individual's work could be clearly perceived, as they rarely could in Europe or America" (*NW* 5).

The portrait of women in the travel narrative is similar to the one found in her Introduction to the translations. A harsh life rapidly ages Somali women. Romantic love, celebrated in the lyric *belwo*, is exceedingly short-lived in the face of a life of drudgery, caring for flocks and children, and setting up and dismantling the huts whenever the tribe moved camp. Both tribal and religious tradition accorded woman a low status, and a sharp tongue was often her only protection. Women appeared to be shy, but proved "meek as Antigone, meek as Medea." Ritual practices at puberty caused many women to have pain and physical problems for life. It was customary for women to be beaten, and a husband who treated his wife with unusual consideration would be suspect (*NW* 18, 78, 111, 216).

*The Prophet's Camel Bell*, like Laurence's African fiction, is remarkable for its handling of language as well as its revelation of character. The style is clean, at times bare. Frequent dialogue reveals the accuracy of Laurence's ear and her ability to portray character through the idiosyncrasies of speech. There are passages of great poetic beauty, such as the description of Zeilah, "place of exile," with its ghost-haunted Residency, or the valley of the candelabra trees (*NW* 61, 130–35). Only extended quotation could do justice to the beauty of either of these scenes, where the atmosphere (whether of the valley's peace or the Residency's anguish) is built through accumulation of detail. The power of Laurence's prose to move a restrained man such as the senior administrator has already been noted.

The style includes wordplay and humorous analogies, some of which will prove characteristic. The sparrow becomes a favorite symbol of cheeky defiance. The starting traveler is "as innocent of the hard earth as the fledgling sparrow." Evening mosquitoes are "thick as porridge," a curious conjoining of cultures. Desert dining involves beetles like croutons on the soup, and the difficulties of distinguishing "insects from onions." Laurence's style has a wide emotional range, and the capacity to move easily between tragedy and comedy, irony and romance. Her descriptions sparkle with paradox, epigram, and insight. George Woodcock's judgment could dispense with its qualifier. This is one of the finest and most evocative travel books ever written.

III   *"Between Yesterday and Today"*

*This Side Jordan* and *The Tomorrow-Tamer* are set in Ghana in the 1950s, in or near its capital, Accra, "this city where you could feel tomorrow being reached for."[7] Both show Africans and Europeans subject to tremendous psychological pressure as the cultural situations that prevailed for their parents or in their youth undergo rapid changes. Laurence's characters are pulled two ways, like the victims of a medieval torture rack. The past commands much of their emotions; the future, their hopes. The mythic equivalents of this social and psychological situation, in the biblical terms which supply many of Laurence's recurring metaphors, are Eden and the Promised Land, the ancient Israelites' goal as they journeyed through the desert wilderness. Nathaniel, the African protagonist of *This Side Jordan*, thinks that the apparently successful whites could not possibly understand "what it was to need a mouthful of the promised land's sweetness now, now, while you still lived" (*TSJ* 208).

The novel's form is traditional. The narrative voice is impersonal, although this third-person voice is broken into by the African protagonist's inner dialogues, introduced with a dash. The chief structural device is parallelism—of two contrasting social groups (African and European), two protagonists, and two narrative sequences, one for each set of characters. Initially, Laurence presents these groups in separate chapters. As the novel progresses, their affairs become intertwined.

Laurence believes that the device of alternating chapters to convey the African and European points of view is not entirely satisfactory, but serves to avoid an omniscient narrator ("that particular method always seemed unworkable for me") and to present the very different viewpoints of the two groups. By 1969, she had come to think that "the novel contains too much of Nathaniel's inner monologues"; that Nathaniel had "a certain authenticity" but perhaps less than she had believed earlier; and that in the end, she was able to understand the Europeans best, "even though my sympathy with colonial Europeans was certainly minimal or even non-existent."[8]

Laurence read Mannoni only after her African novel was completed and on the verge of publication. Nevertheless, her views on the colonial administrators (in this case, members of a British textile firm) are very similar to those of the French ethnographer. Laurence depicts the Britishers as misfits, whose conscious or subconscious sense of inferiority has led them to seek a land, and a situation, where they will be dominant and appear superior. Courage is one of the few virtues she grants them. Laurence's fictional Britishers may enlist our sympathies, but rarely our admiration.

Her colonials are a beleaguered group of exiles who meet in one another's homes, or their club, to talk, drink, and mourn "the lost island home for which they longed but to which they did not want to return until they were old" (*TSJ* 140). James Thayer, the firm's African manager, loves Africa but considers Africans to be children. He has never seen any reason to change his first impressions, formed some thirty years earlier in dealing with illiterate clerks or primitive tribesmen. The rigidity of James's convictions is by turns comic, pathetic, and frightening. Orders from London to speed up Africanization reduce him to "a weird ballet of rage, like something from a Punch-and-

Judy show" (*TSJ* 92). The simile is driven home, two pages later, when his accountant realizes that fear, as well as anger, has been the puppet master. As the noose tightens, James is seen as bumbling and pompous, "a mole-like ledger-keeper, had he stayed in England," but in Ghana a frail and balding Jupiter, "subduing and chastening his erring children" (*TSJ* 179). His wife's story of James's bravery under fire, twenty years earlier, does little to alter this impression.

Cora Thayer is a pathetic creature who hates and fears Africa, has tried to make her home a fortress against it, and collects remnants of brocade to fill the emptiness of a childless existence. In one of those passages which (like Laurence's portrait of the Highlanders' trauma following their chieftains' betrayal of them in the late eighteenth and early nineteenth centuries) reveals a remarkable capacity to identify with the Other's pain, she sketches Cora's future after her husband's premature retirement has driven them back to England on an inadequate pension:

The fall of a dynasty. All at once, he could see her in the hateful flat, too. It would be small, of necessity, and James would clutter it with the ebony heads and the brass figurines she loathed. James, obsessed with Africa's rejection of him, would prophesy doom. . . . James would have no one else to talk to, and she would hear it all, day after day, until he or she died. She would be tired all the time, for physical work was now completely alien to her. The flat would get drabber as she slowly stopped trying. The tines of the fork would be clotted with egg yolk. . . . The sinks would be brown as tea. She would wear shapeless cardigans and heavy shoes, and would cry because she could not get the coal fire lighted. (*TSJ* 130)

The Cunninghams, Bedford and Helen, are an equally pathetic couple. Bedford's military manner has given him the nickname of The Knight, but this armored man is a lead soldier who turns to alcohol to evade problems. His wife reveals that he had been fired from a petty job in England: "He can do a little of everything and not enough of anything." Her own fears are twofold: the fear of staying in a land full of dangers for small children, and the fear of being forced to leave. Despite his disastrous career, the Cunninghams aspire to send their son to an expensive private school so that he can repeat the pattern and become a gentlemanly relic of a dead age.

None of Laurence's imperialists are depicted with religious motivations. This aspect of imperialism is shown through the thoughts of the African schoolteacher. Laurence has separated religion and economics, which were closely linked in the mythology of empire, in order to imply that the links were fraudulent. White hypocrisy on this front is presented through Nathaniel's reflections on the slave trade: "–'take the gold from golden Guinea. Take the gold and bring them to the Lamb. Take the timber and let the light of Holiness shine upon them. Take the diamonds and be sure their souls are saved. Tut, tut, our black bretheren, surely you do not want to lay up riches on earth, where moth and rust doth corrupt?'" (*TSJ* 211–12). Nathaniel's inner dialogues also carry Laurence's conviction that the missionaries tried to destroy African culture, and helped to wipe out indigenous art by forbidding image-making. This recurring charge, or implication, is qualified only once, when Nathaniel thinks he has overstated the case: "Now a hundred details and qualifications came to his mind" (*TSJ* 42).

Curiously, it is Victor Edusei, an African journalist educated at the London School of Economics, who voices the prophecy that there will be less justice under black rule. After Independence, he warns Nathaniel, there will be unbelievable oppression, blacks suppressing blacks. He goes on to blame this situation, by implication, on the colonial administrators who have fostered a slave mentality. Slaves are ruthless, and want only to hold the whip hand. Once again, the psychological analysis of the situation agrees with Mannoni.

Obviously, not all colonial administrators are pathetic misfits, masking fear with bluster. Laurence's anti-imperialist bias is, in some ways, as rigid and semi-rational as the ideas held by her fictional imperialists. In a chapter called "The Imperialists" in *The Prophet's Camel Bell*, Laurence speaks of people so desperately uncertain of their own worth, and of their ability to cope at home, "that they were forced to seek some kind of mastery in a place where all the cards were stacked in their favour and where . . . they could avoid the possibility of being scornful or fearful of anything within themselves" (*NW* 251). Yet her portraits of Britishers such as the top administrative officer in Somaliland and his wife in no way fit her stereotype. Laurence writes, in the travel memoir, of the heroic work done in the *miskiin* (destitute camps) by this Englishwoman, work which required much greater courage than Laurence's own. Carl Berger's study of the intellectual climate of Canadian imperialism in the late nineteenth and early twentieth centuries helps to put the matter in perspective. In a chapter entitled "Mission," Berger analyzes the religious idealism that infused the imperialist mind and that presented the British Empire as "a providential agency, the greatest secular instrument for good in the world."[9] Canadian statesmen such as G. M. Grant and George Parkin saw the white man's burden as a civilizing mission, as great as ancient Israel's, to carry the ideals, peace, and order of white society to "inferior" races. The fact that imperialists with these convictions were wrong in many respects does not carry the necessary corollary that they were hypocritical and inept. Berger's analysis helps us to understand a man like James Thayer, and his comic-tragic beliefs, including his statement that no "decent" white man would work under African administrators.

The chief protagonist in a large cast is Nathaniel Amegbe, the only character whose thoughts are revealed directly. His interior monologues, which were criticized by the publisher's reader and by some critics, are convincing, since their relative formality is consistent both with their serious religious content and with Nathaniel's own research into the history of his people.[10] Nathaniel began life in a village as the son of the chief's drummer, a position equivalent to that of priest. Mission-educated since the age of seven, he is now a tormented young man who possesses two religions, two cultures, and who finds himself "between yesterday and today."

Nathaniel's inner dialogues are both poignant and poetic, and his divided state is shared by almost every character in the novel. Laurence herself has known the pain of wrestling with an inherited faith. Nathaniel finds that he sometimes believes, sometimes disbelieves; that he *mourns* "the gods strangled by my hand"; that he doubts heaven but fears hell, is "the unwilling bondsman of two masters," has "no home," and is a man "over whom both gods had fought and both had lost" (*TSJ* 69, 73, 107, 113, 167, 242).

Nathaniel teaches in a discreditable school with the ironic

name of Futura Academy. His employer takes advantage of his lack of qualifications. After years of penury, and honesty, he accepts gifts in return for recommending two boys for employment in the British textile firm, and is humiliated by the disclosure of the bribes. Ashamed and despairing, Nathaniel decides to return to his village and take the offer of a job as clerk to the local chief. This decision is reversed after the birth of his child in a local hospital. His son Joshua and the city's culture represent the promise of the future. This is imaged, in an evangelical sermon, as crossing the River Jordan to take Jericho. Nathaniel resolves that his God is the God of his own soul, and that his home is "here, here, here" (*TSJ* 275). He is himself en route to the Promised Land, and his son will surely "cross Jordan."

Johnnie Kestoe, the firm's young accountant, is the focus for events among the expatriates and provides the opportunity for Laurence to create much of the novel's parallel structure. Nathaniel's guilt follows the affair of the bribes, and Johnnie's his betrayal of his colleagues to the London partner who comes to investigate the progress of Africanization. Guilt and anger drive Nathaniel and Johnnie to an African nightclub. They fight, and Johnnie, in exchange for a promise to let the matter drop, is given a night with an African girl.

His ambivalence towards Africans, a mingled sexual attraction and repulsion, has been clear from the beginning. Johnnie re-enacts the rape of a continent upon this young virgin from the north of Ghana who speaks no English and who has been sold into prostitution as her ancestors were sold into slavery: "She was a continent and he an invader, wanting both to possess and destroy." The symbolism is blatant here, but the episode has emotional intensity and authenticity. Laurence's themes of freedom/bondage, communication/isolation, and the value and dignity of the Other all converge in this scene. Has she been sold by her family, or stolen, or come freely? With no common language, Johnnie will never know. "She was herself and no other. She was someone, a woman who belonged somewhere and who for some reason of her own had been forced to seek him here in this evil-smelling cell, and through him, indignity and pain" (*TSJ* 233).

In the end, Johnnie faces the prospect of overseeing the firm's Africanization, and of working in close cooperation with his old enemy, Victor Edusei. Johnnie is present in the Ghanian hospital at the birth of his baby. He finds that blood can mean life as well as death, a veiled reference to the tragic abortion that ended his mother's life in a London slum. He asks his wife Miranda to call their baby Mary, his mother's name. The story of Johnnie's youth, given in much less detail than Nathaniel's, suggests that racial hatreds begin in childhood traumas. Earlier, Miranda's slow, painful labor has acted to heal the rift between her and the Amegbes. Nathaniel has not been touched by her liberal goodwill and polite interest in things African, but is moved by the knowledge "that she could feel humiliation and anguish like himself" (*TSJ* 263). The two babies, born at the same time in the same place to African and white parents, symbolize a future where the races will work together in harmony.

The kindly, naive Miranda may remind the reader of Laurence's travel memoir and essays of the author herself as a young woman in Somaliland and Ghana. Miranda urges her husband to promote Africanization in the firm, without visualizing the consequences for the whites or the possible humiliation of the African schoolteacher whose students are ill prepared for business. Walking through the market with Nathaniel, she fails to anticipate that her guide will be the butt of crude jokes. The fetish herbs remind Nathaniel of the death of his small sister, but are simply an object of curiosity to Miranda. She could afford to be fascinated: "she could draw back any time she chose, into the safety of the thousand years that parted them."

Miranda's story may be read in conjunction with Laurence's first published article, "The Very Best Intentions" (1964), an honest and amusing record of the young Laurence in Ghana and of the lessons learned there. The article portrays two Laurences, one a naive liberal, the other an older, wiser self who mocks the first. She speaks of herself in the early 1950s as wearing militant liberalism like a heart on her sleeve. Her initial encounter with a Ghanian intellectual to whom she gives the fictitious name of Mensah proved to be a painful lesson in the inadequacies of liberal goodwill. With heavy irony Mensah taught Laurence that it was unnecessary to belabor the point

that Africans had a past, a history, and artistic treasures; that
their culture, while precious, was deprived in many respects;
that his people needed modern medicine as much as regard
for their heritage. "I could afford to be fascinated," Laurence
writes in a passage that evokes the novel's market scene: "None
of it threatened me" (*HS* 35). The witty, sardonic Mensah is
obviously the model for the journalist Victor Edusei, and for
the artist Danso in "The Merchant of Heaven."

The originality of the novel's technique lies largely in its
handling of metaphor, and of language in general. One type
of image common to *This Side Jordan* and *The Tomorrow-Tamer*
is the grotesquely comic simile. Nathaniel's stout employer,
"slow-moving as a puff-adder," hovers "like an absurd gigantic
mud-wasp vacillating over the choice of nest." James Thayer's
anger at the prospect of Africanization extends his neckveins
"like crimson-black ropes" about to hang him. Other metaphors,
sometimes explicit, develop slowly, such as the suit of armor
seen by Bedford Cunningham in the Tower of London. This is
identified with Bedford through his nickname, and suggests the
masks worn by colonials and natives alike to cover fear and
longing. Another type is the archetypal metaphor such as roots,
dwellings, sojourning, exile, Eden, and the Promised Land. These
patterns recur not only in this novel but throughout Laurence's
fiction.

Her first novel is marred by the occasional use of obvious
symbolism, such as the dead gekko covered with ants which
Johnnie sees after he has betrayed his colleagues, or the portrait
of Nkrumah, captioned "Freedom," in the room where he reenacts
the rape of Africa and recognizes his own servitude. Her parallels, moreover, are sometimes heavy-handed. But most of the
language is fresh and strong, with rhythmic repetitions that
recall the Old Testament Psalms as well as the rhythm of African
drums. The atmosphere of Ghana in the 1950s is rendered with
imagination and realism. Although one may quarrel with aspects
of Laurence's psychology of colonization, her vividly realized
characters are more than credible. They have their own inner
life, the characteristic that will mark her fiction and prove to
be her great strength.

The themes in Laurence's African stories are very close to

those of her first novel. Structurally, the stories are placed
within the collection so that tragic or ironic narratives alternate
with comic ones. Tragic stories, where the search for freedom
is unsuccessful and/or the characters remain largely isolated
from one another and from their chosen society, include "The
Drummer of All the World," "The Rain Child," and "The Voices
of Adamo."

In the opening story, the first-person narrative voice conveys
a double time-frame and, with it, a deep ambivalence. Matthew's
youthful impressions are contrasted with his adult understanding, in a technique that recalls, once again, "The Very Best
Intentions." Indeed, the essay title could serve as a title for
"The Drummer of All the World." The protagonist, son of missionary parents in a fishing village near Accra, is everything his
parents are not. They despise African culture, he reveres it;
they encourage discipline and decorum in their converts, while
Matthew is drawn to the villagers' vitality. When Matthew returns to Accra after ten years away and encounters the African
friends of his youth, he finds he is no longer welcome, despite
his knowledge of the Twi language and his love of the country.

Matthew's idealization of local culture has blinded him to
its deficiencies, to African deprivation, and the need for change.
His period of illusion is over. A sentence near the story's end
recalls the achieved wisdom of the essay: "It was only I who
could afford to love the old Africa. Its enchantment had touched
me, its suffering—never. . . . I had always been the dreamer who
knew he could waken at will."[11] The Africans remain excluded
from opportunity and a decent standard of living, while the
narrator is excluded from Africa's squalor and beauty. Freedom,
here, is the freedom to discard illusion. Laurence's point of view,
in her African fiction, encompasses the full range of Matthew's
adult perceptions, and more. These may be shaped into tragic
alternatives or comic paradoxes, but her treatment is never
simplistic.[12]

"The Rain Child" (1962) prefigures Hagar's experience in
*The Stone Angel,* even to the phrase "Pride has so often been
my demon." Every character in the story save Kwaale, the
beautiful young African girl, is and remains an exile. And even
Kwaale is excluded, by her youth and limited experience, from

the full sharing which her own culture expects and demands. The implacable Kwaale has no pity for Ruth, the African girl who is culturally white but imprisoned in a black skin; Kwaale has not yet experienced alienation and suffering. She has never been a stranger in the land of Egypt, the English teacher thinks, using the archetypal story from the Old Testament which underlies Hagar's name and experience.

Both teacher and headmistress are exiles, and the former's love for the country (like Matthew's) only deepens her sense of exclusion from it. Other exiles include Ayesha, the child prostitute, and Yindo, the Dagomba boy from the northern desert who expects no mercy from strangers in a foreign land. "No got bruddah dis place," Yindo stammers fearfully, when he is discovered with Ruth. The teachers, Ruth, her equally displaced parents, Ayesha, and Yindo are all strangers in a hard land; they are outcasts, rain children. One type of rain is tears. In Laurence's poignant image for the human condition, the English climate and the tropical (the cause of Violet's deformity), the contrasting and excluding cultures, and the resulting human suffering, are brilliantly coalesced.

"Godman's Master" is a favorite from the African collection, possibly because the dwarf's experience is an analogue for the housewife's as well as for mankind's.[13] Whether read as a statement on Women's Liberation or simply as a universal parable, the story is both witty and profound. Moses Adu is the dwarf's first deliverer, who leads the little man out of slavery yet who cannot bestow freedom. *Moses*: the law-giver, who led his people towards but not into the Promised Land; *Adu: adieu,* or *à Dieu; Godman,* called "halfman," the barely human creature or "man-forsaken little god" who aspires to be a free man and who grows into that stature. God-in-man? God's man? Moses' wife is called Mercy. Freedom, in Laurence's fiction, is seen to be a gift which is both a mercy bestowed and also a birthright to be won through infinite desire and struggle, like Jacob wrestling with the Angel, an archetypal narrative which Laurence takes from Genesis and uses repeatedly in her fiction. The witty title suggests the African who refuses to continue as master, and God or human destiny, which includes freedom.

Once free of the village priest who has imprisoned him,

Godman would prefer simply to exchange an unkind master for a kind one. Freedom can be frightening. To work and support himself appears impossible. He is quite willing to keep house. As Moses begins to understand Godman's dependence, even worship, he is horrified: there is more to freedom than not living in a box: "He and Godman were bound together with a cord more delicate, more difficult to see, than any spun by the children of Ananse. Yet it was a cord which could strangle" (*TT* 155).

So the unwilling Godman has freedom forced upon him. And he survives. In Moses' next view of him, a year later, he is robed in scarlet and green. His story is as flamboyant as his costume. "I have known the worst and the worst and the worst," he concludes: "I fear and fear, and yet I live." The story closes with the tiny descendant of court jesters taking his place with the other performers "on the broad and grimy stage": the human comedy, African style.

In "The Merchant of Heaven," an American evangelist comes to Africa to acquire souls. Just souls. Bodies—whether racked with tropical disease, crippled, hungry, or blind—are not Brother Lemon's concern. The metaphors are blackly comic. Brother Lemon, "replete with faith as a fresh-gorged mosquito is with blood," is like his own water-purifier, "sucking in the septic souls and spewing them back one hundred per cent pure" (*TT* 51, 53).

The final metaphor, and the story's focus, is the African artist's picture of the Nazarene as an African: strong, capable of laughter, and surrounded by diseased beggars. Earlier, we have glimpsed Brother Lemon's deprived childhood in an unpainted American farmhouse. His mental and emotional deprivations match the Africans' physical ones. The painting moves beyond the technical limitations of color to an epiphany: "Sometimes, when I am able to see through black and white, until they merge and cease to be separate or apart, I look at those damaged creatures clustering so despairingly hopeful around the Son of Man, and it seems to me that Brother Lemon, after all, is one of them."

The mood is quite different in "The Perfume Sea," where exile is treated comically, without minimizing its pain. The story breathes a spirit of reconciliation, expressed in a pattern of baroque and amusing metaphors. The tall, gaunt Dorée and the plump little hairdresser, Archipelago, are grotesques who nevertheless express the universal pathos and loneliness of human existence. Pigeon and crane, they walk on the African beach "with hands entwined like children who walk through the dark." Each is the other's sanctuary. Their economic and personal freedom has been achieved, as Archipelago puns, "by an act of Mercy," along with their own courage and love.

In the title story, Laurence contrasts the types of freedom afforded by two different cultures. Faith, acceptance, and service lie at the heart of the freedom found within the religious culture of the village of Owurasu. The ironically named Emmanuel typifies the rootless freedom of a secular, technological culture. The bridge builder's life is "to make money, and spend it." His non-community is the society of those like himself who move from job to job. The lack of understanding between cultures is portrayed with humor and pathos.

The language sparkles with wit, wordplay, and exuberance. Brother Lemon's name is contemporary slang for *a failure,* and *leman* is archaic for *lover*: the evangelist's love is more Manichean than the concept of *cortezia* in Provençal love poetry. There are neologisms (Danso "dervished" in), puns (Moses is "the man-forsaken little god," a "god-in-the-box"), baroque similes, and comic reversals: the British anthropologist's fascination with African culture ends abruptly when his own health is threatened by it. The fiction set in Ghana wears frequently a comic and ironic mask.

## IV   *Ancestors and Gods*

In 1966, while working on *The Fire-Dwellers* at Elm Cottage in Buckinghamshire, Laurence began the extensive research required for *Long Drums and Cannons. Nigerian Dramatists and Novelists 1952–1966.* Separate chapters are devoted to the works of Wole Soyinka, John Pepper Clark, Chinua Achebe, Amos Tutuola, and Cyprian Ekwensi; five other writers are discussed more briefly in a sixth chapter, "Other Voices." Laurence's bibliography indicates that she studied Nigerian religious attitudes

and general world view. *Black Orpheus,* a literary journal edited
and published from the University of Ibadan, was one major
resource.

Her travel narrative employs a verse from James Elroy Flecker's
"Gates of Damascus" as epigraph; it begins, "God be thy guide
from camp to camp." Similarly, the Nigerian study begins with
lines from poet Christopher Okigbo: "long drums and cannons/
the spirit in the ascent." As readers of *This Side Jordan* will
remember, the sacred drums are spiritual voices: voices of
gods and ancestors, and voices of the people whose health and
very life depend on communication with them.

Laurence's assessment of the importance of the past to each
new generation of writers is a major motif in *Long Drums and
Cannons.* Part of the psychological damage inflicted by imperial
rulers is the disconnection with the past and with roots. Literature, she writes in the Preface, "must be planted firmly in some
soil. Even works of non-realism make use of spiritual landscapes
which have been at least partially inherited by the writer"
(*LD* 10). She notes that African writers are concerned with
the need to come to terms with one's ancestors and with the
conflicts for each individual caught between old and new values,
torn two ways: "Most Nigerian writers have in some way or
other made an attempt to restore the value of the past, without
idealising it and without being shackled by it" (*LD* 9). Wole
Soyinka, for example, both attacks and praises the old ways
*and* the new. In essays and interviews Laurence has pointed
to an identical concern in her own work.

The past is not simply beneficent, but may become a specter
at the feast: "no one's past is to be dismissed by an act of will"
(*LD* 29, 65). Moreover, the bond between past and present is
inevitable, for the past is within ourselves and shows the
present "its own face" (*LD* 33, 34, 35). Ancestors, she writes
in connection with Wole Soyinka's drama, are continually reborn within us, so that current decisions are made "with deep
emotional reference" to the ancestors and their gods (*LD* 44, 45).
Just as many of the portraits of individuals in *The Prophet's
Camel Bell* are structured around the motif of exile, so Laurence's
analyses of specific works by Nigerian writers revolve around
a small number of thematic concerns, the same concerns which

are evident in the first three works in her Manawakan saga written at approximately the same time. The study of Nigerian writing, like desert life, affords "strange glimpses" of the self.

The ambiguous nature of past experience belongs to Laurence's vision of the psychic journey undergone by every human individual, from bondage towards freedom. The latter is a desired goal, rarely a fully achieved state. Writing of John Pepper Clark, Laurence describes the ambiguity of ancestors, and the necessity to honor and evoke them while simultaneously pointing to the need for change: "Perhaps men cannot any longer be cast in the heroic mould. But this does not mean that the past cannot be drawn upon. It *has* to be, in some ways, as Clark recognises, and it has to be changed as well, according to the writer's own outlook, as he also recognises" (*LD* 96).

Chinua Achebe's fiction draws Laurence's high praise for its ability to handle this ambiguity. Achebe neither idealizes the old society, nor explains it didactically, but recreates it imaginatively through characters "who are shown in all their perplexities and contradictions.... He never preaches or writes in the abstract. His descriptions of the rituals of the old religion are lighted from within by a deep understanding. Almost without realising it, we find that we understand at least some things which we did not understand before. We see the old religion not as a set of distant oddities, not as 'customs,' but as faith, which is a very different thing" (*LD* 123). Laurence sees this gift for character portrayal as Achebe's greatest talent. Since she repeatedly describes her own fiction as taking its form from the characters, her feeling of affinity with Achebe is readily understandable.

A 1978 essay, "Ivory Tower or Grassroots?" shows her continuing commitment to the idea of the writer's political involvement. She speaks of novelists as reflecting the communities where they grew up, and hence providing a social commentary which is both religious and political in a broad sense. All fiction is "about the past," for the present becomes the past in the act of describing it, and even science fiction is a disguised version of the writer's times. The emphasis in the Nigerian study on the need for ancestors and gods is repeated: "Fiction, in the political sense, both binds us to and frees us from our ancestors; it

acknowledges our dilemmas; it mourns and rages at our inhumanity to one another; and sometimes it expresses our faith in
growth and change, and honours our children and our trust
in them."[14]

In this essay Laurence speaks of Achebe and herself as Third
World novelists, members of ex-colonial nations that are struggling to assert their own culture in the face of "overwhelming"
cultural imperialism. Nigerians, during three generations of
colonial rule, learned to despise themselves. Achebe's generation
(here she names Soyinka and the other Nigerian writers discussed in her 1968 study, with the exception of Tutuola) "has
drawn on their relatively newfound sense of self-worth and on
their people's past, and has tried consciously to impart these
values to their own people, to combat the psychic damage done
during the years of domination by British imperialism."[15]

The psychic damage inflicted by missionaries is a recurring
theme in the Nigerian study. Achebe is less scathing than
Laurence in this regard. She writes that he does not condemn
Christianity, nor individual missionaries, but recognizes their
courage and devotion: "What he deplores is their total ignorance
of the people to whom they were preaching, their uninformed
assumption that Africans did not have any concept of God, and
their lack of any self-knowledge which might have made them
question something of their own motives in desiring to see
themselves as bringers of salvation" (LD 106–07). In stories
such as "The Drummer of All the World" and "The Merchant
of Heaven," Laurence (with heavy irony, almost bitterness)
attacks the missionaries' behavior in terms of the ignorance and
lack of self-knowledge noted by Achebe. However, the narrator's
father's stance, in the former story, is preferred to the narrator's
naive idealism. The missionary is described by Matthew's African
friend as follows: " 'Nearly everything he did was wrong. But
at least he did not want us to stand still' " (TT 17).

Laurence notes that Achebe's personal knowledge spans three
eras: the old Ibo society of pre-mission and pre-colonial days;
the mission era of his parents; and the troubled emancipation
of himself and his peers (LD 97). In her essays she has compared
Achebe's three generations with her own knowledge of three
generations in the Manawaka cycle.

Okonkwo, the protagonist in Achebe's novel, *Things Fall Apart,* resembles Laurence's grandparents' generation. She describes Okonkwo as proud, quick to show anger, slow to show gentleness, fearful of weakness: "a man who commits violence against the god within" (*LD* 101, 106). Parallels with Hagar and with Grandfather Connor in *A Bird in the House* spring to mind. Hagar, however, eventually learns to rejoice, whereas Okonkwo remains permanently enclosed within his own fears. This failure of communication, Laurence writes, is portrayed as both a personal and a social problem. Laurence's fictional treatment of the difficulties of human communication is more optimistic than Achebe's.

The protagonist in Achebe's second novel, *No Longer at Ease,* is seen as struggling to achieve an inner independence. He is "torn between what is expected of him and what he himself believes" (*LD* 111). *Arrow of God,* described as Achebe's best, brings Laurence back to her *bête noir,* intolerance, and to the word that Mannoni capitalized in order to show its importance: the *Other.* "The greatest tragedy is that of man's lack of comprehension of the reality of others, his lack of comprehension of the validity of differences" (*LD* 116).[16] Achebe's basic theme is described as human communication: its failures, its difficulties, and its vital importance. His writing depicts "man's general misunderstanding of man" and seeks "to send human voices through the thickets of our separateness" (*LD* 199, 125). The parallels with Laurence's fiction are obvious.

Laurence's epilogue to *Long Drums and Cannons* summarizes the concerns we have been discussing here. Nigerian writers are dealing with cultural conflicts, the impact of Christian missions, and the problems that accompany rapid social change. Nigerian writing exhibits a strong interest in the past, in village life, and in cultural roots. The missions may have helped to sever some of these roots, but were responsible for the establishment of primary education on a wide scale. With the benefit of hindsight, it is easy to blame missionaries for their ignorance of African culture. Laurence acknowledges that Nigerian writers are ambivalent on the subject of missionaries, and does credit them with playing a beneficial role in education. Tribal animosity, strangely, is not a theme in the Nigerian writing of this period, just prior to the Nigerian civil war. Laurence refers only indirectly to the agonies of the civil conflict, and looks hopefully towards the establishment of new forms of government.

She points to rapid social change as a persistent theme in contemporary Nigerian writing, and to the writers' efforts "to maintain a sense of the individual under the deceptive mask of crowds." Nigerian writing is praised for its ability to present social themes through individual characters, "paradoxical, and therefore alive." Despite their concern for change, and for the present, the writers remain aware of the individual's effort "to come to terms with his ancestors and his gods. . . . to free himself from the fetters of the past and the compulsions of the present" (*LD* 203). The photograph on the dustjacket of the book, of a traditional tribal carving brooding sphinx-like over a typewriter, perfectly expresses the need for the writer, a modern Janus, to face two ways.

CHAPTER 3

# The Manawaka Cycle

I  *"Pride was my wilderness."*

MANAWAKA, as Laurence has frequently stated, is both an amalgam of prairie towns and her own private world. It is a mythic territory, mapping universal human experience, and a Scots-Canadian subculture in the Canadian West. Laurence has emphasized that societies need their own myths, generated by their own artists, in order to understand and fulfill themselves as communities. Of Manawaka/Neepawa, Laurence says: "in raging against our injustices, our stupidities, I do so *as family*, as I did, and still do, in writing about those aspects of my town which I hated and which are always in some ways aspects of myself."[1]

Laurence's decision, to turn from portraying Africans to writing about people whose idiom and concepts were thoroughly familiar, was a very self-conscious one. She spoke, in 1969, of her intimate knowledge of Hagar, who belonged to her grandparents' generation: "I felt when I was writing *The Stone Angel* an enormous conviction of the authenticity of Hagar's voice, and I experienced a strange pleasure in rediscovering an idiom I hardly knew I knew, as phrases from my grandparents kept coming back to me. A first-person narrative can be limiting, of course, but in this case it provided an opportunity to reveal to the reader more of Hagar than she knew herself, as her judgments about everything are so plainly and strongly biased."[2]

In the same lecture Laurence suggests that the flashback method is suited to an elderly protagonist, who lives largely in the past; and that the chronological structuring of Hagar's memories provides clarity: the novel may be "too orderly," but the parallel structure gives unity to the whole and immediacy to the past.[3] A more pressing decision than structure concerned the poetic quality in Hagar's voice. Were such perceptions authentic? "I finally came to the conclusion that even people who are relatively inarticulate, in their relationships with other people, are perfectly capable within themselves of perceiving the world in more poetic terms. . . . So I let her have her way. . . ."[4]

*The Stone Angel* is Laurence's best known and most deeply respected work, a novel hailed as a Canadian classic. Ninety-year-old Hagar Shipley of Manawaka is the stubborn angel, a defiant woman filled with a "rage" for life. Her story is presented in two separate but interlocking strands, with present events triggering memories of the past. The two periods gradually converge.

Time present is Hagar at ninety, needing hospital care but stubbornly refusing to leave her home. Time past begins with the memories of six-year-old Hagar Currie, whose father Jason owns the general store. Time past moves through Hagar's marriage to Bram Shipley, a marriage that takes her out of her social class and isolates her from her family; through the birth of two sons, her desertion of Bram, and the deaths of Bram and the favorite son John; to her life in a West Coast city with her son Marvin. As her health fails, Hagar makes a desperate attempt to evade the hounds of fate by a secret journey to the nearby Shadow Point. This jailbreak is a descent into Self which is healing. The novel ends with a death which is also a birth. Hagar achieves a measure of self-knowledge, freedom, and joy: the objects of her life's quest.

Hagar has the speech, the values of Laurence's grandparents. She is clearly a person from the same kind of prairie Scots-Presbyterian background and yet, as the same time, is "an old woman anywhere," forced to come to terms with death (*HS* 16, 18). Hagar may indeed be everyone's grandmother. But in a deeper sense, we recognize in her not our grandmothers but ourselves: proud, stubborn, selfish, generous, fearing love, needing love. Seeking freedom, Hagar forges more chains. Seeking community, she builds psychic walls. Her final self-knowledge accompanies the breaking of these bonds, as Hagar is released into love, death, and the new life suggested by images of rebirth and transformation.

Hagar's name suggests her symbolic journey and the novel's theme. The biblical analogues are found in the Genesis story of Abraham's twin dynasty, and in St. Paul's interpretation of it in Galatians 4:22-27. Genesis tells of the "free" wife, Sarah, and the bondwoman, Agar, "after the flesh." In St. Paul's version, the story of two wives and two sons becomes an allegory of human nature and destiny: "for these are the two covenants; the one from the mount Sinai, which engendereth to bondage, which is Agar. . . . But Jerusalem which is above is free, which is the mother of us all. For it is written, Rejoice. . . ." Agar's son Ishmael, being under the moral law, is self-condemned by his failure to obey it, while Sarah's son Isaac symbolizes the free gift of grace and release. The archetype draws on Laurence's Judeo-Christian background and on her years in Somaliland, which vividly recreated Old Testament narrative.

Northrop Frye shows that the inner significance of Adam's expulsion from Eden is identical with that of the Israelites' desert journey in search of a Promised Land where they could live as free men: "There are thus two concentric quest-myths in the Bible, a Genesis-apocalypse myth and an Exodus-millenium myth. . . . Eden and the Promised Land, therefore, are typologically identical, as are the tyrannies of Egypt and Babylon and the wilderness of the law."[5] This ancient, affirmative myth of bondage, yearning, sojourning, quest, and release is at the heart of Laurence's work.

Laurence humanizes the religious myth, freeing it from its specifically Christian implications. In her work it becomes an analogue for the journey of the human spirit out of the bondage of pride, which isolates, into the freedom of love, which links the lover to other humans. *The Stone Angel* employs images of wilderness, chains, exile, the Egyptian, Pharaoh. The pattern culminates in Hagar's moment of truth, precipitated by the clergyman's song of praise, "Come ye before Him and rejoice." Hagar recognizes that this expresses her deepest need, her life-long desire. The joys she might have held "were forced to a standstill by some brake of proper appearances. . . . Pride was my wilderness, and the demon that led me there was fear."[6]

William New describes Hagar as an essentially tragic figure, and her moment of truth as the deepest point of her tragedy: "Joy is for the Sarahs of the world; but she is Hagar. Her identity will not allow it."[7] This interpretation of the biblical archetype slights the tension in Hagar's character. It also disregards the novel's tragicomic tone and, most important, Hagar's movement towards freedom in the closing chapters.

Tragic and comic, in the sense in which these terms are used above, may be taken as aspects of narrative which precede the ordinary literary genres. Frye defines four narrative categories, linked in opposing pairs: the tragic and the comic, the romantic and the ironic. All are commonly present in a work, but one predominates; and all are episodes in a total quest myth. Tragic narrative ends in the isolation of the protagonist, while comedy depicts the social integration of the individual. Integration includes an advance in self-knowledge. Time, the medium in which conflicts are resolved, plays a redeeming role in comic narrative, which moves towards reconciliation and the formation of a new society.[8]

The closing chapters chronicle Hagar's gradual reconciliation with her world and herself. At Shadow Point, where Murray Lees's story of losing his infant son in a fire releases her memories of John's death, Hagar speaks to Murray the apology she owes to her son. Sensing her confusion, Murray plays John's role just as Hagar's brother Matt had taken on their mother's role when Dan died. In this replaying of the past, Hagar is permitted to tell John/Murray that his lover Arlene is, after all, welcome in their house. Hagar's descent into her shadow self, a kind of *rites de passage*, ends with repentence, confession, and peace: "I could even beg God's pardon this moment, for thinking ill of Him sometime or other" (SA 248).

This peace is not permanent, but Hagar makes further progress in hospital. Two steps forward, one step back. At the end, she recalls doing only two "truly free" acts, which she calls a joke and a lie. Clearly, Hagar refers to fetching the bedpan for the girl in her hospital room; and blessing Marvin, assuring him that he has been a better son than John and stands first in her affection: "Now it seems to me that he is truly Jacob, gripping with all his strength, and bargaining. *I will not let thee go, except thou bless me.* And I see I am thus strangely cast, and perhaps have been so from the beginning, and can only release myself by releasing him" (*SA* 304). Hagar is "strangely cast" as Sarah. But her "lie," if such it be, has been spoken in love. Ironically, Marvin has been a better son than John: Hagar hovers at the edge of this realization.

Her "free" acts are actually far more numerous. They include many small gestures in the closing chapters. Hagar gives her sapphire ring to her granddaughter Tina. She forgives Murray for betraying her hiding place in the cannery. She thanks the clergyman, despised earlier, for singing in the hospital ("that wasn't easy") and tells Doris that he has done her good. This is not to say that Hagar's pride is banished. She calls herself unregenerate: "the same touchiness rises within me at the slightest thing" (*SA* 293).

The bedpan incident ends, significantly with the recurrence of *we* four times in as many lines, as Hagar and her young roommate laugh together at the nurse's indignation. Laurence transmogrifies a hospital bedpan into the grail of medieval legend. The "grail" joins comic structure to comic mood as it unites a dying Canadian woman with an Oriental girl on the threshold of adult life: "Convulsed with *our* paining laughter, *we* bellow and wheeze. And then *we* peacefully sleep" (*SA* 302, emphasis added).

The last scene depicts Hagar's death in terms of transformation images. These are ironically undercut by Hagar's stubbornness. Separated typographically, the section begins with her memories of the birth of her second son, who could not have suspected he was entering a new element, a different kind of life: "Perhaps the same occurs elsewhere. . . . Can angels faint?" Her swollen body, which suggests death and putrefaction, reminds Hagar of flesh in sea water, and then of the stones at Shadow Point, sea-changed into jewels. The cocoon (literally, the effect of narcotics, and the web of memory) is another image of metamorphosis (*SA* 306, 308).

The final lines combine references to water and struggle: read *grace* and *freewill,* or the stubborn quality of the human spirit. Laurence's enduring metaphor for this paradoxical combination is the story of Jacob wresting a blessing from the angel

of God: "I can't help it—it's my nature. I'll drink from this
glass, or spill it, just as I choose.... I wrest from her the glass,
full of water to be had for the taking. I hold it in my own
hands. There. There./ And then—" (*SA* 308). *There, there*: the
"mother-word" (*SA* 66), which occurs at critical points in the
novel, is now rich in ambiguities as Hagar confronts her Self
and her God. Laurence's protagonist brilliantly combines the
inner significance of the twin archetypes, Agar and Sarah.

The universality of the theme, and the intricacy of the images,
make *The Stone Angel* a novel that readily lends itself to textual
analysis along New Critical lines. Students are sometimes surprised by questions on Hagar's prairie environment, as if it were
irrelevant. But Hagar is a Scots-Presbyterian from the Canadian
West, and her perceptions grow from these roots. The starkly
beautiful Manitoba land becomes the analogue for her conflicts.
Manawaka's cemetery, for example, holds formal peonies and
"upstart" ants; wildflowers encroach on its tenuous order. The
theme of pride as an isolating wilderness is caught in the class-
structured guest lists of Manawakan parties. Japanese porch-
lanterns, hung from wooden gingerbread trim, are ironic
reminders of the exclusion of Orientals from full participation
in Canadian society, an exclusion which is the indirect source
of Hagar's West Coast job as housekeeper.[9]

By juxtaposition, Laurence establishes subtle parallels between the town's social hegemony (shanties and brick houses),
its harsh climate (sweltering summers, and winters "that froze
the wells and the blood"), and human pride, masked as meek-
ness and charity. Jason Currie's pride in the size of his contribution to the new Presbyterian Church is echoed in Hagar's
six-year-old pride in her new gloves, while the hymn speaks
of longing for salvation. (*A Jest of God* strikes the same note
of longing, in the opening chant.)

Contrasts in prairie environment suggest paradoxes in human
nature. These include muddy farmyards awash in urine, skeletal
machinery, and lilacs, "a seasonal mercy." Chokecherries sting
sweetly. The "heedless and compelled" sap of Manitoba maples
suggests Hagar's sexual attraction to Bram, but the pride which
makes her conceal her enjoyment of their sexual relation acts,
once again, to isolate her.

Prairie weather provides analogues for pride, passion, fear, and for Puritan culture whose flaws and strengths provoke ambivalent feelings in Laurence (*HS* 18). Bram's beloved horse Soldier freezes to death in a storm; ironically, his fatal freedom stemmed from Bram's fear of fire. As a girl in town, Hagar feels secure during storms, but on the farm storms mean dangerous isolation. Fire and snow, the refrain in Piquette's Song in *The Diviners*, is the culmination of many scenes in the Manawaka books that anchor these images of human pain and passion in prairie weather and culture.

The sight, feel, smell of the land and the culture run through every paragraph. Hagar's arthritic muscles and veins are like pieces of binder twine in her legs. Twenty-four years of bickering with Bram is a prairie river "scoured away like sandbanks." The things Hagar sees as she leaves Manawaka image the death of her relation with Bram: the cemetery; the railway buildings and water tower painted blood-red, black trees, and farms "lost and smothered" in winter landscape. The pain of this departure, and her latent guilt, are suggested through a prairie thunderstorm, where lightning rends the sky "like an angry claw at the cloak of God" (*SA* 161).

The terrible depression of the 1930s, and the drought that compounded its effects in the Canadian West, coincides with Bram's death. Neglected farmhouses and rusty machinery resemble aging bodies; boarded windows are bandaged eyes; warped buildings "wore a caved-in look, like toothless jaws"; sunflowers hang "empty as unfilled honeycombs" (*SA* 169). Air and land are bone-dry, deathly. Hard work and laziness now yield the same result: nothing. This blunt fact of prairie life in the thirties takes on symbolic meaning in Hagar's decision to let Bram and her father share one tombstone: "They're only different sides of the same coin, anyway, he and the Curries" (*SA* 184). Two forms of pride? Biblical analogues spring to mind, such as the parable of the worker who begins his labors late in the day, or St. Paul's reminder that salvation is not bought with works.

One form of pride, or bondage, involves Canada's native people. Indian and Métis compose Manawaka's social rejects. The background to this prejudice, and something of Métis history, will be discussed later. *The Stone Angel* touches lightly on a theme that looms larger as the Manawaka cycle progresses. Its opening scene evokes the native people through the wild, musky things on the edge of the town's orderly cemetery. Such plants had flourished when Cree "with enigmatic faces and greasy hair" were the sole inhabitants of the prairie bluffs.

Examples of racial prejudice are unobtrusive, but form a pattern. Matt would have liked to shoot and set traplines with Jules Tonnerre at Galloping Mountain, but Jason Currie forbids his teen-age son to associate with half-breeds. Bram is initially condemned for having been seen with half-breed girls, and continues to joke and drink with Métis after his marriage to Hagar. She is attracted by his dark good looks ("I thought he looked a bearded Indian, so brown and beaked a face"), but soon comes to share in local prejudices. Hagar despises herself for being forced to serve the threshers, "a bunch of breeds and ne'er-do-wells and Galicians." She refuses to believe John when he describes the Tonnerre shack as passably clean. Her humiliation in Currie's General Store when Bram is suspected of buying lemon extract for resale to Indians triggers her decision to leave. When John tells Hagar, later, of the death of Bram's old Métis crony, Hagar replies (albeit with a bad conscience) "Good riddance to bad rubbish."

John's rebellious nature is expressed in part through his friendship with the Tonnerres. As a child, John trades the family crest-pin to Lazarus Tonnerre for a knife, one which Morag inherits in *The Diviners*. As adolescents, John and the Métis boys dare one another to hair-raising escapades. John's death on the railway trestle bridge is the result of a drunken response to a drunken Métis dare. Indirectly, Hagar is partly responsible, having driven John to desperation and drink by plotting to separate him from Arlene. Symbolically, the tragedy suggests that the destinies of whites and Métis in Canada are conjoined, a theme to be developed at much greater length in *The Diviners*.

Hagar's rebelliousness is expressed in the novel's epigraph ("Do not go gentle into that good night. / Rage, rage against the dying of the light") and the title image. The latter metaphor, like Dylan Thomas's injunction to "rage" against death, catches much of the paradoxical quality of human existence. Hagar's rage, which involves the pride that prevents her from rejoicing, is also her stubborn love of life, her courage, her fighting spirit—qualities lacking in her brothers. The tragic aspect of her experience, her alienation, is thus inseparably united with her admirable fighting spirit. Like the wounded gull in the cannery, Hagar's strength is both her glory and her doom.[10] There is no place for quietism in Laurence's creed.

The image of the stone angel unifies the novel. The actual angel marks the grave of Hagar's mother, who died in giving birth to her stubborn daughter. Purchased to proclaim the Currie dynasty, the angel is "doubly blind," carved without eyeballs by cynical stonemasons (Hagar thinks) who accurately gauged "the needs of fledgling pharaohs in an uncouth land" (*SA* 3). Like Jason's church contribution, the statue is pride made visible, blind to the needs of others and to the deepest needs of self. As the proud product of an Eastern finishing school, Hagar is "Pharaoh's daughter reluctantly returning to his roof" (*SA* 43). As she leaves the town and her husband, Hagar sees the stone angel in the cemetery, sightlessly guarding emptiness and death. Bram's senility fills her with anger at fate, or God, "for giving us eyes but almost never sight" (*SA* 173). John, who has his own blindness, wrestles with the angel in the cemetery while Hagar looks on. Later, it stands crookedly over two men's graves. The irascible Hagar, prisoned by flesh and pride, waits "stonily" for poor Mr. Troy. In this paradoxical image, the stone half (bondage) is more prominent than the linked suggestions of light, love, freedom, and life. The latter culminate in the closing scene: "Can angels faint?" Laurence had difficulty finding the title, despite its apparent inevitability (*HS* 184).

The novel's structure depends as much upon a web of interlocking images as upon its handling of time through flashbacks. Prominent among these patterns are those of houses and birds, archetypal metaphors for human experience which are as old as language itself. Northrop Frye points to two contrasting worlds of metaphoric organization, one desirable and the other undesirable. He calls these the apocalyptic and the demonic, respectively,[11] terms that are useful in analyzing Laurence's image patterns.

The demonic world of bondage, pain, and confusion is suggested in *The Stone Angel* by the wilderness/Pharaoh pattern and by maimed and captive birds. The sight of Silverthreads, a home for the elderly which Hager envisages as a prison, sets her heart pulsing against its cage of bones "like a berserk bird" (*SA* 95). The gull, trapped like Hagar in the old cannery, is wounded by her as it screams their common fear. Horrified, Hagar recalls its free soaring. The gull's broken wing reduces it to the level to which age has reduced Hagar; its strength becomes a hazard as it batters itself "in the terrible rage of not being able to do what it is compelled to do." Two dogs sound like wolfish fiends, merciless. Hagar's curiosity and fear are answered by the arrival of Murray Lees. The wounded bird that drew the hounds off Murray's trail now appears as scapegoat and sacrificial victim: the demonic parody of Eucharist symbolism in the apocalyptic world.

Chickens serve as a frequent form of demonic bird imagery. The Manawaka dump, which figures much more prominently in *The Diviners*, is the stage here for a grotesque and sickening scene in Hagar's childhood. A load of spoiled eggs has hatched in the summer sun. The feeble, foodless chicks are prisoned by their shells and by each other. Hagar, for reasons she does not understand as a child, refuses to help Lottie kill the chicks; at ninety, still puzzled, she thinks it was right to refrain, although her reasons are obscure to her.

We remember the incident when Hagar, en route to Silverthreads, thinks of calves struggling to be born. She has always had a fellow feeling for anything struggling into life. We remember it with new force as Hagar and Lottie Simmons sit plotting the separation of their adult children, pretending it is for John and Arlene's good. The two old women attempt to haggle with fate. They agree that Arlene should be sent East until she and John can afford to marry. Hagar and Lottie see the stifling of John and Arlene's relationship as a mercy-killing. At this point, Hagar remembers the bloody chicks, but Lottie has completely repressed the incident (*SA* 213).

A concordance would reveal the remarkable frequency of bird patterns. Hagar in hospital, in a restraint, is a trussed fowl. In the cannery memories swoop like gulls, and the prospect of confronting herself is imaged as a fearsome storm which might sweep a bird out to sea and drown it in depths "as still and cold as black glass." Discovered by Marvin, Hagar is "an old hawk caught." Hospitalized, her pain beats its wings against her rib cage, while nearby voices "flutter like birds caught inside a building" (*SA* 256).

Birds, with their power of flight, are traditional emblems of freedom and the human spirit. Laurence uses this archetype in her pun *freegull*, which recurs in the Manawaka fiction. The demonic form of the image, the captive bird which in prairie folklore portends death, also recurs. Tht title story of *A Bird in the House* concerns the death of Vanessa's father and the young girl's loss of religious faith. But the larger narrative of Vanessa's maturation restores to the bird image its apocalyptic suggestions of spirit and freedom. The latter suggest the partial and hard-won freedom of the young adult. It includes an understanding and acceptance of her people and her culture, an inheritance which proclaims itself in her veins.[12]

Houses and furnishings form another prominent image pattern. They serve as analogues for human bodies and, by extension, human lives. Lamps and chairs are memories made visible. Laurence's image patterns reflect her wit. Hagar's first experience of sex provides a comical house-metaphor: the bride had not known she has "a room to house such magnitude" (*SA* 52). The henhouse surrounded by chicken wire sags bunchily, "like bloomers without elastic." The abandoned house at Shadow Point, another container for Hagar and her memories, has no lock; this mock castle, like her aging body, affords neither privacy nor defense.

Here, as in the Manawaka cycle as a whole, the beauty and wit of Laurence's language, and the use of setting as human analogue, serve to develop character. Laurence's special talent is the creation of vital individual characters within a vividly realized social group. George Woodcock calls Laurence "a Canadian equivalent to Tolstoy," not in terms of "literary gigantism" but rather "in such terms as a writer's relevance to his time and place, the versatility of his perception, the breadth of his understanding, the imaginative power with which he personifies and gives symbolic form to the collective life he interprets and in which he takes part."[13] Both writers, Woodcock argues, have a panoramic sense of space and history, an ability to preserve lost times and worlds so that outsiders can imaginatively apprehend them:

. . . their characters are as impressive as their settings, and their best revelations are achieved not . . . by the explicit statements of historic themes, but rather by the vivid, concrete yet symbolic presentation of crucial points of instinct in individual lives, such as . . . the moment in Margaret Laurence's *The Stone Angel* when the despised minister, Mr. Troy, sings the first verse of the Doxology to Hagar Shipley during her last days in hospital. . . .[14]

Woodcock concludes that Hagar's recognition of her need to rejoice and her inhibiting pride are intensely personal, yet at the same time one can generalize her situation into a description of the state of mind of a whole generation of English-speaking Canadians.

Hagar Shipley is the first in a series of memorable women. In five closely connected works of fiction Laurence presents universal concerns in terms of Canadian experience over four generations. She allows us to see into the hearts of her individual characters; their society; and ourselves.

## II   *"God's grace on fools."*

Fear is the dominant force in *A Jest of God,* as was pride in *The Stone Angel.* Rachel Cameron's story is a study of anxiety bordering on madness, and of the society that nurtures these fears. Sinclair Ross, a Canadian whose prairie fiction Laurence read during her teens, describes "the exacting small-town gods Propriety and Parity." Manawaka's gods are very similar. As Sandra Djwa notes, "Laurence and Ross share a central vision— a sense of the ironic discrepancy between the spirit and the letter of the religious dispensation. . . ."[15] Manawakan values are work, devotion to duty, "decency," and respectability—above all, respectability. Rachel has incorporated these values, often against her will and better understanding. The town is all-pervasive but is seen at one remove, through Rachel's eyes and through its effects upon her.

Rachel is a lonely teacher who has taught primary school for fourteen years in the Manitoba town where she grew up. The death of her father cut short her university career and necessitated her return to Manawaka to care for her mother. Rachel is afraid of what the townspeople think; afraid of her mother's weak heart and subtle bullying; afraid of the authoritarian school principal; afraid, in essence, of herself and of life. A summer romance with a high school teacher from the city leads to Rachel's conviction that she is pregnant. Her agony of fear and indecision climaxes in an operation to remove a benign tumor and in Rachel's decision to remove herself and her mother to the West Coast city where her sister Stacey lives.

Rachel's quest, like Hagar's, is a search for freedom and joy, caught here in a phrase from the Psalms which runs through Rachel's mind as she is leaving Manawaka: "Make me to hear joy and gladness, that the bones which thou hast broken may rejoice." She wins a partial release from fear, a new understanding of her relation to her mother, and an acceptance of the mystery of human personality: the Other, in Mannoni's phrase.

In "Ten Years' Sentences" (1969), Laurence observes that *A Jest of God* has been criticized as "a very inturned novel." She defends the use of the first person and the present tense as the logical and indeed inevitable method for presenting a protagonist who is a very inturned person. Rachel, in Laurence's words, "tries to break the handcuffs of her own past, but she is self-perceptive enough to recognize that for her no freedom from the shackledom of the ancestors can be total. Her emergence from the tomb-like atmosphere of her extended childhood is a partial defeat—or, looked at in another way, a partial victory. She is no longer so much afraid of herself as she was. She is beginning to learn the rules of survival."[16]

Laurence expands these comments in a lecture from the same period. She attempted, numerous times, to begin the novel in the third person, but "it simply would not write itself that way."[17] The story demanded to be seen through Rachel's eyes. Laurence found that the present tense was essential to convey "the quality of Rachel's pain and her determined efforts to survive."[18]

Robert Harlow criticizes the use of the first person and the present tense in the novel: "Her milieu is a small town, a

cramped set of quarters, and her view of the world is cor-
respondingly, and necessarily, narrow. . . . What is lacking
. . . is objectivity, distance, irony. One simply gets tired of
listening to Rachel taking pot-shots at herself."[19] Harlow misses
the multiple voices of Rachel, who thinks and voices a very
complex self. Rachel is sometimes unconscious of the incongruity in her self. At other times, painfully conscious, she is
embarrassed by her condescension, prudery, and hypocrisy.
Sentimentality issues in her "Peter-Rabbitish voice." A falsely
egalitarian ideal pronounces the verdict "Splendid" on all class
drawings, even the worst. Rachel, adopting her mother's voice,
wonders how the Tabernacle worshippers can bear to make public fools of themselves. She perversely condemns the Tabernacle
decor as gaudy, and the Anglican as insipid good taste. She
seesaws between longing for a life of her own and condemning
herself for begrudging her mother care: "Oh—can I possibly
be this mean?" Most horrible to Rachel is the sound of her own
voice raised unconsciously in the Tabernacle crying the emotions
that are taboo to Manawaka's middle class.

The first-person point of view subsumes the many voices of
Rachel, while the larger fictional form contains an ironic, implicit
commentary through event, image, juxtaposition, and the reactions of the other characters. H. J. Rosengarten acknowledges
this corrective distance within the novel's voice, "the moral perspective that is provided by Rachel's dual consciousness"; con-
finement to Rachel's consciousness does not, he argues, limit the
novel's meaning: "The theme of individual aspiration conquered
by social convention and personal guilt is all the more forcibly
conveyed by this intense concentration on the single sensibility."[20]
George Bowering, another critic who finds that Laurence chose
wisely with regard to voice and verb tense, praises her "uncom-
mon courage" in making the novel "confront social and deep
personal stupidities and fears in the womb of her narrator."[21]

Like other protagonists in the Manawaka cycle, Rachel perceives three worlds with herself caught in the middle, "a weak
area between millstones."[22] The remark has psychological and
social analogues. Psychologically, the first "world" (Rachel's
word) belongs to her pupils and the apparently self-confident
teen-agers they so rapidly become. The third world belongs to

her mother and the mores of Manawaka. Both worlds exclude Rachel, and isolation generates fear.

The children fear authority figures. Their eyes mirror Rachel as a demonic parody of God, "the thin giant She behind the desk at the front," the one with power. Rachel is intimidated by glamorous adolescents, whose piled and lacquered hair (the beehive style of the sixties) suggests a race of strange creatures, Venusians, to whom the planet belongs. She is further intimidated by their easy acceptance of sexuality. Haunted by the memory of a young couple in the deep grass by the river, Rachel is forced to subscribe to the view of her mother, her doctor, and her neighbors that she has no sexual needs.

In the world of Mrs. Cameron and her friends, unmentionable subjects include sex, age, and death. Their world, internalized by a harsh superego, sits in constant judgment of Rachel: "What a strangely pendulum life I have, fluctuating in age between extremes, hardly knowing myself whether I am too young or too old." She does not accept her mother's view, but cannot act on her own (*JG* 57, 90). Rachel sees herself as an anachronism, sole survivor of an extinct species; a fantasy in the mirror; or an invisible woman. She thinks the children look through, not at her. Her cruel self-portraits constitute an attempt to deal with the limbo she inhabits. Rachel sees herself as a skinny sapling servicing a dog, a scampering giraffe, gaunt crane, lean greyhound on a leash, cross of bones, and inhibited ostrich walking carefully through a formal garden.

This fearful suspension between other states perceived as real is depicted in grotesque and macabre images, as Rachel tries unsuccessfully to sleep. The night is a gigantic carnival wheel turning in blackness; glued to the wheel, a paper Rachel is powerless to stop its pointless circling: "I see scratch of gold against the black, and they form into jagged lines, teeth, a knife's edge, the sharpened hackles of dinosaurs" (*JG* 18, 59). The world is microcosm (every detail magnified) or macrocosm, a phallic apocalypse full of pouring, piercing, arching forms.

Rachel's story, and all the Manawaka works, dramatize the plight of women in a male-oriented, chauvinistic society where both sexes are often unconscious of bias and social conditioning. Hagar's experience could be transposed into a male key with relatively minor alterations, but Rachel's is inescapably female. Her basic insecurity and passivity, her financial anxiety, her sexual vulnerability in the event of pregnancy, and her responsibility for her mother (a situation called by some feminists "the compassion trap") are all traditional female dilemmas.[23]

In the opening scene the inner voice hovers on the edge of panic. Rachel is painfully conscious of the social myth that women, especially single women, are prone to hysteria and eccentricity. The ironic omission of any male aberrations illustrates the difference between Rachel's mind and that of the indirect narrator. We note that Rachel thinks young girls are exceptionally anxious to please but fails to apply this to herself. She is nervous with her male supervisor, and tends to think he knows best, despite her observation of his sadistic pleasure in punishing the children. Because she fears losing her job, her objections to his methods and to his interference with her area of responsibility are minimal, and her manner abject: "Probably I would get down on my knees if this weren't frowned upon" (*JG* 45).

Sexual taboos figure prominently in Manawakan attitudes. Mrs. Cameron's cautionary tale of an unmarried mother is received ironically, but Rachel knows how unpleasantly a single woman with child will be treated. Responding to Nick, she is torn between desire and the fear of being considered bold: "Why do people assume it's so different for men? Is he laughing?" She is ashamed to let Nick know she is a virgin at thirty-four, and angry at herself for half-believing her mother's teaching that virginity is a woman's most precious possession. Sex with Nick is the beginning of Rachel's inner peace and self-confidence: the knowledge that he will somehow "inhabit" her gives strength "against all reason" (*JG* 104). Rachel thinks of sex as a deep sharing, a "tender cruelty."

Fear returns with the thought of bearing a child. Nick, casual and irresponsible, leaves all precautions to Rachel. Her conviction that she is pregnant coincides with the discovery that Nick has left. This precipitates Rachel's crisis, her turning point, and eventual release. The idea of abortion is repugnant. Manawaka calls the abortionist "angel-maker." Yet birth would be only the beginning of difficulties, of eighteen years of financial, physical, and emotional responsibility.[24] Rachel imagines her mother's hysterical reaction, wonders how other women manage, and watches the faces of dancing children who will never be hers: "What will become of me?"

Similar situations provided Victorian melodrama with an opportunity for sentimentality and male rescue. In Laurence's handling Rachel's plight becomes an analogue for human alienation and isolation, a crisis which finds its solution in the woman coming to terms with the jests of God, coping with difficulties, and growing stronger in the process.[25] Rachel matures, not by rejecting responsibilities but by transforming them so that she can accept them on her terms. She escapes not *from* society, like some Canadian Huck Finn, but *into* more dynamic forms of community life.

The metal table where Rachel's tumor is diagnosed is as cold as the tables in the mortuary on the first floor of the Cameron house. The life Rachel has anticipated is non-life, but ironically becomes the nucleus for her newfound strength. The gates of her mind clang shut to fantasies of being rescued by Nick: "No way in, not there, not any more. Visa cancelled." Her words, spoken under anaesthetic, are declaration and prophecy: "I am the mother now." Having faced and outfaced her demons, Rachel is discharged from the hospital like a freed prisoner. Her decision to change jobs and move to the coast mirrors her acceptance of the creative opportunities in change and aging: "Anything may happen, where I'm going. I will be different. I will remain the same." She anticipates being lonely, resentful, insomniac, afraid, lighthearted, joyous: "God's grace on fools."

After the apprentice novel, *This Side Jordan,* Laurence's central characters are female. Nick remains a shadowy figure with mysterious problems. Rachel is flanked by her carping mother and her lesbian friend, Calla. Other female roles are implicit in Rachel's married sister, Stacey, and Nick's mother, a "low stone tower of a woman" who lives by her religious faith and provides her family with an emotional and spiritual center (*JG* 146, 187).

Rachel's relation to Calla is marred by fear, as are her other relationships. (Hagar has no close friend; only in *The Diviners*

does Laurence portray mature female friendship.) The stocky
Calla, with her scorn for female fashion, her religious fervor,
and her independent spirit is a perfect foil for Rachel. In Jungian
terms, Calla is both Animus (beloved) and Shadow (the feared
and despised), embodying qualities in Rachel that have yet to
mature. This does not mean that Rachel has latent lesbian qualities, but that her fear of touching, of tenderness in any form,
is part of her prison. At Calla's Tabernacle Rachel tried to make
herself narrower, to avoid brushing against her neighbor: decent people should keep "themselves to themselves." A kiss,
provoked by her confession of fear, sends Rachel running down
the street in flight from Calla, and from herself (*JG* 32, 35, 38).
Rachel turns back to her friend in time of trouble. Calla's non-
judgmental acceptance, unqualified offer of help, and shared
strength help Rachel to discover her own strength.

Stacey, in Rachel's mind, exists in comfort and security:
"Everything is all right for her, easy and open." Those who
have raised children will find Rachel's view unreal, and Stacey's
own turn in court will come, in *The Fire-Dwellers*. In Rachel's
story Stacey provides a focus for Rachel's resentment at being
left alone to care for their mother, and a contrast with Rachel's
lack of confidence. Stacey always knew what she wanted,
Rachel thinks, and this included escaping from Manawaka: "She
was never afraid."

Mrs. Cameron is unconscious of her subtle bullying, which
is comically apparent to the reader. Her weapons are a weak
heart and a culture that enshrines hypocrisy as decency and
order. Her voice "meadowlarks," her appearance is saucy, elfin,
cute: defiant denials of death and aging. Rachel succumbs to
her pressure to attend church for the sake of appearance. Her
mother's religious beliefs seem hollow, but the subject is unmentionable. Mrs. Cameron's character, which might so easily
have remained a caricature, is fleshed out by Rachel's gradual
perception of the pathos in her mother's empty life; she feels
inadequate, and secretly believes her husband thought her
stupid. Mrs. Cameron is both bully and victim. Rachel's shift
in roles, from child to mother, signifies her coming to terms
with her ancestors and with change.

As undertaker, Niall Cameron guarded the town's dead and

its cherished pretensions. Niall's Plutonian domain occupies the dark downstairs of the Cameron house, an analogue for the human subconscious and for repressed knowledge. The transmutation of the name from Cameron's Funeral Parlour to Japonica Chapel amusingly illustrates middle-class mentality: "No one in Manawaka ever dies, at least not on this side of the tracks." The Camerons' attempt to ignore Niall's profession parallels their culture's refusal to countenance ugly truths. In dreams Rachel sees her mild-mannered, alcoholic father as king over silent people with garish clown makeup: "He says run away Rachel run away run away" (*JG* 19).

Rachel descends to the mortuary when she is sleepless with the fear of pregnancy. The new owner's name reminds us of the novel's epigraph from Carl Sandburg's "Losers," a poem about Jonah's descent into the dark and his reemergence into life. Rachel's talk with Hector allays her fears of death and of her father's wasted life. The chapel door reminds her of *an imitation* of a castle prison door, "Ye Olde Dungeon," like a Disney film where even the children recognize the pretense: her anxieties, plainly, are unnecessary. Comic prophet Hector Jonas believes that Niall had the kind of life he wanted. Through his oblique and blackly comic encounter, which is almost a parody of a ritual descent or rites of passage, Rachel realizes that everyone has fears and hopes, that things change, and life moves on. As she must do.

The title, rich in ambiguities, relates to an image-pattern of fools, clowns, jesters. The silent dead on Camerons' first floor wear clown masks. Mrs. Cameron and her bridge-playing friends have clown voices. Rachel continually sees her tall, awkward body as clown-like, grotesque. Nick's father was Nestor the Jestor to the local children when he delivered milk; senile, and mourning for his dead son, Nestor's plight suggests the black joke of a cruel deity.

Laurence's fiction, like Patrick White's, hints at a dark god whose ways are not only mysterious but cruel. One of White's images for this concept is the vivisector. In the novel so named, White depicts human suffering as a kind of vivisection, a cruel surgery which becomes a stage in our transmutation into a more desirable state.[26] Rachel thinks that God, if He exists, must be some kind of brutal joker. She sees her plight as a "knifing" reality, "grotesque, unbearably a joke if viewed from the outside" (*JG* 151). Her life is one long fight with God; she prays, with no certainty of being heard; and speaks of God to her mother, wondering if this is a partial triumph or the last defeat (*JG* 171, 195).

The fool pattern modulates from the demonic to the apocalyptic form. Calla reads from St. Paul: "If any man among you thinketh himself to be wise, let him become a fool, that he may be wise." The word *God* recurs four times in the novel's last short paragraph, composed of thirteen words. The circular sentence structure of the very last sentence, and of the paragraph that contains it, brilliantly identify God with mankind as Divine Fool. They are joined by mercy/grace/pity, the three verbs of the closing sentences. This is the culmination of an intricate pattern on the folly of fear and the fear of folly. Wrestling with it, Rachel is ready to smile at "that fool of a fear, that poor fear of fools"; "I should be honoured to be of that company" (*JG* 181, 198).[27]

Further variations on jests cosmic and human include the speaking in tongues at the Tabernacle, Nick's ambiguously proffered photograph of a boy who resembles himself, Mrs. Cameron's weak heart, and Rachel's confrontation with her mother in the last chapter. Truth is the last thing that Mrs. Cameron expects in reply to her mock apology for being a strain on her daughter; the reversal (tyrant deposed) is high comedy. At the same time, realizing the folly of thinking that she can keep her mother alive, Rachel is released from this responsibility. The speaking in tongues, which has been an object of terror, broadens out into a symbol of the difficulties of human communication, the mystery yet importance of what Mannoni calls the Other. Rachel calls it "God's irony—that we should for so long believe it is only the few who speak in tongues" (*JG* 134). St. Paul speaks of many kinds of voices in the world, none without significance: a statement, Rachel thinks, not of what should be but what *is*.

A jest of history is reflected in Manawaka's cultural composition, half Scottish half Ukrainian. Both groups came because of poverty, and hope. Rachel sees the two as oil and water:

"The Ukrainians knew how to be better grain farmers, but the Scots knew how to be almightier than anyone but God" (*JG* 65). Pride and anger sustained the first few generations of Scots in Manitoba, but by Rachel's time the backbone has "splintered." She thinks that pride is not her problem, but her fears stem partly from a pride of appearance that acts to isolate her.[28] Nick remembers the alienation felt by Ukrainian children in a town where the power structure, the hegemony, was Scottish. To Mrs. Cameron, Ukrainians are Galicians or Bohunks, unfit companions for her children. She is surprised that "the milk-man's son" has achieved a university degree, and oblivious to the related irony that her daughter has not.

In an analysis of the fictional characters as political types, Kenneth Hughes criticizes Nick for his inability to come to terms with his past. Nick's choices suggest that Ukrainians and, by extension, other Canadian minorities, are headed for assimilation and the loss of their cultural inheritance. Hughes also criticizes Nick for using Rachel as a commodity. Rachel, however, never condemns or judges Nick in this way, perhaps because to do so would be to put herself in the role of victim. Laurence has no such melodrama in mind.

Hughes argues that *A Jest of God* is not only a psychological study but a representation of sociohistorical forces within Canada and of that country's relation to Great Britain. In Hughes's reading, the tyrannical Mrs. Cameron is the mother country in its role as imperial power; Rachel is symbolic of "a Canada seeking to free itself from an authoritarian colonial past and to make its own future"; her tumor represents that colonial past and its authoritarian values, while its removal is the end of the colonial state of mind.[29]

Orientals, in Manawaka, fare worse than Ukrainians. The Regal Cafe is owned and run by Lee Toy, a dried shell of a man who seems ageless. Rachel thinks that Lee Toy has spent most of his life in secrecy, living alone above his cafe: "My father told me once that Lee Toy's wife was still in China, still alive and living on the money he sent, but unable to come here, first because of our laws and then because of theirs. Maybe she is there yet, the woman he has not seen for more than forty years" (*JG* 55). Laurence's implicit comment on Toy's heroism and on two contrasting cultures, Oriental and Western, is caught in the two pictures which hang on the walls of the Regal Cafe. One is a Coca-Cola poster, the other, a Chinese scroll with a mountain and solitary tiger.[30]

Other minorities are suggested by Miklos, the Greek owner of the Parthenon Cafe. Hughes's political insights are very suggestive with regard to Laurence's handling of these minor characters, Toy and Miklos. Several textual details, beyond the obvious references in the names of the restaurants, evoke the heroic prototype. Yet Laurence makes the connection between an august past and a petty present without apparent irony. In Laurence's fiction, a classically heroic past becomes an ordinary Canadian present *without the loss of its heroic element.* In Hughes's words, "Laurence time and again sets off the old imperial grand heroic against the democratic, low-key, ordinary and everyday heroic which is her norm for a post-colonial Canadian society. This process of definition is itself one of the dimensions of the political in the novel. . . ."[31] John Watt Lennox makes a similar point about the democratic basis of Laurence's vision, in an article devoted to showing that Laurence discovers "the extraordinary within the pedestrian."[32] Nick's inner demons, Toy's lonely pain, reflect Rachel's fears and ground them in a specific soil.

Laurence's interest in multimedia techniques culminates in the record which accompanies *The Diviners.* In *A Jest of God* it takes the form of children's chants, folk-songs, hymns. All are thematically significant. The chant that introduces the novel evokes time passing, change, and yearning: a yearning for admiration, respect, power, sexual fulfillment, all things denied to Rachel in her view. The cryptic advice to Spanish dancers to get out of town is prophetic with regard to Rachel's decision to leave Manawaka. More important, it hints at her need to transcend the psychic prison of local attitudes. The golden city, Zion or New Jerusalem in biblical typology, suggests a fulfillment which is both physical and spiritual. This is picked up in the Anglican's solo, "Jerusalem the Golden," and in the Pentecostal rendering of "Rejoice! Rejoice! Emmanual/Shall come to thee, O Israel!" Rachel's fears are excluding her from these joyful states.

The metaphors in the opening scene are largely demonic. Time is imaged as a process leading to confined boxes (the school, her classroom) which suggest prisons and coffins. Power is arbitrary (the "thin giant She" can pick any colored chalk, write anything at all on the board) and ultimately illusory. Growing up is a grotesque distortion of the child's body, leading to the final distortion of the undertaker's art.

Conversely, the images at the end are full of hope and affirmation. Heading west, the bus flies smoothly and confidently like a great owl. The possibilities imagined by Rachel are comic, whimsical, but largely pleasurable. Time, in Laurence's comic fiction, is seen to play a redeeming role.

### III  *"Cain and His Brother"*

Stacey's story concerns violence and its many masks. Hagar Shipley and Rachel Cameron are relatively unusual characters, but *The Fire-Dwellers* presents an ordinary housewife with whom many women will identify. Her world is the frighteningly familiar one of a postwar North American city. This is a manipulative society characterized by brutality and deception: masked violence. Stacey's fears, both personal and social, are generated largely by her society: "Doom everywhere is the message I get."[33]

Stacey MacAindra is Rachel Cameron's married sister who has grown up in Manawaka but escaped early. The novel covers several months in Stacey's thirty-ninth year, ending on the eve of her fortieth birthday. Events include her husband taking a sales job with Richalife ("Not Just Vitamins—A New Way of Life"), the death of Mac's best friend, Buckle, and Stacey's brief affair with Luke, a young writer. Much of the action takes place inside Stacey's head as she struggles with herself, her husband, their four children, and their society, to wring a modified victory from besetting difficulties. Without the irony of the narrative voices and the honesty of vision this material would be melodrama.[34] As it is, the novel's ending parodies a serialized soap opera, anticipating the possibilities for the next episode: will the city return tomorrow? We suspect it will, with very similar difficulties.

The violence that blares from radio and television is not simply outside the MacAindra home. Violence, sometimes latent or concealed, permeates their relationships. Stacey's "fortress" harbors a Trojan horse. She is slow to recognize her own capacity for violence and, when she does, is terrified by the idea of hurting her own children: "God, don't let me. Stay my hand. I scare the hell out of myself when I think this way" (FD 212). Simultaneously, she remembers a newspaper story of a divorced mother found in a catatonic state beside her dead child.

The first illustration of MacAindra violence is a fight between the sons, aged ten and seven, over a go-cart. Ian is annoyed by his young brother's mechanical ineptitude: "Cain and his brother must have started their hatred like this" (FD 16). Horrified, Stacey tears them apart and throws them both on the floor. Another newspaper account, this one of a mother smothering her infant, comes immediately to mind. When Duncan cries in his sleep the next night, Stacey feels responsible.

Mac, her husband, is less prone to physical violence, but his icy calm is a different (and perhaps worse) form of rage. Ian inherits Mac's tight-lipped control. He craves his father's approval, yet is suspicious of him: they "knife" one another with words. Mac's Puritan restraint has been bred in him by his clergyman father, who used the whip of iron will and moral superiority to shame his son's exhibition of rage (FD 131).

Mac is seen through Stacey's eyes and through his own words and actions—never from inside. His chief fear is financial. Stacey suspects that this heavy family responsibility has driven Mac "underground" into silence. Guilt at being part of his financial burden is a gun aimed at her head. Mac counters Stacey's objection to the advertising methods of Richalife's manager with the reminder that she wants their children to be able to go to university. Fear breeds guilt, in both Mac and Stacey. He must juggle the claims of personal integrity with financial responsibility. Mac has left an earlier sales job which went against his conscience, but he eventually finds a workable compromise for the problems posed by Richalife.

Violence represents one type of communication, and the failure of other types. One of Stacey's chief fears is of being unable to communicate, or remaining trapped in her skull. The difficulty of peaceful communication, the alternative to violence, becomes a dominant theme. The problem preoccupies Stacey. She moves from the naive view that it can be solved by an honest voicing of thoughts and feelings, to the understanding that whereas this may be a partial solution, silence and concealment are also necessary in human relations, and communication does not depend simply on words.

Two-year-old Jen's refusal, or inability, to speak belongs to this pattern, and one of several optimistic events at the novel's end is Jen's first speech—social words, significantly: "Want tea, Mum?" Stacey's relief, to our amusement, is almost immediately replaced by a new fear, that Jen may never say anything else. The novel opens with Stacey thinking of her efforts to teach "a few human words," followed by her half-conscious recognition that words conceal more than they reveal, and that nursery rhymes are full of horrors.

After nearly twenty years of marriage, Mac and Stacey find it difficult to communicate. Stacey resents Mac's silences. After a day spent alone or with children (the typical situation for the housewife), she looks to Mac to bring her something of the outside world. But he responds to questions with the demand to be left alone. Stacey fears he no longer takes her seriously or finds her attractive: "can you imagine what it's like to live in the same house with somebody who doesn't talk or who can't or else won't and I don't know which reason it could be" (*FD* 197). Her imagination connects Mac's willed isolation with his fear of pain, and with some ancient or Edenic crisis.

Stacey's memories of her childhood in Manawaka revolve around failures in communication. She remembers the "tomb silences" of her parents; her mother's unsuccessful attempts to force Niall Cameron to conform to Manawakan standards; and the pattern of deception between her mother and herself as she placated her mother's fears with false assurances about boys and liquor. Stacey half-knows, half-suspects Mac's similar difficulties with his father Matthew. They are all moles: "Once I thought it was only people like Matthew and my mother who had that kind of weak eyes. Now I know it's me, as much" (*FD* 164).

Tess and Jake Fogler, the MacAindras's childless neighbors,

provide another variant on the themes of concealed violence, fear, and failed communication. Ironically, Jake is part of the euphemistically named communications industry. He is a radio actor, fond of talking of the breakdown of verbal communication. Jake knows nothing of his beautiful wife's fears that he finds her stupid or that he may be attracted to a radio actress, while Tess is equally ignorant of Jake's self-consciousness about his ugliness and short stature.

Tess copes with fear by purchasing objects for which they have no use, and cosmetics designed to vanquish the ravages of time. Her pet goldfish, who devour one another, image her society. Tess forces Jen to watch this cannibalism. Her suicide attempt comes as no surprise, but Stacey blames herself for her failure to see the fears behind the glamorous mask.

Private fears echo public horrors. The epigraph from Carl Sandburg's "Losers" speaks of fiddling to a world on fire, and hints that action is meaningless. This epigraph, and the children's rhyme ("Ladybird, ladybird,/ Fly away home;/ Your house is on fire,/ Your children are gone") reflect the characters' fears. In Stacey's society, death takes many forms: suicide, automobile accident, police bullets, bombing, maiming, napalm. Her city assumes, for an instant, the form of "that other city" (Hiroshima), "glass and steel broken like vulnerable live bones, shadows of people frog-splayed on the stone" (FD 11). A gull is admired for its simple knowledge of survival. Stacey thinks her children will need to know the violence of the city's core.

Newspaper headlines chase through Stacey's mind as backdrop to family activity: " 'Seventeen-Year-Old on Drug Charge.' 'Girl Kills Self, Lover.' 'Homeless Population Growing, Says Survey.' " The radio blares disaster at frequent intervals: NINE O'CLOCK NEWS PELLET BOMBS CAUSED THE DEATH OF A HUNDRED AND TWENTY FIVE CIVILIANS MAINLY WOMEN AND CHILDREN IN. . . ." A story of an ex-soldier with murderous reflexes suggests we have been conditioned into monsterdom. Everyone lives dangerously, Stacey tells Luke; we are all fire-dwellers in a word gone mad. Niall's revolver provides an escape fantasy which she finally abandons. Even the children fear death, having lost one friend in an auto accident.

Lesser anxieties concern the need for a university education;

the need to look beautiful and elegant; the need to be "free" in some unspecified way; and the need to be a perfect spouse. Popular journalism feeds the "tapeworms of doubt" in the social body: "Nine ways the Modern Mum May Be Ruining Her Daughter"; "Are you Castrating Your Son?"; "Are You Emasculating Your Husband?" Conversation at parties reveals the fears of many women at the prospect of an empty house after the children are all at school.

Since people prefer not to see the disasters they help to create, society develops deception to a fine art. The con man is king. Mac's new employer illustrates our will to be deceived. Richalife, promising rejuvenation through vitamin pills, is a secular parody of the religious vision of the Promised Land: "Both Spirit and Flesh Altered." The parody extends from the obvious pun in the name to evangelical testimonials at rallies by those who believe the pills have altered their lives. Thor Thorlakson is the prophet of this pseudo-religion, preaching the good news that "the shackles have been lifted" (*FD* 39). Richalife promises to cure anxiety, depression, and lack of energy. Thor is unaware of the irony that he proposes to replace old addictions (to caffeine, liquor, tranquilizers) with new. His suggestion that they are selling not just pills but themselves sits oddly with his vaunted freedom. Laurence's parody of high-pressure religious evangelism is extremely funny.

Modern business methods and language are also objects of parody. Thor sprinkles his conversation with jargon such as "alertwise" and "caffeine-wise." He sees no hidden intent when Stacey uses this jargon in mock approval, in her parody of a parody of a testimonial: "caffeine-wise I'm like a new woman." The forms of systems analysis and psychological testing are parodied in the Richalife Quiz designed to identify guilt feelings, goals, and family relationships, and in the individual programs based on self-assessment. Mac is shocked when Stacey asks if lies are permitted. However, he and Thor have put themselves on Richalife programs which identify them as younger, happier, and less anxious than they are. The confessional element in the quiz parodies the religious confession. Stacey says it is naive to expect truth on a form, and that the quiz, like much of modern life, "communicates" an attractive lie.

The quiz and the individual charts are manipulation masked as helpfulness. Laurence's portrait of the intrusion of corporations into private lives (the Big Brother is Watching You syndrome) is black comedy: Stacey has trouble with the word *intrusion* when she is drunk. Beneath a jolly, fatherly veneer, Thor is mean and vindictive. He has a "court" of simpering henchmen. The thunder-god is all wind, no substance. But the fears he generates are real.

Deception, the demonic form of communication, goes hand in hand with the anxieties of modern life. Lies, not pills or alcohol, are the chief sedative, and the basis of many relationships. Stacey cannot bear to think of Matthew living in the MacAindra house-hold because his need for constant reassurance necessitates her lies. The "human words" of the opening paragraph modulate into "talking sounds" exchanged amid anxieties.

The Polyglam party is even broader farce than the Richalife rallies, and on the same theme. The "plastic lady" is oracle and trickster magician. She masks her fear of aging beneath garish makeup. Her parlor game fosters anxiety in the housewives, who dutifully follow instructions. Stacey wonders what they are frightened of: "Making a scene? Finding out we're alone after all—" (*FD* 87). Like the Richalife material, the Polyglam booklet offers the attractive lie of peaceful, happy families. Polyglam understands the importance of packaging, as does the hostess, Tess.

Laurence's ironic technique includes Stacey's silent dialogue with a God in whom she does and does not believe. This dialogue is at the core of Stacey's personality. The image of God fluctuates from an authoritarian, omnipotent being to one who shares in our helplessness (*FD* 11, 212). Talking with God is also talking to the unmasked self; questions remain largely unanswered but can be faced with some degree of honesty. God is connected with the destructive aspect of time passing: contemplating her present shape, Stacey decides God has "a sick sense of humour." She attempts to bargain with Him for the safety of her children, like Jacob wrestling with the angel.

The breakdown in communication for Stacey's generation extends to religion. Since she envisages Matthew as a man with no religious problems, Stacey is touched when he reveals lifelong doubt. She pretends to faith for the sake of her children, but suspects that they are not deceived. Like Laurence, she "mourns" her disbelief. Stacey's yearning for a transcendent reality, like Rachel's, is suggested by her singing hymns beloved in childhood, where God is the theme too high "for mortal tongue."

Time, as humans experience it, is one of Laurence's continuing concerns. In *The Fire-Dwellers*, she examines the breakdown in communication in terms of the ways in which we experience time. Stacey wonders if time has imposed layers of masks over too-tender truth (like the circles that tell the age of a tree), or stripped them away. Time passing has turned Mac from a confident extrovert into an anxious, silent introvert. Stacey's change, from a vivid teen-ager who seems to have existed five minutes ago into a plump, dowdy housewife, seems "some monstrous injustice." Yet the vivid young woman survives within the housewife: "*Is* time? How?" (*FD* 12).

Throughout much of the novel, time appears to Stacey as a negative, hostile phenomenon. Her inner self is masked by fat; stretch marks on thighs and belly appear as silver worms, an image of death and putrefaction. Her intelligence has also altered for the worse. Evening courses bore and humiliate her: "Where have I gone?" "Once I was different" (*FD* 72-73).

Personal relations also change. Mac and Stacey, once compatible, have acquired mutually irritating habits. The metaphor of invisible garbage recurs. Problems have ancient roots. Time alienates people, introduces guilt, or becomes a treadmill where one communicates one's own unchanging awfulness to oneself. Like Rachel, Stacey has a sense of inhabiting a middle world, a limbo frightening and unreal: "I stand in relation to my life both as child and parent, never quite finished with the old battles, never able to arbitrate properly the new, able to look both ways, but whichever way I look, God, it looks pretty confusing to me" (*FD* 47). With Luke, the young stranger encountered after a bitter quarrel with Mac, Stacey hopes to shed her accumulated baggage. This escapist interlude is Stacey's last attempt to be eighteen again, and to leave behind the encumbrances of town and family.

The basically optimistic temper of Laurence's vision shows in a series of events late in the novel, where Stacey accepts herself, her responsibilities, and the changes wrought by time, the Black

Joker. Eventually, time plays a redeeming role. One of the first of such events involves Jen's frightening experience with Tess Fogler. In their mutual concern for Jen, Katie and Stacey encounter one another as persons, without the role-playing structures of mother and daughter: they say *we*, like Hagar and the Oriental girl in the hospital bedpan incident.

Other affirmative events include Duncan's narrow escape from drowning, and the accompanying role reversals among the Mac-Aindra males. Ian now exhibits love for Duncan, not jealousy; and Mac is released to demonstrate the affection which his father has taught him to conceal. Duncan is able to face the sea again. Jen begins to talk. Stacey finds she can talk to Mac, as to Luke, but all genuine communication is difficult.

*The Fire-Dwellers* points implicitly to the force of social conditioning on women's consciousness. Stacey has no thought of getting work outside the house; she has neither time nor strength for such aberrations. When Mac suggests that the solution for the painful nervousness of the beautiful girl who testifies at a rally is the lasting love of a good man, Stacey agrees. There is no irony in this encounter, no suggestion that the woman has needs beyond those which might be satisfied by marriage and a family.

The comic narrative structure is buttressed by many techniques for humor, from puns to juxtaposition. *Jen* suggests *genuine*; *Polyglam*, synthetic or false *glamor*; "fishwife, fleshwife, sagging guttily"; "No recriminations. No unmerry-go-round of pointless words." Something unendurable is "Not to be borne. Not to be born would be not to have to die" (*FD* 21). Laurence's wit and love of language runs throughout her work, but *The Fire-Dwellers* is perhaps her funniest novel, albeit the humor is black.

Science fiction is used to suggest grotesque, macabre aspects of society. Stacey perceives a supermarket as a temple with long aisles and chromium side chapels. Votive offerings include dead fish, strawberries on ice, planets of grapefruit, jungles of lettuce, "a thousand bear-faced mouse-legended space-legended space-crafted plastic-gifted strangely transformed sproutings of oat and wheat fields" (*FD* 74). At the hairdresser, mauve-clad priestesses with talonless claws set off one of Stacey's SF sex fantasies. Thor is a wizard, and the Polyglam lady "a slickly sleight-of-handing magician." Convoluted language suggests social deviancy. Luke's

SF story of the Greyfolk in North America, some thousand years hence, is a neat reversal of white colonial policy in Africa. In this connection, we are given the unnecessary hint that SF is an allegory for contemporary human life (*FD* 180, 200).

An imaginative use of typography indicates Stacey's different voices, and separates these from third-person narration. The latter, represented by ordinary type, advances the narrative, and sometimes provides oblique commentary. Stacey's practical thoughts, factual and ironic, are introduced by a long dash, whereas her poetic and romantic daydreams are in italicized passages with regular margins. Memories of newspaper events are in ordinary type, with deep indentation. Snippets of radio news come in unpunctuated capitals like telegrams. Open-ended remarks, without terminal punctuation, accurately reflect verbal patterns, while Stacey's longer inner monologues are in stream-of-consciousness form. As Allan Bevan notes, in his Introduction to the New Canadian Library edition, the introductory dash is essential in conversations interlaced with Stacey's thoughts, and there is constant interaction of memories, thoughts, fantasies, conversations, and actions.

Laurence made three or four false starts on *The Fire-Dwellers* over a ten-year span. She was seeking a form to convey a sense of simultaneity and complexity: "Narration, dreams, memories, inner running commentary,—all had to be brief, even fragmented, to convey the jangled quality of Stacey's life."[35] No single voice could convey the disparity between the inner and outer aspects of her experience, and the frequent contrasts between her thoughts and speech. Problems of voice, Laurence adds, were compounded by the multiplicity of interlocking themes, all inherent in Stacey's situation: the marriage relationship after many years; the relation between generations; the relation with an incendiary world; and the relation with Self, which includes coping with aging and death.

Laurence acknowledges the effect of television on her technique, and her desire to capture sharp visual images, "the effect of voices and pictures."[36] She suspects that readers conditioned by film and television *need* visual variety on the page, hence her typographical innovations. Curiously, she aspired in this novel to write a sparser, more "pared down" prose than she had previously written. Yet *The Fire-Dwellers* is weakened by unnecessary repetition, boring exchanges, and occasionally blatant symbolism. It might profit by deletions. None of Laurence's other work, with the possible exception of *This Side Jordan*, suffers from these weaknesses. Some of the dialogue (such as the conversation between wives at the Richalife parties, or Stacey's bedtime talks with her tired, harassed husband) is realistic but dull. The technical problem of depicting a boring exchange without boring the reader remains unresolved.

Some dialogues sound like a Harold Pinter play, but there are too many relatively futile exchanges. There are repetitions that add nothing, such as the second reference to Katie's long hair which looks as if it has been ironed (*FD* 12, 13). We do not need so many examples of fear, anxiety, and noncommunication. The heavy-handedness here is unlike Laurence's usual style; examples might include Tess Fogler's comment that Jen is "determined not to communicate"; and Jake's fondness for talking about the breakdown of verbal communication. Laurence's theme suffers from overkill.

Stacey's individual crisis, however, requires a social setting, and this necessitates some repetition. The structure in the first three-quarters of the novel is virtually static, with multiple repetitions illustrating a central theme. The kinetic movement of comedy begins near the end of the novel: as she learns from her experience, Stacey grows inwardly. Her growth is paralleled by similarly affirmative movements in the other family members. In a very real sense the protagonist in *The Fire-Dwellers* is postwar Western society.[37] Stacey is a female version of the "little man" in contemporary, antiheroic fiction. She is atypical only in her strongly ironic sense of humor.

Stacey's final, short soliloquy is as comic as Molly Bloom's. She decides that trivialities may be acceptable distractions; that she is unlikely to become thinner, and that this is ludicrous but not tragic: "Give me another forty years, Lord, and I may mutate into a matriarch." The time span is that of the Israelites' desert exile en route to the Promised Land; *mutate* suggests an evolution of species; alliteration adds a comic touch; and *matriarch* suggests a family clan or dynasty, along with a shaping power for its female founder. This mutant joins her family and city in peaceful sleep.

Stacey is one of Laurence's survivors. She wrestles a modest victory from a society which she finally accepts on her own terms.[38] She enjoys debunking hypocrisies propagated by Richa-life, Polyglam, and other advertisers. Violence remains, but "there is nowhere to go but here" (*FD* 259). Stacey learns that the trap is the world, not her four walls, and that it is not without its compensations and pleasures.

## IV  *Jericho's Brick Battlements*

The eight stories that compose *A Bird in the House* reveal a society through its precocious product and critic. All but the last story have been published separately and are, on one level, self-contained. The collection forms an unconventional novel, linked by character, setting, narrative voice, and structure.[39] Taken together, and in order, the stories trace Vanessa MacLeod's growth to maturity, depicted as an understanding of herself and her heritage.

Laurence says the net effect is "not unlike" a novel and that the stories were conceived from the beginning as a related group. She believes the stories are "totally unlike" a novel, structurally, but by this she means that it is unlike a conventional novel or her other novels. She describes themes and events in the average novel as a series of wavy, interlocking, horizontal lines: "The short stories have flow lines which are different. They move very close together but parallel and in a *vertical* direction. . . . Nevertheless, the relationship of time and the narrative voice can be seen just as plainly in the stories, as in a novel.[40]

Vanessa is ten in the first three stories, and eleven or twelve in many others. In briefer incidents she is a small child, an older adolescent, or young adult. The first-person narrative voice in *A Bird in the House* is technically brilliant. It is multiple, representing Vanessa the child and Vanessa the remembering adult. Ingenuity and sophistication blend unobtrusively. Laurence shows us what the child sees, and what she does not see because of her inexperience: "I did not know then"; "I had at the time no idea how much it cost him" (*BH* 9, 84). Laurence describes her handling of voice as follows:

The narrative voice is, of course, that of Vanessa herself, but an older Vanessa, herself grown up, remembering how it was when she was ten. . . . this particular narrative device was a tricky one. . . . What I tried to do was definitely *not* to tell the story as though it were being narrated by a child. This would have been impossible for me and also would have meant denying the story one of its dimensions, a time-dimension, the viewing from a distance of events which had happened in childhood. The narrative voice had to be that of an older Vanessa, but at the same time the narration had to be done in such a way that the ten-year-old would be conveyed. The narrative voice, therefore, had to speak as though from two points in time, simultaneously.[41]

Vanessa's love of writing is another ingenious aspect of the voice. Because she thinks of herself as a writer struggling to understand people, Vanessa is a "professional listener" who eavesdrops unashamedly in plain view or from various posts such as a bedroom air-register. This helps to solve one of the problems of first-person narration, the need for the observer's omnipresence. Vanessa's writings are tragic, romantic, and melodramatic. As she begins to understand the real passions around her, she despises her compositions. Her stories and flamboyant fantasies are ironically juxtaposed with family events so as to serve as indirect commentary. They also allow Laurence to parody popular Canadian romances of the late nineteenth and early twentieth centuries, such as *Annette, the Métis Spy*.

The stories are unified by a steady progression in the type of suffering depicted. The first deals with social exclusion and loneliness; the second, with a past death and painfully aborted dreams. The birth of a baby boy, a new Roderick, effects a bittersweet mood. The third concerns Grandmother Connor's death, the family's grief, and Aunt Edna's lost love. The death of Dr. MacLeod in the fourth story precipitates Vanessa's loss of religious faith. The fifth, sixth, and seventh stories relate individual suffering to massive social failures: economic breakdown, world war, poverty, class friction, and racial discrimination. Laurence shows a development in Vanessa's ability to comprehend both human suffering and the limitations of her understanding in this regard.

Clara Thomas and George Woodcock emphasize the importance of the Depression in these stories. Woodcock calls the evocation of place and time superbly appropriate:

By predicament as well as by place the people of *A Bird in the House* are united, and here—as in *The Tomorrow-Tamer*—the sense of alienation is crucial, though now it is not the transformation of a society so much as the failure of a society that sets the tone. Society in general having failed, the natural social units become important again, and families are willy-nilly reunited, Aunt Edna coming home from jobless Winnipeg, Dr. MacLeod moving in with his widowed mother because his patients can no longer pay him in cash; the depression in fact renews the pioneer intensity of relationships within small and threatened groups, and that intensity Margaret Laurence mordantly evokes.[42]

In the first and last stories the mood is one of modified optimism. Their structure is comic, the narrative driving towards social integration and self-knowledge. *A Bird in the House* is framed by joyous sounds (Uncle Dan's singing, and the bannering horn of Grandfather's MacLaughlin-Buick), as Vanessa, like some new-world Joshua, braves the battlements of her ancestors and comes to terms with them and with herself. These framing stories lighten, and subtly alter, the darker stories of pain and social guilt which they surround.

"The Sound of the Singing" introduces Vanessa's mother's family, especially her stern father. In Manawaka, Grandfather Connor is respected as an upright man: hard-working, thrifty, a strict observer of sabbatarian laws. His brother Dan is a *downright* man, like others whom the townsfolk despise: "They were described as 'downright worthless' or 'downright lazy,' the two terms being synonomous. These *shadows* of wastrels, these flimsy remnants of past profligates, with their dry laughter like the cackle of crows or the crackling of fallen leaves underfoot, embarrassed one terribly . . . . Yet I was inexplicably drawn to them, too" (*BH* 9, emphasis added).

The two brothers suggest Jung's *persona* and *shadow* archetypes. The shadow, the repressed part of the personality, is feared by the conscious, public self. It is usually dark and threatening, immoral in conventional terms. In Laurence's comic version, Grandfather's shadow is profligate, gay, happy as a child—all characteristics that a Puritan culture tends to repress. Grandfather and his brother Dan thus serve as an effective introduction to Vanessa's family, to the town, and to its Puritan values and attitudes. Vanessa's attraction to her uncle, in

Jungian terms, represents the self's need to incorporate the shadow to achieve wholeness.

Brick House, bear, battle, bird, horse, song: the key images here are central to the collection. Grandfather's house, like his person, is dwelling place, monument, and embattled fortress in a heathen wilderness. The opening metaphors hold the ambivalence Laurence has frequently expressed towards her heritage. It is "sternly protective" (like the sweeping spruce branches), yet also threatening and inhibiting. Warlike images include a lawnmower beheading stray flowers. In the last story, opposing Grandfather is like batting one's head against a brick wall.

Grandfather is introduced as "some great watchful bear waiting for the enforced hibernation of Sunday to be over." *Bear* suggests his impatience, temper, strength, and ability to survive. Timothy Connor's early life is sketched in the first and last stories. He has left school early, and come West from Ontario to Manitoba by Red River steamer, like Laurence's Grandfather Simpson.[43] He walked the hundred-odd miles from Winnipeg to Manawaka, finding work as a blacksmith along the way. He saved money, started a hardware business, and built the town's first brick house. He is fond of noting that no one helped him; proud of the financial responsibility he continues to shoulder; and puzzled that thrift and prudence do not earn love.

Grandfather looms as some Old Testament Jehovah, while his gentle wife is mercy incarnate. The image of life as battle belongs especially to the personalities of Grandfather and Vanessa. Like Hagar Shipley, both have warlike natures. She comes to see him as perhaps immortal "in ways which it would take me half a lifetime to comprehend" (*BH* 205).

Daniel's attractive *joie de vivre* is suggested by his Irish songs and his passion for horses. Edna finds the stage-Irish expressions and rebel songs of this Ontario-born Protestant "phoney as a three-dollar bill." The brothers' defects and virtues are comically illustrated and nicely balanced. Vanessa grants the justice of Grandfather's claims, but her sympathies lie with the singer. Like Hagar (and us all) she longs to rejoice.

The image patterns converge in the last story, where the brick battlements are invaded by suitors, grandfather's auto becomes Vanessa's retreat for writing, and the bear of a man is laid to his final rest. The Brick House is prison, and fortress against winter storms. Vanessa's mother feels trapped but her children will escape. Edna finds it "dungeon" and "refuge." "The absolute worst wouldn't happen here, ever. Things wouldn't actually fall apart" (*BH* 187).

At the end, the middle-aged narrator returns to Manawaka to visit the cemetery and the Brick House. She realizes that her grandfather's monument is his living dynasty; more particularly, the granddaughter who has raged against him and his culture: "I had feared and fought the old man, yet he proclaimed himself in my veins." Laurence's emphasis on the necessity for coming to terms with one's ancestors and gods finds its most powerful expression in this beautifully apt and symbolic remark. She calls *A Bird in the House* her only autobiographical work.

The MacLaughlin-Buick is an amusing variant on horses. This form of power, connoting money and pride, suits Grandfather. At twelve, Vanessa remembers riding with him when she was very young. The horn bannered their conquering presence: "*A-hoo-gah*! I was gazing with love and glory at my giant grandfather as he drove his valiant chariot through all the streets of this world" (*BH* 179). Seven years later, Vanessa returns for his funeral and remembers herself remembering driving with him, "in the ancient days when he seemed as large and admirable as God." The incident evokes the dominant metaphor of Laurence's work, of journeying in search of freedom and joy. It reminds us, too, of her insistence that our local roots, our direct ancestors, provide our myths.

Aunt Edna's suitor, the railway stationmaster, belongs to this pattern of journeying. Wes's low-key defiance of Grandfather is extremely funny, and his encounter with the Connors' fiery furnace is a hilarious parody of Saint George and the Dragon. The "monster" is both the overheated furnace and the maiden's father in his basement lair. Edna is a middle-aged lady-in-distress, held in the Connor dungeon. Marriage provides Edna with a kind husband, a house, and the right to travel on Wes's railway pass. Vanessa wonders how long it will be before her own escape.

For comic parody Laurence draws on the St. George myth, and on Homer's *Odyssey*. Grandfather evicts Vanessa's caller,

like Odysseus routing the suitors. Grandfather suspects that
Michael is married; later, Vanessa cannot forgive him for being
right. The disapproving *screee-scraaaw* of his rockers is a form
of battle cry. Myth joins with history in Laurence's fiction, as
in Kafka and Joyce. Vanessa's conversation with a young airman
links the Battle of Britain and Culloden with the Odyssey. War
has claimed many of Manawaka's young Scots and Ukrainians,
Vanessa's friends. She says that war means that people without
choice in the matter were broken and spilled: "Like the clans-
men at Culloden. Or Ulysses' spearmen. Maybe even Ulysses"
(*BH* 197). The young people agree that there are *no more heroes,*
a statement reflected in the irony of the narrative voice, and in
Laurence's use of the low mimetic mode of realistic fiction. At
the same time the characters in *A Bird in the House* are heroic.
*The Diviners* marks the culmination of these techniques.

"To Set Our House in Order" is a beautifully crafted story
of a birth. The event is placed within a web of interlocking
images which contribute to the central theme: of life amid
death, and renewed hope amid failed dreams. The removal of
Vanessa's mother to hospital leaves the child with her stern,
aristocratic paternal grandmother and her practical Aunt Edna.
The child's fears are expressed; the grandmother's, repressed,
as the culture dictates. Grandmother tells Vanessa that the
MacLeods do not tell lies; that they accept what happens as
God's will; and that she has survived the loss of her son Roderick,
killed at the Battle of the Somme. The story reveals ironically
that living involves lying, and lies can be loving.

The story sketches the aborted dreams of three characters.
Grandmother MacLeod wishes to live as an aristocrat, like her
Scottish ancestors. In pioneer conditions, and a depressed econ-
omy in the 1930s, she struggles to maintain her imagined world
of silver, lace, and tea parties. Her husband, a country doctor,
read Greek tragedies in their original language. The thwarted
scholar's son, Vanessa's father, wanted to enter the merchant
marine. His library is filled with travel books and copies of
*National Geographic Magazine.* Vanessa's final thoughts about
order link these failed dreams with the newborn life.

The strangeness of these diverse viewpoints is suggested in
the circular rose window in the MacLeod house. Its many-

colored glass permits the viewer to see the world under very different aspects, "as a place of absolute sapphire or . . . a hateful yellow." The multiple colors (all components of light), the perfect shape, and the traditional connotations of the rose in Christian iconography combine to make the window the kind of image Northrop Frye calls anagogic, an image which seems to contain the cosmos. Vanessa rejects Grandmother's version of God's will, yet the image patterns point to some transcendental order, suggested by the rose window and the golden poplar leaves in the bluff.[44]

The theme of inner freedom is represented by bird imagery. Grandmother MacLeod's hair is "*bound* grotesquely like *white*-feathered *wings* in the *snare* of her coarse night-time hair*net*" (*BH* 40, emphasis added). Vanessa's dream of a captive bird mingles with the sound of her mother crying and the voices of dead children. The reference is to an earlier baby born dead; metaphorically, it evokes the failed dreams and stillborn hopes of the fictional characters and of people everywhere. Human ambivalence is expressed through Vanessa's reaction to her new brother, towards whom she feels "such tenderness and such resentment."

Vanessa's imagination is drawn to stories of death and love, but she finds a disturbing difference between exotic versions and home truths. "Mask of the Bear" depicts love and death through relationships in the Connor household. Before Grandmother's death, Vanessa is unable to understand that her grandfather loves his wife; before Vanessa overhears Edna crying, she is ignorant of her loneliness. Vanessa is appalled by the pain she glimpses. The older narrative voice alerts us to the suffering concealed behind the masks.

This story is unified by the bear-mask metaphor, symbol of lonely, bewildered rage. Literally, the mask is thoroughly appropriate: not only are bears indigenous to Manitoba, but the bear is a totem for the Canadian Indian and his socioreligious art. Grandfather's heavy bear coat suggests the family responsibilities he has shouldered for half a century and his stern Puritan culture. Vanessa thinks of him as the Great Bear, not simply because of his surliness but because he is caged by his unbending personality and his strict code of ethics. Sabbath laws

reduce Grandfather to the level of a caged bear, and unwanted
visitors drive him to his basement lair, where his displeasure
is expressed by growling rockers. Edna's mask is an acidic wit.
She is more like her father than she cares to admit, and finds
it difficult to express tenderness.

Bears also suggest Great Bear Lake. Humorous images are
balanced by poetic ones. Vanessa imagines a vast, watery blackness with jagged rock and eternal ice, a place that annihilates
human voices and warmth. This chilling image of pride and
death, envisaged after her father's death, runs prophetically
through "Mask of the Bear." Vanessa is "chilled" by her childhood, as the "freezing burden" of inexperience blocks her from
those she would console. Similar images of coldness, of landscape
utterly alien to human feelings, shape what she sees from her
window just before she overhears Edna's sobbing.

Death moves closer to Vanessa in the title story, which deals
with her father's death and her own loss of religious faith. The
central image is a captive bird which has strayed into the house
and which the servant girl (who becomes the target of Vanessa's
rage) succeeds in setting free. The story opens with Manawaka's
Remembrance Day parade. Vanessa cannot bear the sight of
the elderly veterans, who resemble imposters, "caricatures of
past warriors." Like Stacey, she fears time's power to alter
human beings. She is horrified by her father's tale of her uncle's
death in the mud at the front. To comfort her, he hints of brief
pleasures for rural youths unexpectedly in strange lands.

The MacLeod's hired girl has rarely been off the farm, and
their efforts to modify her habits of grooming, dress, and decorum are comically ineffectual. Vanessa is fascinated and repelled by the baroque religious beliefs of Noreen's congregation,
the Tabernacle of the Risen and Reborn. Vanessa interprets as
poetry and myth what Noreen takes literally. Here, as in "The
Merchant of Heaven," Laurence suggests that the spectacular
splendors of the fundamentalist imagination stem from deprivation, and compensate for it. Noreen's farm life has been "endlessly drab," but she dwells in a world of technicolor splendors.

Dr. MacLeod succumbs to pneumonia. Vanessa, like a prisoner
attempting to escape, flails out at Noreen with physical and
psychological blows. She denies the existence of heaven and of
the spirits of the dead: *"Rest beyond the river.* I knew now

what that meant. It meant Nothing. It meant only silence, forever. . . . It mattered, but there was no help for it" (*BH* 110). Entrapment includes the human soul in a vast, uncaring universe. Rejecting what she understands as Christianity, Vanessa is temporarily isolated from her society: her ancestors and gods. The story has an epilogue in which Vanessa, age seventeen, discovers a 1919 letter and photograph. Recalling her conversation with her father, she hopes the French girl has meant some momentary freedom for him. Burning the souvenirs, she reexperiences her loss.

"A Bird in the House," "The Loons," and "Horses of the Night" depict existential alienation, *angst*, but these tragic stories are contained within the comic framework of Vanessa's growth. The emphasis in the fifth, sixth, and seventh stories is on the individual in society, on social conditioning and social guilt. Laurence's characters exhibit personal responsibility and qualified free will: qualified, because of heredity and environment. Each story is unified by a dominant image.

"The Loons" concerns Piquette Tonnerre, daughter of Lazarus and granddaughter of a Jules who fought with Riel. The Métis settlement is a chaos of lean-tos built from materials from the dump. There is an unbridgeable gulf between the Métis, whose children peddle wild strawberries from door to door, and the townsfolk, secure in brick houses. Piquette has failed several grades through illness and disinterest. Dr. MacLeod decides a summer with his family at their cottage might help her tuberculosis. Vanessa is disappointed to find that Piquette does not share her romantic attachment to wilderness terrain, or her fear of the loons becoming extinct: "as an Indian, Piquette was a dead loss."

Four years pass. Vanessa is astounded by Piquette's violent gaiety and flamboyant beauty. Later, she learns that Piquette has married an English Canadian; and still later, that she has returned alone with two youngsters, and been burned to death in a shack fire. This event recurs in *The Diviners*. Piquette's alienation is reflected in the loon's eerie call: "Plaintive, and yet with a quality of chilling mockery, those voices belonged to a world separated by aeons from our neat world of summer cottages and the lighted lamps of home" (*BH* 121).

Piquette remains a reproach and a mystery. The adult Vanessa remembers "the terrifying hope" in Piquette's eyes when she spoke of her fiancé. Like Piquette's people, the loons have disappeared: "Perhaps they had gone away to some far place of belonging. Perhaps they had been unable to find such a place, and had simply died out, having ceased to care any longer whether they lived or not." Laurence connects the loons with Piquette's ancestral past: "the older Vanessa can see the irony of the only way in which Piquette's people are recognized by the community, in the changing of the name Diamond Lake to the more tourist-appealing Lake Wapakata."[45]

Rural poverty in scattered northern settlements, widespread hardship in the 1930s, and World War II (the ironic end to the decade's unemployment) form the background to "Horses of the Night." This story of psychic depression and breakdown depicts social madness through the personal disorder of one casualty. Vanessa's loss of religious faith is a related phenomenon. The title suggests the four horsemen of the apocalypse, and the terror of Chris's inner world. Horses also suggest power and freedom, like the fantasy horses of his youthful imagination. The very different way in which Vanessa reacts to stress introduces a measure of freedom and hope.

The story spans thirteen years in Vanessa's life, from six to nineteen. It deals, through her eyes, with an older cousin's experience. Chris stays with the Connors to attend high school. She visits his farm after her father's death; and gets news of him in later years. Like Piquette, Chris harbors a terrifying hope. He wants to be a civil engineer. Lacking money to attend college, Chris turns salesman, only to find no buyers. He retreats to his squalid family homestead up north; into the army; and, eventually, into madness. Chris is sensitive, gentle, poetic. Given different circumstances, he might be bridge builder and wordsmith. In the Canada of the 1930s and 40s, his sensitivity turns inward to destroy him. Vanessa sees his madness as an extension of "that way he'd always had of distancing himself from the absolute unbearability of battle."[46] His imaginary horses and his optimistic schemes to make money appear to her as "the brave and useless strokes of fantasy against a depression that was both the world's and his own" (BH 153).

The northern lake images fears felt by both youngsters. The

lake was once home to prehistoric monsters, whose fossilized footprints survive. Vanessa sees it as alien and threatening, like the view of God she has held since her father's death: "Distant, indestructible, totally indifferent." Beside this monstrous lake, Chris speaks of his inability, in the face of social misery and war, to believe in a God who is both omnipotent and good.

"The Half-Husky" deals with sadism in the context of small-town poverty and class feelings. The Connors acquire a puppy whose friendly nature is transformed by cruel teasing. Harvey Shinwell's ingenious torments include pointed sticks, pepper, and lighted matches. The dog becomes wolfish, dangerous to strangers. When Harvey steals from the Connors, Grandfather and Vanessa go to the Shinwell's house in Manawaka's North End. The area's squalor prepares us for the squalor of the house, and both are analogues for relationships. Harvey's aunt treats him with a brutality calculated to humiliate and degrade. (She, in turn, has been brutalized by others: the story hints at her street profession [*BH* 167, 171].)

The denouement seems inevitable. The dog has to be destroyed. Vanessa learns that Harvey is in jail, for beating and robbing an elderly Chinese. Ada is still "on the street" and considered "safe to go free," although she shares the responsibility for Harvey's twisted nature. The story brilliantly identifies the half-husky not only with Harvey and Ada, but with Vanessa, who has learned from Harvey how to hate. Half wolf, half dog; half vicious, half loving: read Everyman.[47]

As a feminist statement, *A Bird in the House* is subtle, never didactic. It shows three generations of women coping with inherited myths and changing conditions. Vanessa's mother, who stood first in the province in high school graduation, was denied a college education. She and the indomitable Aunt Edna remain admirable models. "Escape" for their generation usually meant marriage. In the last story Vanessa sets out for college and the city feeling *less free* than she had expected: higher education is no panacea. Laurence's female protagonists continue to wrestle with difficulties in the battle that is life. As Robert Gibbs notes, the real freeing is still in process where the book leaves off.

## V   *"River of Now and Then"*

*The Diviners* is a sprawling, brawling epic with tremendous energy and power. It expresses a mature and profound understanding of human nature and destiny. As local reaction indicates, it is disturbing. What great novel is not? A strong case can be made that this novel, rather than the universally appealing narrative of Hagar Shipley, or the beautifully crafted stories of *A Bird in the House,* is Laurence's masterwork.

Novelist Marian Engel, who reviewed *The Diviners* for *Chatelaine,* remembers reading the proofs with the excitement that is generated by a major work; four years later, a rereading evoked "the same galloping eagerness and enjoyment and admiration. . . . Some things bothered me about it still, some things impressed me, but its greatness was there like an object." Engel discovered that some of the local academic critics were reluctant to review the book: one called it "big and sloppy" in comparison with the "almost perfect" *A Bird in the House.* Engel concludes that Toronto critics are terrified of the monumental, particularly in the works of women. Unlike the Vanessa MacLeod stories, *The Diviners* is untidy: "There are signs in the text of blots and erasures, spilled ink, thumbprints and tears. Tut, tut, Ms. Laurence, girls should be neat. It is unladylike to achieve apocalypse."[48]

Clara Thomas also finds the structure epic in intention and techniques. Laurence's longest, most complicated prose narrative incorporates traditional epic conventions such as stories of heroic battles, lists, heightened descriptions, oral techniques, "and one magnificent epic simile."[49]

The essential unity of technique and vision has been discussed by critics as diverse as Jean-Paul Sartre and Wayne Booth. *The Diviners* illustrates this literary axiom particularly well. The creative vision that underlies the work is located in Laurence's understanding of the way in which humans experience time. Simple-minded notions (such as the one-way flow of time, or the idea that individual pasts consist of clearly verifiable sets of events) are invalidated. In *The Diviners* the technical brilliance of voice and place, the handling of narrative, and the structuring of human experience are correlatives for the vision: an understanding of time as a living river incarnate in human generations, *a river which flows two ways.*

The narrative joins history to myth. *The Diviners* is the story of forty-seven-year-old Morag Gunn, a writer from Manawaka. It is the story of her lovers, her daughter, her neighbors, and her inner growth. Morag moves from the small prairie town to Winnipeg, Toronto, Vancouver, London, and McConnell's Landing, an Ontario town even smaller than the Manitoba town of her childhood. On one level, the novel is a *kunstlerroman*, the story of the education of an artist. It is also the story of two peoples whom destiny has brought together in Canada, the Scots and the Métis. Each has its own ancestors, gods, and inspirational myths. Morag's daughter, fathered by Métis Jules Tonnerre, carries in her veins a heritage that she does not yet understand but is unwilling and unable to reject.

The novel is framed by the river seen from Morag's desk, a river whose current runs counter to the prevailing wind, and which thus appears to flow both ways. The phenomenon fascinates Morag, and becomes the central metaphor for the way in which we experience time and life itself. As the novel opens, this phenomenon introduces Pique's departure, and the apparent contrast between her daughter's way of life and Morag's own. At the beginning of Part 4, the two-way flow is linked with Morag's sense of order, and Pique's reversal of this order by staying up at night and sleeping by day. Pique's reversal is also expressed through her unsettled nature, her difficulties in finding a vocation, and her lack of what Morag's generation would call ambition. At the novel's end, the river has cumulative force. The water at its edge is clear, while beyond, it deepens and keeps its life hidden. River depths suggest mysteries in time for individuals, generations, and nations. The novel's ending, like its beginning, evokes the mysterious core of human experience, and its unity in diversity.

For individuals, the two-way flow means that relationships are being continually altered as events are reinterpreted. This can be frightening and painful, yet carries with it creative possibilities for growth. Morag's neighbor, an old man with the gift for water divination, tells her of his early married life. Royland's story incorporates several voices or viewpoints, all

of which are Royland's at different times. His transformation
from a self-righteous, aggressive evangelist, who unwittingly
destroys his wife, into a kindly grandfather-figure is credible
and touching.[50]

History and legend merge in Morag's pictures of herself as
a small child with her parents. The faded photographs are
jumbled together in a large envelope lifted from the dump.
Morag's skull is another container for Louisa and Colin Gunn,
whose people came to Canada during the Highland Clearances.
Morag remembers herself as an older child composing the interpretations of her parents and herself which answered to her
emotional needs.

Strangely suggestive is the adult Morag's desire to converse
with her dead mother, coupled with the realization that she is
now more than ten years older than her mother was when she
died: "she would seem so young to me, so inexperienced" (D 9).
A Jest of God effects a similar reversal, as Rachel realizes that
she is now responsible for her mother. Morag remembers their
deaths, not their lives: "yet they're inside me, flowing unknown
in my blood and moving unrecognized in my skull" (D 15).

Despite its brevity, Part 1 establishes the middle-aged Morag,
loving, anxious, ironic, defiant, "born bloody-minded"; the suc-
ceeding generation's rebellion; the preceding generation's battle
with poverty, drought, and disease; their ancestors' trials in the
Scottish Highlands; and the river metaphor, identified with the
generations, genes, instinct, blood, memory, cultural values, and
individual experience.

For much of Morag's story Laurence has rejected the first-
person voice which serves for Hagar's, Rachel's, and Vanessa's
narratives. Yet never has one individual's point of view been
conveyed with more immediacy. "Where is the Voice Coming
From?" Rudy Wiebe poses the question implicitly, in a story
with this title. John Fowles calls voice the most difficult problem
for a writer.[51] It is a primary consideration for novelist and critic
alike. In The Diviners a third-person voice combines Morag's
thoughts and language with those of another narrator. "Third
person" is inaccurate here. As Clara Thomas notes, "we are
captured by the illusion of Morag describing herself."[52] Morag's
voice is distanced, with no loss in intimacy. Sherrill Grace writes:

Although Morag does not technically speak in her own voice, the third-person narrative voice, in the past tense for the fictional present and in the present tense for remembered sequences, is always extremely close to her, presenting events through her eyes, constantly adopting her mannerisms until we feel we are listening to her thoughts. Laurence uses this third-person voice brilliantly. . . . The third person allows a minimal distance from Morag creating, in addition, the sense that there are two Morags, one who experiences and remembers while the other writes, a doubling phenomenon quite common in artist-hero novels.[53]

This third-person voice, Grace adds, emphasizes that this is the story of a people and a country, not simply an individual.

A first-person voice, Morag's, is used less frequently, usually signalled by italics. There are also two major variations on the flashback narratives that form much of the novel. These are tagged "Snapshot" and "Memorybank Movie." A static description of a photograph is interrupted by Morag's current thoughts (italicized) as she self-consciously interprets her own memories: *"All this is crazy, of course, and quite untrue. Or maybe true and maybe not. I am remembering myself composing this interpretation in Christie and Prin's house"* (D 7). Laurence assaults the reader's assumptions that time flows one way, that events are what they seem, that people's memories are reasonably objective.

Memorybank Movie scenes have action and dialogue, like film scripts. E. J. Pratt shaped much of his poetry around parallels between modern communication systems and the human brain and nervous system. Laurence flanks her organic river metaphor with mechanical metaphors, computer and camera, suggesting twentieth-century forms of man, toolmaker and wordsmith. Language is itself the Memorybank Movie upon which our survival depends. The movies may be introduced by the third-person voice before a subtitle and the shift to dramatic form. The subtitles are usually ironic, and frequently blackly comic. In The Law Means School, Morag learns the authoritarian and hypocritical structure of society; power and justice are not synonymous, and courage is needed for survival.

Morag is adopted by Christie Logan, the town's garbage collector, and his obese wife Prin. They live on Hill Street, which the adult Morag remembers as the Scots-English equivalent

of the other side of the tracks. As the adopted child of a couple
despised by the establishment, Morag experiences blatant discrimination. Like Adele Wiseman's *Crackpot, The Diviners* portrays class prejudice in an ostensibly democratic society. Attempts
to humiliate Morag only encourage her inner toughness. She
hates the Logans for exposing her to pain, and hates herself
for her failure to respond adequately to their goodness. Pique's
mixed feelings for Morag are paralleled by Morag's for Christie
and many others.

The long second part juxtaposes Pique's current rebellion
with Morag's childhood in Manawaka. Morag reminds herself
that Pique sees differently, that time changes not only one's relation to others but to oneself: "What happened to me wasn't
what anyone else thought was happening, and maybe not even
what I thought was happening at the time. A popular misconception is that we can't change the past—everyone is constantly
changing their own past, recalling it, revising it. What really
happened? A meaningless question. But one I keep trying to
answer, knowing there is no answer" (*D* 49).

Morag's unfinished university career and her marriage to
Brooke Skelton are related in Part 3. Its ironic title suggests
the idealistic hopes with which the average girl approaches
marriage. "Halls of Sion" chronicles the birth, growth, and bitter
failure of this relationship, as Morag's strength grows. The
English professor is drawn to her mask of joy, as a counter to the
fears generated by his childhood. Morag conceals from Brooke
her dark self, the anger and guilt of her Highland inheritance and
personal past. She plays princess to Brooke's prince: "we were
living each other's fantasy," Morag tells Jules. Brooke considers
his bride a child, an attitude Morag accepts initially as romantic
but which becomes intolerable. His refusal to have children
and, worse, his inability to take her writing seriously stem from
this misconception of Morag as child and princess. She becomes
a trapped princess in an elegant apartment tower in Toronto.
Adultery with Jules, after Brooke has insulted him, is a joining
that is also a severing of the chains which have separated her
from part of herself.

Morag's leaving is a desperate necessity and a kind of death.
She and Brooke will continue to inhabit one another, a sexual

metaphor which covers feelings and parallels the continuation in
Morag of her Manawaka experience. As she heads west, the
prairie winter reflects her emotional state, and hints at rebirth.
Small, tough prairie trees survive terrible winters: "a determined
kind of tree, all right." Prairie flowers are similarly sturdy. Morag
thinks that strangers would find the landscape dull, bleak, empty:
"They didn't know the renewal that came out of the dead cold"
(*D* 231).

Part 4 takes Morag through the next two decades, covering
Pique's birth and growth to young adulthood, Morag's development as a writer, and her growth towards self-acceptance and the
hard-won maturity that is in the narrative voice from the beginning. Its title gives an ironic turn to a phrase from anthropology
which is usually applied to ceremonies where an adolescent, after
undergoing rigorous rituals, is accepted as an adult member of
the tribe. Morag's rites must be discovered by her, and extend
over her adult life.

Royland's gift for water-divining is linked with Morag's writing, and with the songs and ancestral tales of Christie and Jules.
Art, like the ability to locate water, is a mysterious gift which
is given for a time and may be withdrawn. Both the Old Man
of the River and Morag are very conscious that they hold their
gifts by grace, that "things remained mysterious, his work her
own, the generations, the river" (*D* 4). Royland's penchant for
fishing, and his name (*roi*, king), evoke the Fisher King of the
Grail legends described in Jessie Watson's *From Ritual to
Romance*. Yet Royland is also solidly realized as cracker-barrel
humorist and kindly neighbor.

Morag has tried divining, without success. She is gifted differently, and her goal is more cryptic, since the value of water
is undeniable. She thinks of language as a living flow, and loves
the magic in words: "A daft profession. Wordsmith. Liar, more
likely. Weaving fabrications. Yet, with typical ambiguity, convinced that fiction was more true than fact. Or that fact was
in fact fiction" (*D* 21). She wonders what will happen to her,
economically and spiritually, when the gift is withdrawn. Words
haunt her, through their suggestive power, and the memories
they evoke. As a child, her imagination earns her the tag
"mooner." She is shamed by the realism applied to her Christ-

mas poem, and deeply moved by a line from Hilaire Belloc which
shows the reader the folly of this standard. Her high school
teacher praises her for not opting for an easy ending. By this
age, Morag knows that her gift can be neither denied or refused.
A strong hand has been laid on her shoulder: "Strong and
friendly. But merciless" (D 100).

Royland's divining, Morag's writing, Christie's gift for "gar-
bage-telling" and ancestral tales are all analogues. The Scavenger's booty includes the Highland tales, and a Gaelic Bible
rescued from the "Nuisance Grounds." The implicit parallel
between the dump, with its euphemistic name, and the subconscious, seen by Freud as a dump of repressed childhood memories, is witty, like Marshall McLuhan's dictum that art is formed
from the garbage of the past.

Christie—grimacing clown, fool, hero, and religious prophet—
is a complex creation, one of Laurence's best. His adages include
"One man's muck is everyman's muck," and "By their garbage
shall ye know them." His view of life has been shaped by his
profession, or his profession chosen (after the carnage of World
War I) because it concurs with his views. He tells Morag that
people of any class are "only muck"; the remark is illustrated
in the cruel scenes that follow (D 25). Gus Winkler's sadistic
beating of his son brings on a recurrence of Christie's shell
shock. Meanwhile, "nice" people in Manawaka pretend that
cruelty, class discrimination, and the dump itself do not exist.
Manawaka's cemetery adjoins the dump. Morag observes that
the "dead stuff" is together on the same hill, "except that the
cemetery is decent and respectable" (D 57).

Christie despises this hypocrisy. The dump's contents include
aborted babies wrapped in newspaper, mute evidence to pride
and pretense. Christie has few delusions about human nature,
yet is himself generous and loving. His gospel of muck is not
materialism, but resembles Christ's teaching that we are defiled
by inner, not outer filth (D 32). He would have preferred to
bury Prin himself, in the Nuisance Grounds; in the same spirit,
Morag thinks Christie should really be buried there. Analyzing
the images of cemetery and dump in the Manawaka cycle, David
Blewett writes that Christie's compassion is a life-giving force,
a means of grace: "Paradoxically, the garbage dump, for all

its sordid associations, by the end of the cycle stands for an humanity, which we see in Christie Logan, and which is the very reverse of the inhumanity earlier associated with Jason Currie, the cemetery, and the Currie Memorial Park."[54]

Laurence is conscious of an affinity between her fiction and that of Chinua Achebe and Patrick White. Nowhere is the link with White so clear as in the figure of Christie Logan, the Good Fool. His name, little Christ, underlines Laurence's intention. The loving simpleton, or foolish sage, points to the limitations of reason and to a supra-rational vision. The fool figure, in White and in Russian novelists such as Dostoyevsky, is generally a mystic, whose simplicity and honesty is interpreted by conventional society as stupidity, even madness. Blewett calls Christie "one of the greatest fools in modern literature, but for that reason a channel and an image to divine grace."[55] The fool is also a prominent device in *A Jest of God*, where Rachel and Calla are God's fools. Patrick White uses drunkenness and delirium as a prophetic device, as Laurence uses incoherent remarks that puzzle Prin: "Oh what a piece of work is man oh what a bloody awful piece of work is man     enough to scare the pants off you when you come to think of it     the opposite is also true hm        hm" (*D* 71).

Christie teaches Morag his clan's motto, "This is the Valour of My Ancestors," with the formal description of their crest badge, "a passion nail piercing a human heart, proper." In words that blend romance and legend, history and myth, he tells of the unspeakable Highland Clearances, and of her ancestor, Piper Gunn, who led the Sutherland crofters into a new life in Manitoba. Two sentences haunt Morag's memory. These refrains describe Piper Gunn, "a great tall man, a man with the voice of drums and the heart of a child and the gall of a thousand and the strength of conviction"; and his strong woman, Morag, "with the courage of a falcon and the beauty of a deer and the warmth of a home and the faith of saints" (*D* 41).

The Hudson Bay landing is only the beginning of trials en route to the Red River Valley. Laurence gives nothing but the barest bones of the historical material, yet manages to create the illusion of a detailed account. Her concern (and Christie's) is with the truth of human experience, not with facts. Christie's language, like himself, is a marvelous mixture of spirituality, humor, poetry, and obscenity: "Cold as all the shithouses of hell"; "Weather for giants, in them days." In a letter near the novel's end Morag tells Ella that Christie said the Highlanders walked about a thousand miles to York factory; it was actually about one hundred and fifty miles, but must have felt like a thousand. She adds that Christie knew things about inner truths that she is only beginning to understand; and that she likes the thought of history and fiction interweaving (*D* 341).

Laurence shares Morag's sentiment in a letter expressing her ideas about the nature of history and fiction. She begins by acknowledging that she read W. L. Morton's *Manitoba: A History* for the first time, the summer she began writing *The Diviners*; and that Morton's history gave her not only many needed facts but also a sense of "the sweep of history, the overview":

> The novelist (at least, this is true in my own case) seeks to bring characters to life as much as possible and to place these individuals within the historical context of their time and place. What I think I share, most of all, with Morton is the sense of my *place*, the prairies, and of my *people* (meaning all prairie peoples) within the context of their many and varied histories, and the desire to make all these things come alive in the reader's mind.[56]

In "Myth and Manitoba in *The Diviners*," Thomas shows the importance of narrative, and of narrative order, elements frequently dismissed as relatively unimportant aspects of criticism. Narrative reveals structure; and structure, theme and vision.

Morag's personal growth illustrates the concept Laurence stresses in her Nigerian study: the need to come to terms with one's ancestors, to understand their experience in order to be released from its bondage. Christie introduces Morag to the ballads of Ossian in Gaelic, as an antidote to the cultural imperialism of Wordsworth's "Daffodils." Ossian stimulates Morag so that she is able to imagine Piper Gunn's woman building a chariot with materials and motifs drawn from the Canadian prairies: her imagination has been repatriated. Thomas notes that folk literature becomes myth when it is deeply accepted by an individual as personally relevant. It then assumes power to shape that individual's identity. After Christie's first tale Morag goes to sleep comforted by a bravery she now feels as her own.

*The Diviners* contains three sets of myth: Christie's tales of the Highlanders and of Morag's father in World War I, Jules Tonnerre's tales and songs, and the adult Morag's imaginary reconstruction of Catharine Parr Traill. Shortly after Morag's introduction to Ossian, she talks with Jules and begins to learn of his heroic ancestors, Grandfather Jules and Chevalier "Rider" Tonnerre. By the time of Christie's second tale, she has begun to worry about historical accuracy and is unable to accept Indians and Métis in the simple role of villains *vis-à-vis* the Scottish settlers. Christie's gift of the hunting knife which a boy has traded to him for cigarettes symbolically joins Morag to the Tonnerre family. The history of the two icons, plaid pin and knife, begins in *The Stone Angel* and concludes in *The Diviners*. The knife that Jules uses to shorten his agony becomes part of his daughter's inheritance, along with his songs. Christie's third and last tale, about the settlers taking the fort from Riel and his "gang of halfbreeds," meets with fifteen-year-old Morag's scepticism. The Métis were losing their land, she tells Christie. Riel wanted them to have their rights.

Morag hears Jules's stories after their sexual encounter in his shack. The two adolescents, one bound for the front, are "like children away from home with the night coming on," an image of isolation and mutual dependence which recalls the little hairdresser and his assistant in "The Perfume Sea." After the casualty lists, Morag replays Jules's tales: of the Chevalier and his magical white stallion; of the Prophet, who took the fort in Manitoba; and of the war "Out West" at Batoche (the Northwest Rebellion of 1885). Both sets of tales, and Morag's childhood, are terminated by the fire in a Métis shack which kills Jules's sister Piquette and her two small children. Morag, sent to cover the event for the *Manawaka Banner*, returns to cry "as though pain were the only condition of human life."

Thomas sees this event as Morag's passage from innocence to experience. Certainly it marks a stage in her development, but Morag is still remarkably innocent when she marries Brooke. The Métis deaths provoke a temporary mood of cynicism. Torn with anger and guilt, Morag sees Christie as a fraud and his tales as "a load of old manure." She is eager to leave Manawaka and her past behind, still ignorant of the fact that she carries them inescapably within her.

Despite its deep religious humanism, *The Diviners* has been attacked as pornographic. The controversy centered, in 1976 and 1978, in attempts to have the novel removed from Ontario's Grade Thirteen English curriculum. The 1976 attack was organized by the Reverend Sam Buick of Peterborough's Dublin Street Pentecostal Church. Reverend Buick and his Citizens in Defence of Decency appeared to see in the novel little but blasphemy, immorality, adultery, and fornication.[57] The decision by Peterborough's Board of Education to approve *The Diviners* as a Grade Thirteen text sparked public meetings, petitions, and an ugly ideological battle in the heart of the area where Laurence has lived since 1973.

Teacher Robert Buchanan, who was responsible for putting the novel on his senior English course, was one of its able defenders. John Ayre reports that Buchanan realized it was not simply a good novel but, with its echoes of the Bible and Milton, a great one. Buchanan had taught, previously, in Brantford under Jim Foley, who pioneered the study of Canadian literature in Canadian high schools, and who had created Canada Day in Port Colborne, where authors could meet and talk with students on a personal basis. Buchanan saw in the novel a superb opportunity to show his students that literature is being written here and now. Morag's dialogue with Catharine Parr Traill (who, like her sister, Susanna Moodie, had cleared land in the Peterborough area one hundred and thirty years earlier) was one point of connection. Laurence, moreover, had turned their own Otonabee River into a symbol of time and life.

A second scandal erupted in 1978 in southwestern Ontario. The Huron County School Board had been under pressure to remove three novels from Grade Thirteen English: J. D. Salinger's *Catcher in the Rye*, John Steinbeck's *Of Mice and Men*, and *The Diviners*. William French, book editor of *The Globe and Mail*, describes a dramatic, highly emotional public meeting in Clinton, Ontario. He observed a strong hostility towards what he calls "common" four-letter words and "taking the Lord's name

in vain." French suggests that parents, confused by rapidly
changing values, are clinging to the old verities and trying to
impose them. Both French and Ayre note the attackers' failure
to distinguish between advocacy and description, and both compare the Ontario incidents with the "Scopes monkey trial" in
Tennessee in the 1920s.[58]

Part of the explanation for the irrational and bitter attacks
on *The Diviners* lies in the conservative mood of the times.
The hedonistic, revolutionary 1960s gave way in the seventies
to a moralistic backlash and a movement to the Right. This wave-
like movement is a common historical phenomenon. Late in 1978
a conference was held in Toronto to plan for a Centre for
Human Freedom and Sexuality. Planners included therapists,
academics, physicians, and other professionals. Symptoms of the
current Canadian conservatism were recounted: the confiscation
of books by reputable Canadian authors; the banning of certain
films in Ontario; the widening of obscenity laws; the seizure of
magazines at the border.

The Toronto conference was concerned with the politics of
sexuality. University of Toronto sociologist, John Alan Lee, said:
"Society's attitude toward sex is a real touchstone. There are
two taboos rarely open to discussion or challenge: *sex and power.*
It's only in the last ten years we realized that they are related."[59]

This insight is particularly relevant to *The Diviners*. Morag
Gunn and the novel which embodies her attitudes constitute
a threat to many people. *Her sexuality is threatening, her independence is threatening; and her language is threatening.*
These interrelated aspects will be developed below. Laurence's
protagonist flouts social conventions and structures, from fashion
to marriage and formal religious affiliation. Morag also holds
deep ethical and religious convictions. But the witch-hunters,
unaccustomed to interpreting literature, fail to see or understand
this. It is far easier to spot an objectionable word or scene, and
cry foul. This reaction permits an individual to avoid ideas that,
consciously or unconsciously, appear threatening. In the Lakefield controversy, many students saw themselves as pawns in a
struggle with an older generation wrestling with the ghosts
of its own moral inhibitions.

Morag's sexuality offends ancient, firmly entrenched stereotypes of women as much less highly sexed than men. The well-bred Victorian woman had to conceal hunger for food, let alone sexual appetite. Morag's need for sex, her frank enjoyment of it, the ease with which she climaxes and her means of solitary relief are attributes of women that have become topics for public discussion only in the last decade, in conjunction with a new wave of feminist writings. Morag's brief encounter with Chas during her lonely Vancouver years is doubtless one of the passages that attracted Reverend Buick's yellow pencil. Yet this encounter, prompted by her sexual hunger, is ethical *within context*. Chas's sadism, and Morag's fear of becoming pregnant by a man she despises, should be nemesis enough for the moralists. Morag determines that this will never occur again. She has learned that body and spirit cannot be divorced, and that her flesh carries responsibilities. The earlier encounter with Harold is black comedy, as two solitudes attempt mutual consolation. As Marian Engel observes, Morag's attempts at casual sex are disastrous because she is not a casual person.

Sex and power: Morag's inner growth is partly a coming to terms with her own strength. She learns early that weakness attracts bullies. Her humiliated friend Eva, sterilized by a bungled abortion, illustrates what happens to a lower-class girl without Morag's determination: "Morag is not—repeat *not*—going to be beaten by life. But cannot bear to look at Eva very often" (*D* 92).

Eva attracts boys at dances because her conversation consists of monosyllables designed to flatter. The adolescent Morag is torn between pride and the longing to be popular with boys. She succumbs to peer pressure and wears makeup, which separates her from herself. At university it is not loneliness that makes it unbearable to lack dates, but the sense of being "downgraded, devalued, undesirable." One Morag, the product of North American social conditioning, wants to be glamorous and adored, get married and have children; another Morag wants something not yet fully understood: "All I want is everything" (*D* 147).

So Morag marries her prince, and the relationship becomes a prison and a lie. Symptoms are Morag's eager agreement to go out with Brooke when she feels like writing; her attempt to conceal her black moods; her acceptance of his demeaning game before they have sex: "Have you been a good girl?" Repressing knowledge of the lie adds to her feeling of being separated from herself. It is only when the decision to leave is irrevocable that Morag can acknowledge the chains, now broken.

Brooke has felt that he *owns* his wife. When she leaves, he wants legal proof of what is and is not his property. Morag makes no financial claims. The novel depicts, with ironic humor, the high cost of independence. It also shows that psychological and economic independence are closely linked. One suspects that it is really this portrait of a woman who does not need male shelter, financial or emotional, that disturbs many readers of both sexes. Yet Morag is no superwoman, no monster of self-sufficiency. Catharine Parr Traill's innumerable talents make her feel inadequate. But Morag copes. She survives, with a little help from her friends.

In connection with the 1976 Peterborough School Board affair Laurence spoke to John Ayre of her intention in the novel: "One of the major themes, of course, is the maturing of a woman, to show how she ultimately becomes an independent person, not just in an external way but how she eventually achieves a sense of inner freedom. In that sense, Morag moves further ahead than any of my women characters. I think it is an extremely positive book."[60]

In an analysis of Morag as outsider Marian Engel sees an intimate connection between her psychological stance and class:

The conflict in *The Diviners* is between an intense desire to belong to a rejecting and constricting society, and a desire for a life of one's own. This theme could not have been handled through the lives . . . on the other side of the tracks. In Morag, Laurence has created an arrant outsider, and stripped her of the solid family ties that gave Canadians, like good ships, the steadying characteristic known as "bottom." Morag has to find her own steadiness. . . . The great and the gothic are narrowly separated. It is easy for an author to slide from grand emotions into mawkishness. But Laurence keeps her balance. . . . She is one of the few heroines who achieves the apocalypse of knowing what her life has been about, not through the agency of a man, but through her own experience.[61]

Engel adds that Laurence's casting of Prin as vegetable cipher
rather than termagant is proof of her understanding of women's
lives.

Morag's language, the third factor connected with the furor
raised by the novel, is offensive to many readers. One obvious
defense, if such were needed, would be that her vocabulary is
in character: it is realistic for someone with her background.
David Blewett observes that the narrative perspective here,
unlike the earlier works in the Manawaka cycle, is not that of
the respectable middle class but of the socially disreputable.
Joe Hogan, chairman of the Peterborough schoolboard's review
committee in 1976, advised the board of his committee's unani-
mous support of the novel, stating that sex and profane dialogue
represented "two narrow and insignificant aspects of the novel."[62]

To call the rough language insignificant, however, misrepre-
sents it. Language reflects values as well as class. People swear
*by* what is important to them. For the postwar generation, the
switch from religion as a source of obscenities to sexuality indicates changing social values. Morag's language draws on both
areas. Moreover, people swear *at* what is important to them.
Morag and Pique, like rebels in the 1960s who termed the
Vietnamese war an obscenity, are repelled by human suffering
and degradation. This concern sometimes finds expression in
four-letter words. Jules's oaths, similarly, express anger over the
mistreatment of his people, or the ironies of fate which facilitate
their self-destruction. Christie's language is an intimate part of
the man.

Indecent language is also a source of black humor. Six-year-
old Morag conveys fear, courage, and defiance in her "Hang
onto your shit and never let them know you are ascared" (*D* 28).
The adult Morag's explosive anger, when her husband insists on
treating her as a child, issues in some of Christie's choicest
terms. Just prior, her grief and guilt over Prin's death and
Christie's loneliness induce in Morag "the mad and potentially
releasing desire to speak sometimes as Christie used to speak,
the loony oratory, salt-beefed with oaths, the stringy lean oaths
with some protein on them, the Protean oaths upon which she
was reared" (*D* 209). Normally, Morag's language is strong and
ironic, but far from obscene.

Language as the expression of character is illustrated by Morag's dialogue with Catharine Parr Traill, a nineteenth-century pioneer who lived and wrote in the Peterborough-Lakefield area which inspires the fictional McConnell's Landing. Catharine's formal language, innocent of humor, contrasts comically with Morag's inner voice: "In cases of emergency, it is folly to fold one's hands and sit down to bewail in abject terror. It is better to be up and doing" (*The Canadian Settler's Guide*, 1855). Traill serves as a model of women's experience in an earlier century, just as Pique suggests future generations. Again, myth and history join hands. Morag takes what she needs from "C.P.T.," mythologizing the historic character.

Morag's temptation is to see herself as a weak successor to the tradition of strong Canadian women represented by Traill: "Morag Gunn, countrywoman, never managing to overcome a quiver of distaste at the sight of an earthworm. . . . Detestor of physical labour. Lover of rivers and tall trees. Hater of axes and shovels. What a farce" (*D* 46). Morag prefers to buy food from supermarkets and travel by taxi. She worries incessantly about Pique, and suffers from sexual loneliness, a problem unmentioned by the venerable Catharine: "Too tired."

Morag's version of Traill's energetic pursuits, in the form of directions for filming, is pure slapstick:

*Scene at the Traill Homestead, circa 1840*

C.P.T. out of bed, fully awake, bare feet on the sliver-hazardous floor-boards—no, take that one again. Feet on the homemade hooked rug. Breakfast cooked for the multitude. Out to feed the chickens, stopping briefly on the way back to pull fourteen armloads of weeds out of the vegetable garden and perhaps prune the odd apple tree in passing. The children's education hour, the umpteen little mites lisping enthusiastically over this enlightenment. Cleaning the house, baking two hundred loaves of delicious bread, preserving half a ton of plums, pears, cherries, etcetera. All before lunch. (*D* 79)

Morag's life would be considered easy by the formidable C.P.T.

In her second dialogue, Morag describes herself as caught between the old pioneers and the new. Maudie appears too good to be true, like Catharine. Morag envies "Saint Catharine" her

religious faith, and the unspoiled land which in her day was a
visible analogue for Jerusalem the Golden. Pollution threatens
the very survival of Morag's world. Her third dialogue with
the ghost indicates an advance in self-acceptance. Morag promises Catharine that she is going to stop feeling guilty. She
has her own work, and her garden of wildflowers and human
relations: "I'm not built like you, Saint C., or these kids, either.
I stand somewhere in between" (D 332). Morag bids Catharine
farewell.

Clara Thomas describes the pioneer matriarch as a friendly
adversary, a means of self-testing, and reminds us of Laurence's
belief in the importance of assimilating local history. Ontario's
past is "equally necessary" for Morag's patriation.[63]

Challenges for a new generation of women are suggested
through Morag's daughter. Pique is sometimes sentimentalized.
Her search for self seems narcissistic at times. Morag's conviction, that conditions for her daughter's generation are infinitely
more difficult than they were for herself, is unconvincing: "When
I was her age, beer was thought to be major danger. Beer! Because it might lead to getting pregnant. Good God, Royland. . . .
The world seems full of more hazards now. Doom all around"
(D 22). Laurence's statement that Neepawa was "Belsen writ
small, but with the same ink," or Hagar's, that the plagues go on
from one generation to another, is closer to the vision found
throughout the Manawaka cycle.

Pique's restlessness reflects contemporary social problems.
Morag links it with threats to the environment from pollution
and other man-made horrors: "No wonder the kids felt themselves to be children of the apocalypse" (D 4). River-slaying
now appears to Morag's imagination as a crime worse than
murder. Pique, who lacks the ambition Jules noted in Morag,
mocks her mother: "Do. Do. Always that. Do I have to *do* anything? Don't worry. I'll get a job" (D 195). Her freedom is a
catalyst for the repressed anger of solid citizens, who resent her
life style. Pique feels their anger, when she hitchhikes with a
guitar. In Ontario she has been taunted for having Indian blood,
and for having a mother who fails to fit a conventional social
slot. The old patterns recur, Morag thinks. She remembers
similar humiliations, and wishes she could spare Pique.

Like the river, Pique is drawn in two directions. She inherits two mythologies. Her ancestors, represented by Jules's songs, and by Christie's tales as retold by Morag, contain her future and her past. Music is the medium for Pique's generation. She treasures the Métis ballads from her father, and writes one of her own that begins "There's a valley holds my name." She was named after Jules's sister Piquette, who died in the shack fire. At the novel's end, Pique intends to join the communal life of her Métis uncle's family at Galloping Mountain. This journey "home," like the rest of life, is a backwards/forwards process. Pique hopes to share in their life, and contribute to it, for an unknown period. Her generation accepts unstructured situations.

Women and Métis, two central concerns in *The Diviners,* are natural partners in a modern Canadian setting. An American equivalent of politically disadvantaged groups might be women and blacks. The Métis were actually called *black* in the nineteenth century by some Scots settlers in the Red River Valley.[64] Pique is the child of Canada's founding races (Indian, French, Scots, and English) and symbolizes Canada's future. The symbol might easily have been melodramatic, forced, or pat. In Laurence's handling it is none of these. As a Manitoban, Laurence grew up in the area where Métis had hunted buffalo only a few generations earlier. There were Métis in her town, her school. Her experiences in Africa, and her experience as a woman and a writer, made the themes in this novel natural and inevitable.

The Manawaka novels as a whole contain a composite portrait of four generations of Canadian women, of their problems, challenges, aspirations, and achievements. They range from the ordinary to the extraordinary, from housewives to artists. *A Bird in the House* and *The Diviners* depict woman as artist, in youth and maturity. These aspects of the cycle will be considered at greater length in the concluding chapter.

*The Diviners* is Laurence's most political novel, and her most spiritual one. She is writing, here, about the disinherited, the dispossessed. She is writing of psychic and economic alienation; of struggle, growth, and hope. In his editorial for the Margaret Laurence Issue of the *Journal of Canadian Studies,* Michael Peterman objects to what he calls the "explicit political qualities" of the novel. Peterman's argument owes more to his observation of Laurence's activities in the 1970s, and to his implicit conviction that good novels avoid political issues, than to any concrete analysis of *The Diviners*.[65] His charges—that the novel has didactic elements, and that it involves an unfortunate shift to the right in what William New describes as the delicate balance between artistic skill and public purpose—are unsubstantiated.

The critical consensus is that Laurence does balance the elements of art and politics. Indeed, the novel's success *as* art is inseparable from the very human social concerns (political in the widest sense) that animate it.

In the Manawaka cycle Laurence creates a continuous, multidimensional world, an entire society, complete with hegemonic patterns. This portrait of a society is one of the great values of her fiction. It follows from her method of allowing characters to gestate in her mind for years, and of rooting them solidly in the society she knew so well. Laurence has said that she would like the five Manawaka works to be read, essentially, as one work. This is understandable since all five are religious pilgrimages: "the affirmation of faith and the finding of grace," as Clara Thomas describes *The Diviners*.[66] In a similar vein, Denyse Forman and Uma Parameswaran speak of "sacramental overtones" in the cycle's first three novels, of a search for identity which is also an indirect search for a relation to God.[67]

Manawaka is, of course, Laurence's prairie town, transformed by her imagination. Through it, she has come to terms with her ancestral past, a task she believes essential for every human being. For Laurence, one of the most difficult aspects of this process was to accept her deeply resented grandfather as a part of herself. Grandfather Simpson models for Vanessa's Grandfather Connor, and forms parts of Hagar and Morag. She speaks of him to Thomas as part of "our myths ... our history": "He was a pioneer. He was a very strong, authoritarian old man—I never remember him as anything but an old man. He seemed to be as old as God right from the moment I first had a memory of him. I don't remember the old man expressing any emotion but anger except once—that was when my grandmother died and, horrifyingly, he broke down and cried. This was like having a mountain crumble."[68]

Manawaka was Laurence's time and place, and she set herself to get it "exactly right." Her success fulfills the prophecy of the closing line in one of her undergraduate poems: "this land will be my immortality."

VI *The Dispossessed: "Freedom is a word our hearts both sing"*

Two of Laurence's essays, collected in 1976, deal directly or indirectly with the Canadian Métis, whose problems occupy an increasingly important place in her fiction throughout the Manawaka cycle. "Man of Our People" reviews George Woodcock's biography of Gabriel Dumont, the Métis military leader in the Northwest Rebellion of 1885. On the dustjacket of Woodcock's book, Laurence speaks of repossessing, through knowledge of the Métis and their tragic confrontation with white civilization, "a crucial part of our past." Her article has a brief preface:

The whole tragic area of Canadian history which encompasses the struggles, against great odds, of the prairie Indian and Métis people in the 1800's is one which has long concerned and troubled me. This article has a great deal of relevance to my own life-view ... seen in its broadest sense in my novel, *The Diviners,* and more narrowly and politically (as a study of another nomadic tribal society in conflict with an imperialist power) in "The Poem and the Spear" in this collection. (*HS* 204)

Laurence sees Somalis and Métis as victims of technology, in the form of vastly superior weapons.[69] The battle of Culloden, with its massacre of the Highlanders and the subsequent repression of the remnant that survived, belongs to this pattern. Laurence notes that many of the settlers who came to Canada came as oppressed or dispossessed people. She urges readers to become aware of the "soul-searing injustices" done to the Indians and Métis.

Some background to the tragic history of the Métis in Manitoba and Saskatchewan may help the reader to appreciate Laurence's concern. Indians originally provided much of the labor force for the fur trade in the Canadian West. Gradually, white traders and *voyageurs* began to marry ("after the fashion of the country") with the native population, principally the Cree, the Salteaux, and Assiniboine. The mixed-blood population increased, and acquired a sense of cohesiveness. When fur traders were discharged, many remained in the Northwest with their Indian wives and families. Because of their dark complexions, the French half-breeds often called themselves *bois-brules* (literally, burnt wood), but generally the French group was referred to as *Métis* and the English, as *half-breeds*. The Métis were largely migratory or nomadic, whereas many of the English half-breeds settled down to agricultural pursuits.[70]

For nearly two hundred years prior to 1869, Rupert's Land, the vast drainage basin of Hudson Bay, was ruled like a feudal fiefdom by the Hudson Bay Company. Their charter gave them complete control, political and economical: one citizen of the Red River Valley, writing in 1856, called the Company an incubus which had buried the area in apathy.[71] By 1869, a sizable group of half-breeds, French and English, lived in the Valley near Fort Garry (now Winnipeg). Their livelihood centered on the buffalo hunt, an enormous enterprise which required a military type of organization and which supplied the dried meat and pemmican on which the traders depended.

Indian and Métis had common bonds, including languages; and both claimed territorial rights as aboriginal people. But the Métis, unlike their Indian cousins, were never accorded legal status by the Canadian government. Faced with overt discrimination and violence, they were forced to abandon the name of Métis; politically, they were nonexistent. They inherited all the Indian problems, and their tragedy "climaxed and epitomized the whole struggle of red man, or brown, against white."[72]

In 1869, the Hudson Bay Company, without informing the people of the area, surrendered their charter 'and sold the Canadian West to the government in Ottawa (newly confederated, two years before). White settlers had been slowly increasing for half a century, and trade between the Métis and the Americans, just to the south, was rapidly increasing in the 1860s. The Métis feared for the security of title to the lands on which they lived, on the banks of the Red and Qu'Appelle Rivers, while the Canadians, in central and eastern Canada, feared for the security of Rupert's Land against American encroachment. Louis Riel led the Manitoba Métis, first in passive resistance to the Canadian surveyors, and finally in an armed rebellion. His provisional government stopped entry of the Canadian representatives in December, 1869, seized Fort Garry, and composed a list of constitutional demands, most of which were made law the next year when Manitoba became the fifth province to enter the Dominion of Canada.

For Riel and his people it was a Pyrrhic victory. His provisional government had executed Thomas Scott, an Ontario Orangeman, after a court-martial. This act, and Riel's unfortunate links with American supporters, were largely responsible for the military force which took Fort Garry in the spring of 1870, and forced Riel into exile in the United States. As for the Manitoba Métis, some received title to their farms and subsequently lost it to unscrupulous land speculators and white settlers. Ontario settlers (Laurence's ancestors among them) poured into Manitoba in the next few decades and altered its social makeup from a large proportion of French-speaking Roman Catholics (the Métis) to a predominantly Protestant, English-speaking majority. The Métis were the tragic heirs to centuries of hostility between these groups in Canada.

After 1870, many of the Manitoba Métis moved westward to the area of Batoche on the South Saskatchewan, where the Dumont family had lived, and helped to lead the buffalo hunt, for two generations. Between 1870 and 1885 (the second rebellion, and the one which sealed the fate of this people), the Saskatchewan group was enlarged by Métis who had lost their land in Manitoba or who preferred the greater freedom of the Northwest Territories and access to the remaining buffalo. It was a tortured time for Indian and Métis alike, as Joseph Kinsey Howard writes: "—a time of war, famine, disease, moral dissolution. It was a time when smallpox, whiskey, prostitution and the slaughter of the buffalo did more to win an empire than bullets could; and perhaps the bullets could never have done it alone."[73]

The disappearance of the buffalo, and the inevitable spread of white settlement westward, doomed the way of life of Métis and Indians, both of whom depended on the buffalo for food and other necessities. By the late 1870s and early 1880s, the Saskatchewan Métis were in fear for their land rights, while

pleas on their behalf from white intermediaries and their own
petitions went unanswered by Ottawa.

The Métis story leads deep into the heart of Canadian history
and the Canadian psyche. Other major writers, especially the
Western Mennonite novelist Rudy Wiebe, have made these
events the basis of fiction and drama. Excellent biographies of
Riel and Dumont, the central figures in the events of the 1800s,
are Howard's *The Strange Empire of Louis Riel* (1952) and
George Woodcock's *Gabriel Dumont* (1975). But readers of
these biographies will find the neglect and delays by the Canadian government almost incomprehensible, even in terms of
self-interest. A third biography balances the picture and makes
that neglect comprehensible in terms of another culture and
another dream, an English-Canadian dream of a united nation
from sea to sea—a British North America. Riel's vision of a
Métis nation ran aground on the shoal of Sir John A. Macdonald's vision of " 'an immense confederation of free men,
the greatest confederacy of civilized and intelligent men that had
ever had an existence on the face of the globe.' "[74]

Donald Creighton's two-volume biography of Canada's founding father and greatest political leader explains the forces in
central Canada which doomed the Métis to extinction as a
people for the next eighty years. Sir John A. Macdonald, from
his early years in a border community which had been threatened
by American raiders in 1838 after the rebellions in the Canadas,
and again in the 1860s by Fenians after the American Civil War,
had a lifelong fear of American encroachment. As a lawyer,
Macdonald had played a leading part in the military trials which
followed the 1838 invasion and battle, near Kingston; as a politician, he had felt the weight of American pressures through two
generations. The Métis fell between the Scylla of a vision of a
British North America, and the Charybdis of American Manifest
Destiny.

Macdonald held consistently to four policies. These were,
first, the need for a strong central government, and the de-
sirability of maintaining the British connection as the only realistic counterweight which might ensure Canada's survival as an
independent nation; after confederation in 1867, he envisaged
the settlement of the West with white immigrants and the build-

ing of a transcontinental railway. The latter made the former possible. Only settlement, and the railway, could tie British Columbia to the federated eastern provinces of Canada, and defend the entire Northwest against encroachment from the south. The British connection was more, of course, than a political counterweight. It was also a deeply held ideal. For Macdonald, British institutions and culture were the epitome of human development. Ethnicity was not a Victorian value; military valor was. The Métis *as a separate people* were almost literally invisible to Sir John, and were doomed by the forces that had formed him. He and his colleagues saw the Canadian West as empty, with the exception of the Indians who had been conveniently consigned to reservations by a series of treaties with their chiefs. Yet Macdonald was no bigot. He stoutly opposed Protestant extremists who attacked French Catholic interests. His moderate coalition policies made confederation possible, and held the country together through half a century of political crises.

Ironically, the neglected Métis and their armed rebellion in 1885 solved the financial crisis of the Canadian Pacific Railway Company and Sir John's government. By using the unfinished railway to get troops to Saskatchewan to put down the rising led by Riel and Dumont, the central Canadian provinces were convinced of its value, and a previously balky parliament voted money for its completion. A flood of patriotic enthusiasm in the East temporarily united its warring factions.

There is little doubt, today, of the justice of many of the Métis claims, especially with regard to land. Riel's hanging, in 1885, aggravated ancient rivalries between Ontario and Quebec; and was used to turn Quebec against the Conservative party for generations to come. As Woodcock puts it, Macdonald "very unwisely placed political tactics above humanity and in the process permanently alienated Riel's fellow francophones in Quebec."[75]

The state of the Métis, after 1885, was pitiable: "not only had many Métis not received the land grants which the government had promised, but after their defeat many of them were so poor that they had neither the means nor the heart to cultivate any land that they might be graciously given."[76] Many retreated north (their ancient pattern in the face of a threatening white civilization) to marginal lands where some semblance of the old free hunting life could be maintained. (Pique's Uncle Jacques, in *The Diviners*, represents this trend.) Others became unwilling, impoverished farmers. All had become "a people without standing in the new world of the future, and without rights in the old world of the past...."[77]

Laurence's fiction accurately depicts the general contempt with which the Métis were regarded in the latter part of the nineteenth century, and the twentieth. In a primitive or frontier society their invaluable abilities won the Métis a fair degree of social acceptance. As the fur trade declined, white civilization spread westward, and the buffalo became almost extinct, Métis usefulness to white society declined, and with that change came a growing contempt for an illiterate, nomadic group.

With typically imperial arrogance, the whites saw the Métis as not merely uneducated but *improvident*. One is reminded of Laurence's jibe at the British in Somaliland, who found the Somalis stupid because they did not speak English fluently. What Woodcock and Howard see as evidence of generosity, hospitality, and general disrespect for money, was seen by Victorian travelers (and by the thrifty Scots settlers of Manitoba) as prodigal.[78]

The Métis maintained a strong sense of individual liberty and egalitarian democracy, such as existed among the great Indian tribes of the plains. Alexander Ross, an early nineteenth-century historian, praised the splendid organization of the buffalo hunt, where mutual aid and mutual restraint was necessary if the animals were not to be frightened prematurely. Woodcock describes the Métis attitude as one of anarchic egoism, tempered by mutual respect among the strong and by generosity towards the weak. The "uneducated" Métis could often speak half a dozen languages (French, English, and different Indian languages). They could ride and shoot better than their Indian cousins. They were superb hunters, trappers, guides.

In their prime Métis helped to protect the white settlers of the Red River Valley from hostile Indians; and constituted a formidable antagonist to the Canadian militia in 1870 and 1885. One is inclined to agree with Woodcock's thesis, that if Dumont had been allowed the free exercise of his military judgment at that time, the Métis, by guerilla warfare tactics, could have brought the confrontation to a stalemate and consequently won infinitely better terms for their people. Such was not to be. Nor was Riel's dream of a new nation in the Northwest, where Métis would live in harmony with a united Canada.[79]

After roughly eighty years, Métis reappeared as an ethnic group in Manitoba. In the 1960s the political climate was particularly favorable to the kind of pressures the group could bring to bear, and group cohesiveness could be used to improve conditions for its members. Modern Métis are radically different from the prairie horselords of the 1800s. Joe Sawchuk, who worked with Métis in Manitoba in the 1970s, objects (like Laurence) to the kind of Social Darwinism that sees European culture as superior to primitive cultures and thus entitled to preempt the "inferior" people's land. Sawchuk speaks of a "white settler mentality" which helped to destroy the Métis sense of self-worth.[80] Laurence's fiction depicts their struggle against this psychic aggression.

One of the political structures that has helped the Métis in the 1960s and 70s is the Manitoba Métis Federation, a non-profit, voluntary organization dedicated to achieving recognition of the Métis and their problems, to educating them in social action, and to bettering their economic position. This new political process is very different from that manifested by the nineteenth-century Métis who stressed their independence and organized around a feeling of separateness. Since this is no longer possible in Canada, their current political strategy has been described as "fighting the white man with the white man's weapons," the weapons of institutionalized political process. In the 1800s the Métis were organized around the buffalo hunt; today, they are organized around a lack of occupation and the need to improve their social and economic position.[81]

Laurence's review of Woodcock's biography closes on three main points: along with the injustice done to Métis and the necessity of redressing that injustice, she stresses their "rediscovered sense of self-worth and the ability to tell and teach the things needed to be known" (*HS* 211). By the latter, Laurence means the Indian respect for and closeness to the earth and its creatures, an intimacy lost by the greed and exploitative nature of industrial culture. We have forgotten, she says, our need to pay homage to the earth and its creatures. Pre-industrial societies were not ideal, "nor can we return to them, but they knew about living in relationship to the land, and they may ultimately be the societies from whose values we must try to learn" (*HS* 212). In *The Diviners* the haunting ballads of Jules Tonnerre, Lazarus, and Piquette catch the pain of this prairie people, while through Pique, child of Morag Gunn and Jules Tonnerre, Laurence expresses her belief that white Canadians are inextricably joined to Indians and Métis in Canada's future as in her past.[82]

## VII  *Where the Soul Meets History*[83]

Laurence has frequently spoken of her "eyes" being formed in the prairie town of her youth, and of the "voice" which the novelist finds through a kind of surrender to the fictional characters. These influences, this talent, have combined to make her fiction a powerful portrayal of interrelated characters: of individuals, and of the society in which they share.

Edward Sapir writes of the intimate relation between language and society: "We see and hear and otherwise experience very largely as we do because the language habits of our community predispose certain choices of interpretation."[84] Laurence makes exactly the same point in a 1978 article, quoted earlier. In general, her comments on language show the social and religious coloring of her vision: "I have had, if any faith at all, a faith in the word. *In the beginning was the Word, and the Word was with God, and the Word was God.* . . . we must communicate with what is almost the only means we have—human speech. . . . this imperfect means is the only one we have" (*HS* 203).

Her twin themes, of the search for freedom and the struggle for human communication, are nicely balanced and inevitably connected, expressing her concern for the individual and the group of which he or she forms part. This concern for community belongs to the themes of Canadian literature and history, where the individual has traditionally found "his or her greatest freedom in an enlightened alliance with society and the social order."[85] English Canadians' rejection of the American Revolution in 1775, and French Canadians' rejection of the French Revolution, were rejections of anarchic individualism in favor of a community orientation which continues to find expression in contemporary Canadian society. In a recent essay Laurence refers to the generation of Canadian writers who preceded her. Exhibiting a strong sense of kinship, Laurence calls these writers "sod-busters" and "literary heroes," who revealed their particular Canadian communities and whose writing influenced her own.[86]

One important literary influence has been the fiction of Sinclair Ross. Laurence first read his *As For Me and My House* when she was eighteen. In her Introduction to a collection of Ross's stories Laurence comments on the realism of Ross's portrait of small, ingrown prairie towns, a realism that is nevertheless "illuminated with compassion."[87] His treatment of the land, "violent and unpredictable," sometimes suggests a harsh and vengeful God; his concern with the problems and difficulties of human communication is also hers. In Ross's fiction the outer situation mirrors the inner; the empty landscape reflects the inability to speak, to touch: "The patterns are those of isolation and loneliness, and gradually, through these, the underlying spiritual goals of an entire society can be perceived. . . . Hope never quite vanishes. In counterpoint to desolation runs the theme of renewal . . . man emerges as a creature who can survive—and survive with some remaining dignity—against both outer and inner odds which are almost impossible."[88] Like Laurence, Ross depicts an often agonized search for freedom and communication.

Numerous critics remind us of the centrality of *the land* in prairie fiction, a land (and climate) of extremes which provokes deep emotional responses.[89] In the first few decades of this century, a generation of Canadian writers (Ralph Connor, Robert Stead, Nellie McClung) saw the West in terms of Edenic or regenerative possibilities. They emphasized the heroism of man's imposition of order upon the land, a land given by God and holding His presence. Donald Stephens links Laurence's work with the feeling for the land found in Western literature in general: "Though Margaret Laurence concentrates on people, the prairie emerges as an essential background to her portraits

of them. The sensual appeal in the landscape is always felt."[90]
And Henry Kreisel, after noting Ross's uncompromising portrait
of prairie Puritanism, links the theme of the conquest of the
land with the theme of the imprisoned spirit, in the writings
of Frederick Philip Grove, Martha Ostenso, Sinclair Ross, and
Laurence.[91]

Laurence's literary tradition is also concerned with the treatment of *time*. Rudy Wiebe writes of the prairies as a place
where people live not by clock-time but by the cycles of their
bodies and the seasons.[92] His fiction, like that of Adele Wiseman
(another Manitoban), reflects a feeling for the continuity of
generations, of a future unfolding from a past and a past that
continues to inform the present.[93] Laurence's view of the time-
continuum owes more to her prairie roots, and to the literary
tradition she has inherited, than to the work of European philos-
ophers such as Henri Bergson.

The concept of the frontier belongs to American rather than
Canadian patterns. The concept, as proposed by Frederick
Jackson Turner, has been given a Canadian application by some
historians, notably Arthur Lower. Turner's theory involved the
place where civilization met savagery or wilderness; it fostered
individualism, since it saw the individual as the only source of
law and order in a disordered or loosely organized milieu. Writers
and historians such as Wallace Stegner and Carl Berger have
pointed to the folly of applying the American frontier thesis to
the Canadian West, where events promoted very different conditions for society and hence for literature. Fur traders and
missionaries operated in the Canadian West long before the
settlers arrived, and with or before the latter came the Royal
Canadian Mounted Police, the railroads, and the Law. Dick
Harrison, who calls the attempt to live with foreign myths "cultural insanity," contrasts the frontier tradition with the Canadian
Garden myth, seen in the works of Ralph Connor, Nellie
McClung, and Robert Stead. The two myths embody two contrasting visions of order, inductive and deductive: the first
dependent on the individual in relative isolation; the second, on
the acceptance of a tradition of law and order emanating from a
remote center.

Laurence's work portrays the Garden myth in its ironic form.

The earlier, romantic forms of the myth fostered the sense of an empty land, lacking in history prior to the arrival of the Europeans. Indian and Métis were rarely depicted, except as "degenerate creatures destined for a merciful extinction."[94] Moreover, the early Western writers of this century, many of them originally from central Canada, fostered the idea that the majority of the settlers were of British stock. It remained for writers like Ross and Grove, and (later) Wiebe, Wiseman, and Laurence, to redress the balance: to focus attention as much on cultural patterns as on the land; and to repopulate the Canadian literary West with Indians, Métis, Ukrainians, Germans, and Jews. Yet despite their realistic knowledge of evil, these writers exhibit the basic idealism and the social concerns of the earlier generation of Western Canadian novelists.

The 1978 essay in which Laurence declares that the novelist must be a sociopolitical being builds upon an earlier one by Hugh MacLennan ("The Writer *engagée*," 1976), using many of the same terms. MacLennan argues that the problems of our time should be faced by our artists, that the novel is capable of becoming a powerful instrument of human communication, and that the novelist "must be involved emotionally with the world he inhabits."[95]

Laurence points, here, to the social influences that helped to form her, from her early exposure to anti-colonialism, through the Leftist politics of her Winnipeg period and the culture shock of Africa, to the Women's Movement of the 1960s and 70s. The quest for freedom, for relationships of equality and understanding, for the survival of the spirit with dignity and love—these Laurentian themes reflect the emotional involvement with sociopolitical problems which MacLennan and Laurence believe to be essential for the novelist. As Laurence puts it, "the themes of freedom and survival relate both to the social/external world and to the spiritual/inner one, and they are themes which I see as both political and religious. If freedom is, in part, the ability to act out of one's self-definition, with some confidence and with compassion, uncompelled by fear or by the authority of others, it is also a celebration of life and of the mystery at life's core. In their varying ways, all these characters experience a form of grace."[96]

Dispossession, she adds, is one of her significant themes, through the Highland Scots of Christie's tales and the Tonnerres:

Like love, like communication, like freedom, social justice must sometimes be defined in fiction by the lack of it. I believe this to be so in many instances throughout my fiction—the plight of the Métis; the town's scorn of such people as Lazarus Tonnerre, Christie Logan, Bram Shipley, Lottie Drieser, to name only a few; the depression years of the thirties; the way in which the true meaning of war comes to some of the town's men in the trenches of World War I, and again later to many of the townsfolk with the tragedy of Dieppe in World War II.[97]

Georg Lukács, the great analyst of alienation applied to the arts, helps us to understand the significance of Laurence's work. Alienation, like dispossession, is a psychic phenomenon with socioeconomic foundations. In "The Intellectual Physiognomy of Literary Characters" Lukács argues that great fiction contains living characters whose feelings can be shared by the reader; that these unique individuals are also types who embody their particular society; and that their personal problems reflect in a significant way the general problems of their age: "In all great writing it is indispensable that its characters be depicted in all-sided interdependence with each other, with their social existence, and with the great problems of this existence."[98] Laurence's characters embody the vitality, the uniqueness, the mental and emotional energy, and the close relation to their society which Lukács defines as "intellectual physiognomy" and which he considers characteristic of great novels. When Lukács speaks of literary characters' capacity for awareness of self, one is reminded of Laurence's comment, that the fictional characters control the handling of time in the work. Characters such as Laurence's Hagar, Grandfather Simpson, Morag, and Christie Logan have the inexhaustible depth and vitality that we associate with great fiction. It is Laurence's avowed goal to portray the individual in all his contradictions; and it is the ability to evoke "all the paradox and conflict and warmth of a living man" that elicits her praise of Nigerian writing (LD 74). Lukács notes that great fiction expresses sociohistoric situa-

tions through individual characters; that it raises the individual
to the universal through intensified or poetic form; and that
this requires strange, grotesque characters and situations, not
commonplace ones: "The more profoundly an epoch and its
great problems are grasped by the writer, the less can his portrayal be on a commonplace level." Romantic writers, he argues,
may depict extreme characters and situations as ends in themselves, but the classic realists "choose the extremely accentuated
person and situation merely as the most suitable means of
poetic expression for portraying the typical in its highest form."[99]
It is not merely Laurence's secondary characters (Prin, Fan
Brady) who are "extreme" in this sense, but her protagonists:
Hagar, obese and strong-willed; Rachel, awkward and patholog-
ically nervous; Stacey, concealing her gin and her dreams, dancing by herself in mid-afternoon; Christie Logan, Scavenger, loony
prophet. These are all extreme characters; and all are raised, in
Lukács's phrase, to the poetic universal or "intensified typical."

Woodcock's comparison of Laurence's fiction with that of
Tolstoy stems from a similar conviction, that great fiction catches
the living interaction of social contradictions, that it exhibits
great social problems in all their diversity. Laurence's depiction
of war, depression, class conflict, ecological hazards, social injustice, or colonial oppression is couched, always, in terms of
inner human realities such as love and hate, pride, loneliness,
defiance, courage, and longing. This is indeed "political in a
different sense," as Laurence remarked to Bernice Lever in 1975.
Like Achebe, Patrick White, and the Canadian writers whose
work she admires, Laurence sees man as *a social being*. All her
work reflects this primary perception.

Laurence has been called a religious writer; this study strongly
supports that view. Her Manawaka cycle of fiction, taken as a
unit, moves with a "rhythm of reconciliation" which expresses
a sense of design and of beneficent purpose in the universe.[100]
David Blewett accurately defines the meaning of Manawaka, that
fictional Manitoba town, as the embodiment of Laurence's vision
of human nature. As a symbol of human divisiveness, whose inhabitants are separated by pride and greed, Manawaka is an
inner and outer world, and an inescapable one: "The achievement

of each of the protagonists is that, finally, she stands and faces, and so triumphs over, the Manawaka within."[101]

Laurence's use of the four elements of earth, air, fire, and water in the Manawaka cycle further illustrates the religious nature of her imagery.[102] Faith and love lie at the core of this literary vision. To Simone Weil's definition of faith as intelligence illumined by love, George Grant adds that "love" is attention to otherness, receptivity of otherness, consent to otherness. We have seen the centrality of the latter concept throughout the body of Laurence's writing. The major critics of her work interpret it as a search for spiritual understanding and reconciliation.[103]

It is one of the continuing paradoxes of literature that it achieves universality through the depiction of specific regions and cultures. William Faulkner's Yoknapatawpha County is a well-known example. Hugh MacLennan illustrates the paradox, and historical resistance to it, by tracing fashions in national literature over the last two thousand years. Writing in what we now call the Golden Age of Latin literature, the poet Horace believed that his own work would last because he was the first to have brought Greek poetry to the Italians. English literature was not taken seriously in France until the eighteenth century. German literature was accepted towards the end of the eighteenth century; Russian and American, in the nineteenth; and Irish, in the twentieth.[104]

By the mid-twentieth century, tremendous contributions to the tradition of literature and the poetic use of language were being made by countries such as Australia, Africa, the Caribbean, and Canada. Their writers sought to voice their developing aspirations and self-understanding—what Laurence has called their ancestors and their gods. Laurence uses, without apology, the rhythms of the Canadian speaking voice to recreate her regional roots. By celebrating her region she helps us to better understand our own.

## EPILOGUE

# *Her Final Years*

The voice was unmistakable. Strong, gutsy, caring, and full of laughter. Life was far too serious a business not to be laughed at. The voice belonged to Margaret Laurence, to her life as to her writing. It had been formed, over three continents, as her intelligence, curiosity, compassion, and courage reacted to the hand which Fate had dealt. It was the voice of a small, mid-Western Canadian town. It was also uniquely Laurence's own. And why not? Her belief that every individual is unique and valuable was one of the cornerstones of her very personal creed.

This memoir is concerned with her last thirteen years, the years between the publication of her master novel, *The Diviners*, and her death on January 5, 1987. Why did this highly talented woman write no further fiction, with the exception of three short works for children? What was she doing with her time during years which are for many artists their most productive ones?

The unity of her life, especially during these final years, is striking. In contemplating her primary concerns—friendship, peace, women's issues, the writing community (which she tagged "the tribe")—one is impressed with the fact that a close look at any one of these areas leads inevitably into all of the others. Where to begin?

Anyone reading a record of activities in these years cannot fail to be impressed by her deep concern for the welfare of people everywhere, and for the earth itself. Her impassioned appeals on behalf of world peace, battered women, anti-pollution, and the charitable way in which she reacted to the public attacks of those who misunderstood her writing or condemned it unread, convey the image of a saintly woman, heroic and dedicated. The temptation to canonize Margaret is very strong.

Most biographers, however, have little respect for hagiography. As for Margaret, she would have hooted with laughter at the prospect. In writing to Clara Thomas in 1969 to express her pleasure in Thoma's sympathetic treatment, she noted that such a viewpoint tended to overlook her worst characteristics. These included her fierce temper and might, she conceded, be dealt with more easily after her death. She was, she claimed, more like her fictional character Stacey (in *The Fire-Dwellers*) than like the person called up by Thomas. Avoiding canonization, however, requires effort. Margaret remains a formidable figure with which to reckon.

From 1969, Margaret's life was divided between southern Ontario and Elm Cottage, England. During the last few years of the decade spent in England, ties with Canada began to reassert themselves; from the spring of 1974, for the remainder of her life, she would live in southwestern Ontario in the village of Lakefield, eight miles north of the city of Peterborough.

She was now a public figure. Calls on her time and presence steadily increased as she became well known through publications and awards. She served for two terms as Writer-in-Residence at the University of Toronto, beginning in the fall of 1969. In the same year she bought a cottage on the Otonabee, a short drive to the south of Lakefield. "The Shack," as she called the small cedar cabin, was destined to play an important part in her life for the next decade, and would provide the setting for *The Diviners*. Margaret called this cabin the most loved place of her later years. It was a haven where she could write, watching the birds and the river: "every time I lift my eyes from the page and glance outside, it is to see some marvel or other."[1] A sense of gratitude and religious awe emanates from her description of the pair of great blue herons which nested nearby, or the migrating flocks of Canada geese. They moved her deeply.

The yellow brick house in Lakefield, a former funeral parlour, was acquired in 1973. That fall Margaret served as Writer-in-Residence at the University of Western Ontario in London; and, in the same capacity, at Trent University during the winter term. (Trent University lies on the Otonabee River between Lakefield and Peterborough.) Her children were now aged twenty-two and nineteen, and Margaret was entering the final phase of her wide-ranging life. One suspects that she knew and accepted this fact. The village she had chosen was in many ways not unlike the Manitoba town of her youth. Lakefield is smaller than Neepawa but equally gossipy and friendly. Margaret lived at 8 Regent Street, just off the main thoroughfare. A short walk brought her to stores and the post office, the object of a daily pilgrimage in search of her beloved mail. She was an "inveterate letter-writer," self-styled, and "an addicted receiver of letters."[2] Mail provided vital links to beloved friends, a lifeline which was necessary to her well-being.

Let us return to the question of what Margaret was doing during these years in Lakefield. As time passed without the publication of new fiction–and most of the essays in *Heart of a Stranger* (1976) had been written years earlier–her casual friends were puzzled. One sent a clipping on "Writer's block," which made her angry. Her close friends knew that she worked every day, hard and long, at an amazing variety of tasks that grew out of her career, her multiple links with the writing community, and her concern for the precarious state of the world. No sooner had she accomplished one such task than it was replaced by two more. She soldiered on, convinced that these activities mattered.

One copy of a form letter composed by Margaret around 1980 was sent to Anne Woodsworth, librarian at York University. She begins with the point that she has had virtually no time for her own work for some years because she has been asked to do so many activities, and has been glad to do them. Now, however, she is giving notice that she cannot undertake to do any of the following: read manuscripts; write book reviews; provide quotes for book jackets; give readings or conduct seminars; participate in writers' workshops or panels; give advice on essays or theses; provide photographs, biographical information, or copies of her books; receive visitors, attend conferences, give interviews or appear on television or radio; give speeches, lectures, or graduation addresses; judge writing contests; or reply personally to readers' letters. She is, she adds, most grateful for the latter.

The warning was hollow, although the momentary defiance that it represented obviously gave her pleasure. She celebrated her mock-release by boldly writing *Whoopee!* beside the list of items supposedly banned. (She was still doing many of these chores in 1986.) To Enid Rutland in March, 1983, she wrote that she was trying desperately to get some of her own writing done despite constant interruptions of this type and that, ironically, she had actually had more time when her children were small. In those years she had not been involved with Trent University, anti-nuclear groups, Energy Probe, etc. Since she had freely chosen her current activities, she should not (she added generously) complain.

The list in the form letter is far from complete. Joan Johnston remembers Margaret being endlessly busy, working long and hard for peace and for various charities such as the Three Guineas, a group devoted to helping women in various fields. Journalist John Fraser called her peppery public letters "a sub-species of her craft" which deserved to be collected. Archivist Phyllis Platnick, of York University, observed that one gets from her letters of the 1980s "a feeling of desperation" in relation to the tasks which were being asked of her and the time available. Clearly she was pulled in many directions and felt continually short of time. Her correspondence shows how accurate the summary in the form letter was of the endless calls on her time and strength.

Throughout her adult lifetime, "work" to Margaret meant, solely and simply, her serious writing and her care for her children. Nothing else really qualified for the term. Her concern for peace and a nuclear-free world stemmed naturally from these two central loves. Without peace there would be no future for coming generations; no libraries, no readers. Painter Helen Lucas recalls that peace was the most important thing to Margaret during the years of their friendship, the last ten years of the writer's life. Lucas tells of a dinner party at her home with Margaret and two other guests. A banker voiced his conviction that war was helpful to nations' economics: "Margaret was so angry she raised her voice, she was defending the human race, she went to her purse and found a recent speech of hers and read it aloud while pounding on the table! This very cool man sat there with a slight smile and said nothing. She probably didn't change his mind, but she gave it a really good try. She was *great*."[3]

Project Ploughshares, based at the University of Waterloo, was one of several anti-nuclear groups to which Margaret gave support. She was a board member of Ploughshares and of Energy Probe, and considered the former group, which explores problems in militarism and their impact on development, to be one of the most effective advocates of peace working in Canada. To the June, 1980, issue of its publication *The Monitor*, she contributed an article sent earlier to the editor of *The Toronto Star*. It voiced her concern about the world's apparent drift toward World War III. She called the drift "absolute lunacy," as was any acceptance of the idea of war as inevitable: "Am I thinking selfishly of my own children? You bet I am. And by extension of our children everywhere." To Margaret, global war was "unthinkable." We do not bear and raise and love our children, she urged, in order to see their lives thrown casually away. Her quick temper was usually turned on appropriate targets.

Margaret's sense of responsibility, her conviction that each of us should be a responsible citizen of the world, was established early. In December 1942, as editor of her high school magazine *Annals of the Black and Gold*, she had reminded her fellow-students that it would be their task to build up the world after the war. This sense of civic responsibility was also evident at university. Theologian and activist Lois Wilson recalls that she and Margaret were both active in student politics, working for the general well-being of United College, Winnipeg.

In the 1970s and 80s these concerns came to the force. "My Final Hour," a frequently reprinted talk originally presented to the Trent Philosophy Society on March 29, 1983, expresses her love and reverence for this planet, our home: "I have always believed I had to live as well as to write, to be a citizen and a person and a mother and a friend as well as a writer." She describes our current world situation as hurting, endangered, *terrifying*, yet she calls for hope, proclaiming her belief in the social gospel as a Christian and as a member of humanity, "a sharer in a life that I believe in some way to be informed by the holy spirit." No one should rest, she urged, with individual salvation, despite her central belief that every individual matters, that no one is ordinary. We are called to love our neighbours as ourselves.[4] In her powerful appeal, disarmament is not simply a political matter but a spiritual one, the most pressing of our time. Her work for peace stemmed directly from her religious faith.

It was Margaret's imagination (a gift obviously lacking in many of our religious and political leaders) which enabled her to envisage holocaust in human terms, a dead and putrefying world: "All children are our children.... In a nuclear world there would be nowhere to hide, and nowhere except a dead and contaminated world to emerge back into. I profoundly believe that we must proclaim that this must not happen." And again: "We cannot afford passivity.... Our aim must be no less than human and caring justice, and peace .... *for all people that on earth do dwell.*"[5] In her polemics as in her fiction, Margaret drew on the language of the King James Version of the Bible. It was at her core.

Meanwhile, throughout the last ten years of her life, Margaret was waging a very personal battle of her own, a war of words and nerves which took a terrible toll and may well have hastened her death. In "Living Dangerously.... by Mail," Margaret refers rather flippantly to her first "anti-fan" letter drawing "psychic blood." In general, this essay turns letters from hostile readers into high comedy. It was, however, no joking matter when the minister of a Pentecostal church in Peterborough attacked *The Diviners* as immoral and blasphemous, indeed little short of pornography. His goal was to have Margaret's books, especially *The Diviners*, removed from the curriculum of senior high school English courses. The 1976 and 1978 incidents have been documented and discussed in chapter 3 in connection with an analysis of the novel. A third wave of attacks began in 1984, again in the Lakefield/Peterborough area.

What concerns us here is how this very public campaign in the media and in her hometown affected Margaret, and what it cost her in spiritual, emotional, and physical terms. In a speech on censorship given in Peterborough (June 2, 1983) to Ontario provincial judges and their wives, she said, "I have been burned by the world-be book censors–scorched mentally and emotionally." Describing her attackers to the judges as born-again fundamentalists who were doubtless sincere within their own scope, she spoke of the trauma she had suffered over the controversy, her obsession with it for many years, and her "anguished defense" of the novel in question. She described *The Diviners* as fiction with "a strong sense of the worth and value of the human individual, of caring relationships, of social injustices done to the poor and to such groups as the Métis." With one exception, its sex scenes depicted tender love between consenting adults. Margaret believed that she had suffered *slander*, using the Oxford English Dictionary's definition of a false report maliciously uttered to a person's injury. The whole affair, she added, was "a pretty awful experience" for her. To David Staines she wrote that she was miles behind in everything, owing to huge amounts of time in recent months spent battling the vigilantes nearby (22/2/85). Anger and humour, her typical responses, barely masked the pain.

In the same talk, Margaret defined her novels as a celebration of life and of the mystery at the core of life, a portrayal both of human love and of man's tragic inhumanity to man. She described herself as a serious writer, answerable to herself, her people, and "to God." By contrast, pornography was a *denial* of life, a statement of misogyny, and a depiction of violence as socially acceptable, even desirable. In letters to friends, Margaret marvelled that the writing which she knew to be religious in intent and expression could be seen by some readers as blasphemous. She mourned the barriers to communication between generations and individuals, barriers which left walls that could never be scaled. It overwhelmed her, she wrote, but she was trying to learn to be calm.

When she was charged with degrading the Métis by showing them in an unfavourable light, she replied that she had shown them as a suffering and courageous people to whom great injustice had been done by white society. Privately, she suspected that some of the opposition to *The Diviners* stemmed from its depiction of a love affair between a Métis man and a white woman.[6] She may well have been correct. Racism dies hard.

During the 1980s, Margaret was working on a novel based on these attacks. She eventually abandoned the attempt, convinced that the material did not lend itself to fiction, or would not do so for her. Curiously, she contributed a preface in 1982 to a collected volume of Gwen Pharis Ringwood's plays. One of the

plays concerned a young female teacher's dilemma when faced
with puritanical attacks and an attempt to censor the reading list
she provided for her students. Margaret called "A Remembrance
of Miracles" (1980) both contemporary and timeless, and found
it "almost unbearably poignant" because of its personal relation
to her own experience.[7]

Several friends, Hugh MacLennan and Timothy Findley among
them, are convinced that the stress connected with these current
attacks actually shortened her life. Given Margaret's particular
make-up, it seems a reasonable hypothesis. MacLennan made
the suggestion at Kingston, May, 1987, in giving the Margaret
Laurence Memorial Lecture at the Annual General Meeting of
The Writers' Union of Canada. She must, he argued, have suffered *some* psychological damage from it, "and it is quite possible
that if this outrage had not occurred, she would still be alive."[8]

In Findley's view, the matter hung on Margaret's exceptional
sensitivity, the same sensitivity that made her writing possible:
"Margaret is the Black Celt, that's the core that delivered the
writing. She's a walking nerve-end."[9] The sensitivity which fed
her writing made her extremely vulnerable. Another writer, a
*different* individual, might have laughed at the attackers and
responded with cutting satire. Not Margaret. In the 1970s she
allowed others to defend her, and was greatly heartened by the
support of the writing community and by many of her neighbours
in Lakefield. Following the 1984 attack she spoke up herself, but
never to defame the attackers. Throughout all the controversies
she bled inwardly.

In times of stress (and, given Margaret's emotional make-up,
this meant much of the time) she turned first to words and to
people she loved. Cigarettes and alcohol also became necessary
forms of relief. She smoked heavily throughout the Lakefield
years, despite valiant efforts to cut down. She wrote to Adele
Wiseman (2/84) that she was seeking help to stop smoking but
feared it might be too late. She was frightened, but she accepted
responsibility for herself. Besides, why should she want to live
forever? She had done, she believed, what she was *meant* to do:
raised her children, done the writing that was somehow inevitable for her to do. Her work. With the aid of a physician she
had cut back to one package per day before the fresh attacks on

her work began in 1984, but while visiting a friend for two days in 1986 she smoked many times that amount. Obviously cigarettes offered release from nervous strain; cigarettes, and the whisky which was her regular companion during the long lonely evenings after her day's work was done.

Margaret was far from being physically strong during her last years. Her numerous health problems included severe back pain which hindered her ability to travel and hampered life in general; arthritis, which made it difficult to type; carpal tunnel syndrome, affecting the nerves in her right wrist; and the growth of cataracts on her eyes.

She had always been short-sighted, with one eye much worse than the other. By 1985 she was suffering the terrifying fear of losing her sight. In August she underwent cataract surgery on her right eye. June Callwood, in a short article, catches the drama of the event and something of its profound significance for Margaret, who had given to her heroine Morag Gunn her own paradoxical mixture of extreme short-sightedness and passionate love of colour and natural beauty: "Margaret's great themes of loneliness, spiritual quest and compassion, were played against backgrounds that she described vividly, lingering over colour like a landscape artist."[10]

Margaret spoke of her various health problems in letters to friends, never in public. To Wiseman, prompted by anger over a letter to the *Globe and Mail* (February, 1984) which had pointed out that she had not published anything for ten years (a gross inaccuracy), she wrote to say that she had reared her beloved children and written seven books of adult fiction along with a great deal of other writing, including some books for children. She was annoyed that the latter were rarely included in lists of her writing. She was tired, she continued, and tired of being expected to be eternally strong. These gloomy comments were quickly followed by a disclaimer. All was well.

The writer of the letter to the paper, irked by William French's assessment of Laurence as Canada's finest novelist, had apparently confused quality with continued productivity. As for Margaret, at fifty-eight she could admit to being tired. She had matured early and had been extraordinarily productive for some twenty years, the same years during which she had given birth to her children and had raised them primarily alone. In her forties, she had the wisdom one associates with old age. Seen from a distance, her life appears to have been speeded up and condensed, as if she had lived for seven or eight decades within a three-score span.

Margaret's own experience naturally gave her an understanding of and affinity with women. In her later years she became a strong spokeswoman for feminist concerns, although she never ceased to sympathize with men and the human condition in general. Her writings and her life made her a role model for many women, and an inspiration for other women artists. Alice Williams, quilt-maker, has written of the inspiration and encouragement she received from Magaret.[11] The model was many-faceted but included motherhood, family values, independence, caring, courage, and the integrity to be true to one's own particular gifts. Wilson called her an important mentor for young writers and a woman "whose stunning articulation of what it means to be a woman has been and IS a watershed in our collective understanding of what it means to be an authentic human being."[12]

Her letters to women often celebrate the breed in a comically mock-heroic tone which is nevertheless in earnest. To Marian Engel, early in 1985, she wrote to praise Jane Austen as a strong and subtle feminist, and to observe that women have always had difficulties such as Austen depicts. However modern women such as Engel and herself had raised their children without servants and with very little help of any kind. They were, she insisted, *heroic* (4/1/84). Also to Engel, she had written that their lives had been difficult but that at least they had had some true choices. Many women writers, their friends and acquaintances, had chosen to combine raising a family with doing their writing. They deserved to be called heroines (1/12/85).

Similar references are scattered thickly through her letters to Engel. Austen, she wrote in 1984, would have loved modern women writers but might have been a bit in awe of them, since they had coped with rearing children, writing books, and earning their livings. They were hardly the type to hide a manuscript when the vicar came to call. Emily Bronte, she felt, would not have understood the practicality of modern women. After meeting Australian writer Coral Howells, Margaret wrote that Howells, being a woman, understood what it was like to raise children, run a house, and still pursue a profession (11/17/84).

Like many reflective women of our century, Margaret knew that the female element in the Godhead had been grossly neglected and misunderstood. During a talk in Chalmers United Church in Kingston, 1979, she said: "I have a feeling there has to be more recognition of the kind of female principle in God.... after centuries of thinking of God in strictly male, authoritarian terms.... I think many women nowadays, and many men, feel the need to incorporate that sense of both motherhood and fatherhood in the Holy Spirit."[13]

Her religious faith, her fight for justice on many fronts, and her defence of women are all connected. Wilson writes: "Her relationship with the Christian Church as institution was some- what ambiguous for years. Two events reconnected her: one was the strong support from both Anglican and United Church con- gregations for her over the censorship issue in Peterborough. The other was the mounting of the sculpture *Crucified Woman*, which now stands outside Emmanuel College in Toronto but which was first displayed in Bloor Street United Church. As Wilson observes, the sculpture says publicly and eloquently that women have been the victims of violence and injustice.[14] To Margaret, the crucified woman–like the historic Christ–expressed *all* human suffering and the vulnerability of God.

Margaret was indeed writing during her last years. She wrote constantly. She no longer cared, however, whether her writings were collected in book form. And because she wrote slowly, with numerous revisions, even short articles and introductions could take weeks. An article published in 1985 in *Canadian Woman Studies* examines the relationship between women and technol- ogy. Margaret writes here that for over thirty years manual type- writers had served her well. She had no desire for a word processor, although by 1984 she had succumbed to an electric typewriter, and would later acquire an electronic one.[15] Over those thirty years she had often typed two or more fair copies, with carbons, because a xerox machine was unavailable or because she could not afford xerox copies. She notes that women writers tend to have less money and less time and strength for their writing because many of them refuse to choose between career and children, opting for both. Her description of the experience of many women writers is, in fact, a description of her own life: "Women writers, like women in other areas of work, have usually had numerous other jobs–child-rearing with its vast emotional needs, gladly given, shopping, cleaning, cooking, laundry, and a host of others, including doing their own business correspondence, without the access to typing and secretarial services that male writers, especially if associated with a university, have frequently enjoyed."[16] Margaret added that she was still her own housekeeper, secretary, and business manager and that, for most women, lack of time remained a persistent problem.

The reference to being sometimes unable to afford xeroxing picks up another facet of Margaret's life, one shared with many women. Letters and interviews confirm the anxieties she suffered in connection with money, especially in the 1960s. Separation from her husband was her decision, the most difficult (one suspects) that she ever had to make. She chose to be true to her writing, the gift and burden that was uniquely hers. The relationship was not helping it. As Lucas observed, "the marriage had to go because the work had to come. It was her calling."[17] Economic struggles and a deep loneliness were part of the price paid.

Margaret was mildly technophobic. When Johnston suggested an electronic typewriter, Margaret replied, "Kid, you're dragging me kicking and screaming into the twentieth century."[18] Two points in her article on women and technology are particularly well take. She noted that women have always operated machinery–especially when it was to the advantage of society for them to do so–and have always received less pay and prestige for such jobs than men have.[19]

Margaret's friendships were legendary. Her many letters bear witness to the warmth with which they were nurtured, and to the sharing which meant so much to her. In March, 1986, she wrote to the editor of *Lakefield Chronicle* to mourn and celebrate her beloved friend and neighbour Evelyn Robinson, who had lived next door for twelve years and was, in Margaret's phrase, the best neighbour she had ever known. She believed that

Robinson had lived by what Margaret called our Lord's new commandment, to love one's neighbour as oneself. It is obvious that that command was close to Margaret's heart. This letter to the *Chronicle* is typical, not unique.

Letters, which were as necessary to Margaret as breathing, formed the lifeblood of her human relationships. Her addiction to the written word (she once told Engel that she wrote better than she talked) had its drawbacks. To Sister Janice Ryan she wrote that she answered some twelve hundred letters a year. It was becoming impossible, but she hated not answering letters which came from people's hearts (2/9/84). She told Joan Johnston that she answered twenty-five hundred letters a year.[20] To Wiseman, she once confessed that she had written thirty-two letters on the previous day and was caught up for the moment. She had resolved not to answer them all anymore, but rather doubted her ability to maintain this stance (10/2/84).

A few weeks later she bolstered her resolution by a blow for freedom. Temporarily oppressed by some three dozen unanswered letters combined with several unread manuscripts from publishers, Margaret threw the entire lot into the garbage in a plastic sack. As she wrote to Wiseman, something snapped (3/6/84). The limit to her tolerance and ability had been reached. *Tra-la-la!*

Her act of rebellion was celebrated in letters to other friends, but the writing to admirers was soon taken up again, and her letters are dotted with references to the pleasure which correspondence from her readers had given to her. As for the manuscripts, they had been sent in hopes that Margaret would read them and provide comment for dust jacket copy. That unpaid work was done frequently, lovingly, generously. Margaret called her contributions to jacket copy her "Tender Messages," *t.m.*'s for short.

The garbage affair, and an anecdote which Findley loves to tell, demonstrate that Margaret's practicality extended to self-defence, and that her compassion (great though it was) did have limits. Findley's tale comes out of literary politics and gossip at the time when he was serving as Chair of The Writers' Union of Canada. Margaret knew of the troubles which the Union executive had had with a certain male writer with a reputation for being impossible to please: "Well, this man–he's dead now–goes unannounced to Margaret in Lakefield, and she saw him coming through her front window. She knew how boring he was, and she was trapped. She got down on her knees in her kitchen, and *crawled* to hide. He wouldn't stop ringing the door-bell for a long time, and she was terrified she'd cough and reveal herself. It was a minor dishonesty, but in essentials she had a ruthless honesty."[21]

Margaret believed that practicality was a female characteristic, but hers doubtless stemeed from growing up in the Canadian West during the great depression. Her fiercely democratic attitudes partnered the practicality. To Engel, she wrote to denounce a dinner given by the office of the Secretary of State for the executive members of a Canadian academic journal on whose board Margaret served. She thought poorly of the pheasant, and worse of the fine china: it was all a shocking waste of the tax-payer's money (5/13/84). Engel replied, cheerfully and with equal practicality, that foreign heads of state would be insulted by bad china, and that Margaret had as much right to pheasant off good plates as Mrs. Thatcher.

Letters meant communication, always a major theme in her writing. And they meant fun. To Lucas, Margaret described herself as a lover of fiction and other word-arrangements, despite her sharp awareness of the limitations of words (8/15/85). She had had the good luck, as she put it, to be born into a family of readers and a house full of books, ones that had "influenced, enriched, disturbed and changed" her life. Many of the books were provided by women–her step-mother, Neepawa's first librarian, and her strong-minded aunts–and some were by women authors. As a child, Margaret loved Anne and Emily, L.M. Montgomery's spunky heroines; and Nellie McClung's *Sowing Seed in Danny*, with the "indomitable Pearl." She writes that these fictional girls gave her the sense that a woman could be intelligent and independent, that women could pursue vocations as well as being wives and mothers.[22]

When Margaret's writing was going well, she experienced a form of grace, an ineffable joy. At such times she would say or think, "Thank you God, dear Sir or Madam."[23] The phrase expressed her joy when the words were coming well, and her feeling of harmony with the cosmos.

Music was her second art after language, another source of joy. She loved simple but good music, popular songs, ballads. She could identify with the African love of rhythm since it was in her own bones. Margaret (she had been told) had perfect pitch, and was a talented whistler. Lucas remembers her dancing with herself in her own house to band music, and encouraging her guest to do the same.[24]

The two had met in 1977. Their friendship had deepened through co-operation on Margaret's nativity book, *The Christmas Birthday Story* (1980), which Lucas had illustrated. Margaret had originally written the story in 1960 in Vancouver, when her own children were small. She had wanted to emphasize the aspects of the family, she told Lucas, such as joy in the birth of the child, and the connection with all creatures. She had confidence that her friend's illustrations would be tender, but not sentimental.

Incredibly, this beautiful book was the basis for yet another attack by Evangelicals, some of whom took exception to the suggestion that Mary and Joseph would be happy to have either a boy or a girl: "Either kind would be fine with them. They just hoped their baby would be strong and healthy." Findley remembers that the book was charged with being subversive, since it suggested (to the attackers) that "Christ could have been female."[25]

In July, 1986, a beautifully orchestrated irony took place in Johnston's garden beside the Otonabee River near Lakefield. Margaret's sixtieth birthday celebration, a grand affair for over fifty guests, with clowns and balloons, was paid for by a cheque from York University in exchange for a hefty collection of clippings dealing with the attacks on her.[26] The nemesis was relished quite as much as the food and drink.

On August 22, Margaret was admitted to hospital with breathing difficulties. One week later she was given the verdict: lung cancer. With this, she resumed smoking, asked for her typewriter, and set to work in earnest on the book of memoirs which she had been writing for some years. Her goal, which Johnston helped to realize, was a typewritten draft to be edited by her daughter. The work is a celebration of motherhood and of the women who have been central in Margaret's life: her mother, her step-mother/aunt, her mother-in-law, and herself as a mother.

Margaret's energy was now very limited. Johnston's offer to transcribe tapes was accepted, and Margaret began to dictate. Johnston also helped to care for her in her own home through September and October, until reinforcements arrived on October 31 in the form of her son and daughter. An incident in mid-October expresses the quintessential Margaret, full of courage and fun. Johnston had taken her to hospital for further tests: "I suggested to her that now she had the memoirs as far as we could go with them, perhaps she could ask the doctor if there wasn't something that could be done. I feared that perhaps she may have refused treatment in order to get her work finished– her all-important work. Margaret said, 'Oh, kid, you've seen all the flowers and cards and letters. I'd be too embarrassed not to die now!'"[27]

Margaret's last weeks were made even more painful and difficult by a broken leg, the result of a fall. The cast covered her entire leg, toe to hip. She continued to do what she could for herself, hobbling to bathroom and kitchen with the aid of a walker fitted out with a cloth bag which held cigarettes, a thermos of coffee she had made herself, a newspaper, perhaps mail. "You never saw anyone manage a walker like she did," Johnston recalls.[28] One of her lasting impressions of the writer is of her indomitable spirit.

Very early on the morning of January 5 Margaret died, alone. A family funeral in Lakefield was followed by a memorial service in Toronto at Bloor Street United Church on January 9, led by the Very Reverend Lois Wilson. She and Margaret had been friends since their student days. Margaret had chosen the readings, from the Old and New Testament, and three hymns: "Unto the Hills," "Guide Me O Thou Great Jehovah," and "All People that on Earth Do Dwell." She had also asked for the Scottish pibroch, "Flowers of the Forest." Wilson had fleshed out Margaret's requests and structured the service according to her wishes: "So it's not quite like Tom Sawyer–planning your own funeral–Margaret was not such an egotist."[29]

The service expressed Margaret's family values, her strong sense of community, her deep religious faith, and her joy. Wilson spoke of her "believing and doubting, freely acknowledging the grace of God in her life, but also carrying on vigorous conversations with God about just that." She spoke of their public dialogue in Kingston in 1979. It was here that Margaret had called for more recognition of the female principle in God, and had affirmed that all her novels constitute "a celebration of life itself and of the mystery at the core of life." She had also insisted that her work is informed by hope: "I don't think any of it is optimistic. One would have to have a very simplistic, or very narrow view of life to be optimistic in a world such as ours. Hope is different. Hope is something I couldn't live without. And given God's grace, somehow one feels the planet and its creatures will survive.[30] This passage was one of the ones selected for the "Notes on the Service." Margaret had never presumed to define God, but terms like *grace* and *the holy spirit* came readily to her lips and were expressed in her daily life.

The puzzle as to what Margaret "did" with her final years has been answered. The puzzle as to why she wrote no more adult fiction after *The Diviners* will always remain. Findley, for one, is not satisfied by the theory that her time was consumed by community demands, her sense of civic responsibility, her love of letters, and her genius for friendship. He credits a mysterious loss of confidence, along with an intellectual decision made during the writing of *The Diviners*: "If a piece of creative writing had started to happen, she would have put aside the letters and polemics."[31]

Margaret's own answer, as mysterious as any delphic oracle, is given near the end of her last novel. Like Morag, she had received the gift, the strong hand laid on her shoulders ("Strong and friendly. But merciless"). And like Royland–mirror within mirror–Morag feels that the gift is leaving, is being transferred to others. This was the old man's lesson to her and the meaning, for us all, of *inheritance*: "the gift, or portion of grace, or whatever it was, was finally withdrawn, to be given to someone else." Margaret explained to Helen Lucas that *it was all there* in the novel's last sentence: "Morag returned to the house, to write the remaining private and fictional words, and to set down her title." Puzzled, Lucas begged, and was given, a further explanation: "She said it meant that someone else would write the next book, the next novel–she was leaving things all set up and waiting for the next writer."[32]

This novel includes a heart-rending description of what writing meant to Morag, and no doubt to Margaret: the wrenching up of guts and heart, to be carefully set down on paper in order to live (p. 78). It meant laying herself on the line as a target for snipers. Neepawa residents, for example, were far from pleased by what they took to be her fictional portrait of them, and decided to "forgive" their famous citizen only after her death.[33] Obviously Margaret would have known, during her lifetime, of the hostility and misinterpretations on this front. She had continued to do what she believed had been *given* her to do (as she told Helen Lucas): to write out of her lifeview as a Christian social democrat, a view that had been chosen for her from earlier than she herself could understand.

The high cost to Margaret of fulfilling her special task is known to her friends, and to careful readers. She was a woman of great strengths and surprising weaknesses. The latter included her fear of driving, and of city traffic. Lucas stresses her loneliness, her vulnerability: "The smoking and drinking were symptoms of her self-destructive part, the Black Celt, not *causes* of her death but *symptoms.*" Johnston's verdict is light-hearted: "I think she enjoyed her vices. She'd done what she *had* to do, so she deserved a break."[34] Findley also spoke of Margaret as the Black Celt, and of her vision being inseparable from the nervous system that matched it: "with that sensitivity, the world may be unbearable, yet [artists] are expected to give up their bad habits." He found it difficult to forgive her attackers.[35]

We come back, then to the voice. *Oh, kid. . . . . Shoot, honey, we're heroic. . . . . God's pity on God. . . . .* Like her fictional hero Piper Gunn, Margaret had "the faith of the saints and the heart of a child and the gall of a thousand and the strength of conviction." Her fiction stands, and will continue to stand among the best work that has been written anywhere in this century of great novelists.

Patricia Morley,
Manotick, 1990.

# Notes

## Chapter One

1. See my article, "The Long Trek Home; Margaret Laurence's Stories," *Journal of Canadian Studies* 11, no. 4 (November, 1976), 19–26, for a discussion of this metaphoric pattern in Laurence's African and Canadian stories.
2. Margaret Laurence, *Heart of a Stranger* (Toronto, 1976), pp. 145–46. Further page references are in the text as *HS*.
3. Clara Thomas, *Margaret Laurence*, Canadian Writers Series, (Toronto, 1969), p. 6.
4. Susan Warwick, "A Laurence Log," *Journal of Canadian Studies* 13, no. 3 (Fall, 1978), 75.
5. Thomas, p. 7. For further information on the Wemyss and Simpson families, see Clara Thomas, *The Manawaka World of Margaret Laurence* (Toronto, 1975), pp. 6–9. See also Joan Hind-Smith, *Three Voices. The Lives of Margaret Laurence, Gabrielle Roy, and Frederick Philip Grove*, Canadian Portraits Series (Toronto, 1975), p. 4.
6. Donnalu Wigmore, "Margaret Laurence. The Woman Behind the Writing," *Chatelaine* (February, 1971), quoted in Hind-Smith, *Three Voices*, p. 6. *This Side Jordan* is dedicated to "my mother Margaret Campbell Wemyss."
7. Thomas, *Margaret Laurence*, p. 6.
8. Ibid., p. 8.
9. Conversation with the author at Lakefield and at Laurence's cottage, called "The Shack," July 25–26, 1976.
10. Margaret Laurence, *New Wind in a Dry Land* (New York, 1964), p. 6. Further references are in the text as *NW*, but the work is called *The Prophet's Camel Bell*, Laurence's preferred title.
11. Conversation with the author, July 25, 1976, and *NW*, p. 275.
12. Ibid.
13. Donald Cameron, *Conversations with Canadian Novelists, Part 1* (Toronto, 1973), p. 99.
14. Conversation with the author, July 25, 1976, at Lakefield; and *Margaret Laurence. First Lady of Manawaka*, Director Robert

172 *Notes*

Duncan, Producer William Weintraub; Distributor, National Film Board of Canada.

15. See Graeme Gibson, *Eleven Canadian Novelists* (Toronto, 1973), pp. 189–92.

16. Margaret Laurence, "Ten Years' Sentences," *Canadian Literature*, no. 41 (1969), rpt. in William New, ed., *Margaret Laurence*, Critical Views on Canadian Writers Series (Toronto, 1978), pp. 18–19.

17. "A Conversation about Literature: An Interview with Margaret Laurence and Irving Layton," taped by Clara Thomas, *Journal of Canadian Fiction* I, no. 1 (Winter, 1972), 67.

18. See Bernice Lever, "Literature and Canadian Culture. An Interview with Margaret Laurence," *Alive*, 41 (1975), in New, ed., *Margaret Laurence*, p. 25.

19. Valerie Miner, "The Matriarch of Manawaka," *Saturday Night* 89, no. 5 (May, 1974), 19.

20. Ibid., p. 18.

21. Ibid., p. 17.

22. Ibid., p. 20.

23. Margaret Laurence, "Ivory Tower or Grassroots?: The Novelist as Socio-Political Being," in *A Political Art. Essays and Images in Honour of George Woodcock*, William H. New, ed. (Vancouver, 1978), p. 15.

24. Margaret Laurence, *Jason's Quest* (Toronto, 1970), p. 167. Further references are in the text as *JQ*.

25. Clara Thomas, *The Manawaka World of Margaret Laurence* (Toronto, 1975), p. 108. See also p. 113, where Thomas notes that *Jason's Quest* plays variations on Laurence's "central concerns."

26. See Patricia Morley, *The Mystery of Unity. Theme and Technique in the Novels of Patrick White* (Montreal, 1972), pp. 187, 250, with regard to the quaternity in the work of White and of Jung.

27. Adele Wiseman, *Crackpot*, New Canadian Library 144, Introduction by Margaret Laurence (Toronto, 1978), p. 3.

28. Micere Mugo, "Visions of Africa," M.A. Thesis, University of New Brunswick, 1973, p. 20, quotes from p. 5 of Laurence's unpublished article, "Half War, Half Peace."

29. See George Woodcock, *Gabriel Dumont. The Métis Chief and His Lost World* (Edmonton, 1975), p. 19.

30. Wole Soyinka, *Myth, Literature and the African World* (Cambridge, 1978), pp. 59, 144–45.

31. Margaret Laurence, "Time and the Narrative Voice," in *Margaret Laurence*, William New, ed. (Toronto, 1977), p. 156.

32. Ibid., p. 157.

33. See Sherrill Grace, "Crossing Jordan: Time and Memory in the Fiction of Margaret Laurence," *World Literature Written in English* 16, no. 2 (November, 1977), 330. In *An Introduction to Metaphysics*, Bergson defines inner duration as the continuous life of a memory which prolongs the past into the present. Coleridge's "secondary imagination" is "essentially vital," like Bergson's *élan vital*.

34. Percy Janes, *House of Hate*, New Canadian Library 124, Introduction by Margaret Laurence (Toronto, 1976), p. vii.

35. Margaret Laurence, untitled review of *Surfacing* by Margaret Atwood, *Quarry* 22, no. 2 (Spring, 1973), 63.

36. Soyinka, *Myth, Literature and the African World*, p. 153.

37. Laurence, review of *Surfacing*, p. 64.

## Chapter Two

1. See Clara Thomas, *Margaret Laurence*, Canadian Writers Series (Toronto, 1969), p. 14. Thomas quotes from a letter in which Laurence speaks of the diaries as being unusable in the form in which they had been written. Laurence writes that she had to "recreate the situation while also trying to understand it at a distance of ten years."

2. O. Mannoni, *Prospero and Caliban: The Psychology of Colonization*, trans. Pamela Powesland, Foreword by Philip Mason (London, 1956), p. 13.

3. Ibid., p. 34. Cf. Ibrahim Tahir, "Anthropological Curiosity," *West Africa* (November 9, 1963), p. 1273: Laurence understands that "the basic human truths" are true of Africans. See also Anthony Babalow, review of *This Side Jordan*, *British Columbia Library Quarterly* 25 (July, 1961), 34: "the novel ... gives the reader a highly informed insight into Africa today."

4. *A Tree For Poverty. Somali Poetry and Prose*, Selected by Margaret Laurence (Hamilton, 1970), p. 9. Subsequent references are in the text as *T*.

5. George Woodcock, "Many Solitudes: The Travel Writings of Margaret Laurence," *Journal of Canadian Studies* 13, no. 3 (Fall, 1978), 6.

6. Ibid., pp. 3, 4, 9–10.

7. Margaret Laurence, *This Side Jordan*, New Canadian Library 126 (Toronto, 1976), p. 268. Further references are in the text as *TSJ*.

8. Margaret Laurence, "Gadgetry or Growing? Form and Voice

in the Novel," unpublished lecture delivered at the University of Toronto, Autumn, 1969, pp. 3–4.

9. Carl Berger, *The Sense of Power. Studies in the Ideas of Canadian Imperialism 1867–1914* (Toronto, 1970), p. 217.

10. G.D. Killam mounts a similar defense of the monologues in his Introduction, *This Side Jordan* (Toronto, 1976), p. xvii.

11. Margaret Laurence, *The Tomorrow-Tamer,* New Canadian Library 70 (Toronto, 1970), p. 18. Further references are in the text as *TT*.

12. Laurence never refers to Frantz Fanon, the black psychiatrist whose *Black Skin, White Masks* postdates, in the English translation, her African work. Fanon agrees with Mannoni's analysis of the pathology of racial conflict in colonized nations as largely due to Adlerian overcompensation, but takes issue with Mannoni's views that the black man's dependency complex predates colonial invasions and that racism does not reflect an economic situation. Mannoni states that colonial racism is different from other racisms, whereas to Fanon, all forms of exploitation resemble one another, all being based in the treatment of other humans as objects rather than persons. See Frantz Fanon, *Black Skin, White Masks,* trans. Charles Lam Markmann (New York, 1968), pp. 83–108, "The So-called Dependency Complex of Colonized Peoples."

13. Henry Kreisel, "A Familiar Landscape," *Tamarack Review* 55 (Third Quarter, 1970), 91, describes "Godman's Master" as a microcosm of the human condition . . . my favorite among the African stories. . . ."

14. Laurence, "Ivory Tower or Grassroots?: The Novelist as Socio-Political Being," in *A Political Art,* William New, ed., p. 16.

15. Ibid., p. 17.

16. Frantz Fanon, *Black Skin, White Masks,* pp. 217, 229, disagrees with the theory of the black man's "dependency complex" but agrees with Mannoni's emphasis on the importance of recognizing the value and dignity of the *Other.* Paraphrasing Hegel, Fanon states that one goes beyond oneself by recognizing the Other, and that failure to do so imprisons both parties within themselves: "The only means of breaking this vicious circle that throws me back on myself is to restore to the other, through mediation and recognition, his human reality, which is different from natural reality"; "I have one right alone: that of demanding human behaviour from the other."

## Chapter Three

1. See George Woodcock, "The Human Elements: Margaret Laurence's Fiction," *The Human Elements. Critical Essays,* David Helwig, ed. (Toronto, 1978), p. 138, Cf. Clara Thomas, "The Novels of Margaret Laurence," *Studies in the Novel* 4, 2 (Summer, 1972), 156: "The stone angel ... is woven into a culture-pattern that is entirely authentic, Protestant, nineteenth-century, and English Canadian."

2. Margaret Laurence, "Gadgetry or Growing? Form and Voice in the Novel," Lecture at the University of Toronto, Fall, 1969, pp. 4–5.

3. Ibid., pp. 5–6.

4. Ibid., pp. 6–7.

5. Northrop Frye, *Anatomy of Criticism. Four Essays* (New York, 1967), p. 191.

6. Margaret Laurence, *The Stone Angel,* Introduction by William H. New (Toronto, 1968), p. 292. Further references are in the text as *SA.*

7. Laurence, *The Stone Angel,* p. ix.

8. See Frye, *Anatomy of Criticism,* pp. 44, 162, 215, and *Fools of Time. Studies in Shakespearean Tragedy* (Toronto, 1967), pp. 15–16, 80, for an analysis of tragic and comic narrative structures.

9. See *SA* 156 for a description of Hagar's employer: "He'd been in shipping and said they used to bring Oriental wives here, when the celestials were forbidden to bring their women, and charge huge sums for passage, and pack the females like tinned shrimp in the lower hold, and if the Immigration men scented the hoax, the false bottom was levered open, and the women plummeted." See also *A Dream of Riches. The Japanese Canadians 1877–1977,* Japanese Canadian Centennial Project (Vancouver, 1978), *passim.*

10. Cf. Clara Thomas, *The Manawaka World of Margaret Laurence* (Toronto, 1975), p. 70: "Throughout the novel a world of dualities is constantly with us, in the juxtaposition of the physical Hagar young and old, and also in the contrast between a Hagar who is supported and ennobled by her enduring pride and the same Hagar, ruined by it."

11. See Frye, *Anatomy of Criticism,* p. 139.

12. Cf. *Eleven Canadian Novelists,* Interviewed by Graeme Gibson (Toronto, 1973), p. 205, where Laurence describes Vanessa: "She herself was partly a bird in the house who wanted to get out."

13. Woodcock, "The Human Elements," pp. 134–35.

14. Ibid., p. 136.

15. Sandra Djwa, "False Gods and the True Covenant: Thematic Continuity Between Margaret Laurence and Sinclair Ross," in *Margaret Laurence*, Critical Views on Canadian Writers Series, William New, ed. (Toronto, 1977), p. 67. Djwa claims that Laurence's fiction, especially *A Jest of God*, "leads us to believe that she would not have written the way she does, using Biblical allusion to provide a mythic framework for an essentially psychological study of character, if Sinclair Ross had not first written *As For Me and My House*" (p. 69).

16. Margaret Laurence, "Ten Years' Sentences," in *Margaret Laurence*, ed. New, p. 21.

17. Margaret Laurence, "Gadgetry or Growing? Form and Voice in the Novel," Lecture at the University of Toronto, Fall, 1969, p. 7.

18. Ibid., p. 8

19. Robert Harlow, "Lack of Distance" (1967), in *Margaret Laurence*, ed. New, pp. 189–90.

20. H.J. Rosengarten, "Inescapable Bonds" (1968), in *Margaret Laurence*, ed. New, pp. 192–93.

21. George Bowering, "That Fool of a Fear. Notes on 'A Jest of God,'" in *Margaret Laurence*, ed. New, p. 162.

22. Margaret Laurence, *A Jest of God* (Toronto, 1966), p. 94. Further references are in the text as *JG*.

23. Kenneth James Hughes, "Politics and *A Jest of God*," *Journal of Canadian Studies* 13, 3 (Fall, 1978), 46, insists on the asexual universality of Rachel's experience: "Laurence is a liberationist, not simply a women's liberationist." Laurence has said she is "90% in agreement with Women's Lib," but men have problems too, and changes should benefit them as well: see Margaret Atwood, "Face to Face," in *Margaret Laurence*, ed. New, p. 36.

24. See *JG* 169. Cf. Elizabeth Smart, *The Assumption of the Rogues and Rascals* (London, 1978), p. 122; Smart puns on birth and its attendant responsibilities as "twenty years' hard labour."

25. Cf. C.M. McLay, "Every Man is an Island," in *Margaret Laurence*, ed. New, p. 177: "Yet Rachel's acceptance of life is attributable to her acceptance of her central predicament, her essential aloneness."

26. See Patricia Morley, "Doppelganger's Dilemma: Artist and Man in 'The Vivisector,'" *Queen's Quarterly* 78, no. 3 (Autumn, 1971), 409.

27. See Bowering, "That Fool of a Fear," for a good analysis of this pattern.

28. Laurence told Graeme Gibson, *Eleven Canadian Novelists* (Toronto, 1973), p. 202, that Rachel's problem is similar to Hagar's: "Because anyone who is desperately afraid of having human weakness, although they feel very unself-confident, as Rachel did, is in fact suffering from spiritual pride."

29. See Hughes, "Politics and *A Jest of God*," pp. 50–51, where the Camerons are characterized as "the type of the Canadian independent petty bourgeois family in decline," representing "the fall of the petty bourgeoisie in Canada as a whole in the twentieth century." This seems to divorce the novel not only from the author's stated intentions, but from the novel's realized form.

30. For further fictional portraits of the experience of Chinese immigrants in Canada, see W.O. Mitchell's novel, *Who Has Seen the Wind?* (1947), and Gabrielle Roy's story, "Where Will You Go, Sam Lee Wong?" in *Garden in the Wind,* trans. Alan Brown (Toronto, 1977).

31. Hughes, "Politics and *A Jest of God*," pp. 46, 42. See also *Land of Pain, Land of Promise. First Person Accounts by Ukrainian Pioneers 1891–1914,* trans. Harry Piniuta (Saskatoon, 1978), for a description of Ukrainian experience in Manitoba which concurs with Laurence's portrait.

32. John Watt Lennox, "Manawaka and Deptford: Place and Voice," *Journal of Canadian Studies* 13, 3 (Fall, 1978), 24.

33. Margaret Laurence, *The Fire-Dwellers,* New Canadian Library 87 (Toronto, 1973), p. 59. Further references are in the text as *FD*.

34. Cf. Phyllis Grosskurth, "Wise and Gentle," in *Margaret Laurence,* ed. New, p. 194: "Mrs. Laurence . . . never condescends to her frowzy housewife. Stacey is no tragic heroine, but she is a person worthy of respect." See also F.W. Watt, "Review of *The Fire-Dwellers,*" *Margaret Laurence,* ed. New, p. 198: "The ground occupied by *The Fire-Dwellers* . . . is on the borderline between art and soap-opera." Naim Kattan writes, "Sa vie est semblable a mille autres," but adds that Laurence's characters *live,* and illustrate courage ("Une Femme de Quarante Ans," *Margaret Laurence,* ed. New, pp. 200–02). Cf. Diana Loercher, "Her Price for Coping," *Margaret Laurence,* ed. New, p. 203: "we've heard it all before, but not said quite this well. What is captivating about Stacey is her incisive analysis of her conflicts . . . with a relentless, and often hilarious, honesty."

35. Laurence, "Gadgetry or Growing?" p. 10.

36. Ibid., p. 12.

37. The minor motif of Sophoclean tragedy supports this emphasis on society. Stacey thinks of her husband as Agamemnon, and has

178 Notes

attempted a course in Greek tragedy. William Rose Benet speaks of Sophocles' portrait of the individual's search for truth and self-knowledge *in relation to the existing moral order: The Reader's Encylopedia*, 2nd ed., II (New York, 1965), p. 947.

38. Laurence told Gibson (*Eleven Canadian Novelists*, p. 202) that Stacey's real self-discovery was that she was a survivor who had come to terms with her past. Cf. Allan Bevan: "The novel, then, ends on a note of low-keyed optimism" (*FD*, xiv).

39. Cf. George Woodcock, "Jungle and Prairie," *Margaret Laurence*, ed. New, p. 148: "... it is hard to know whether to define *A Bird in the House* as a collection of tales or as a loosely knit and unconventional novel." In his Introduction to *A Bird in the House*, New Canadian Library 96 (Toronto, 1974), Robert Gibbs finds the stories "not inseparable parts of a novel" but organically unified. Further references are in the text as *BH*.

40. Margaret Laurence, "Time and the Narrative Voice," in *Margaret Laurence*, ed. New, p. 158.

41. Ibid., pp. 158–59.

42. Woodcock, "Jungle and Prairie," p. 148. He adds that *voice* is handled even more skillfully: "Laurence has shown the lives and emotions of older people through a child's eye, until in the end the child moves into the age when those emotions became identified with hers, and the perceiver becomes the perceived." Cf. Clara Thomas, *The Manawaka World of Margaret Laurence*, p. 97.

43. See "A Conversation About Literature: An Interview With Margaret Laurence and Irving Layton," taped by Clara Thomas, *Journal of Canadian Fiction* I, no. 1 (Winter, 1972), 67, concerning the close parallels between the fictional Grandfather Connor and Laurence's maternal grandfather.

44. See Margaret Laurence, "Time and the Narrative Voice," p. 159: "It is actually a story about the generations, about the pain and bewilderment of one's knowledge of other people, about the reality of other people which is one way of realizing one's own reality about the fluctuating and accidental quality of life ... about the strangeness and mystery of the very concepts of *past, present and future*."

45. Ibid., p. 160.

46. Robert Gibbs, introducing the novel, sees this insight as crucial to the narrator's own freedom and growth (*BH*, v).

47. See also Patricia Morley, "The Long Trek Home: Margaret Laurence's Stories," *Journal of Canadian Studies* II, no 4 (November, 1976), 19–20.

48. Marian Engel, "Steps to the Mythic: *The Diviners* and *A Bird in the House*," *Journal of Canadian Studies* 13, no. 3 (Fall, 1978), 72, 74.

49. Clara Thomas, *The Manawaka World of Margaret Laurence* (Toronto, 1975), pp. 132, 169.

50. Margaret Laurence, *The Diviners* (Toronto, 1974), p. 196. Further page references are in the text as *D*.

51. John Fowles, "Notes on an Unfinished Novel," *The Novel Today*, Malcolm Bradbury, ed. (Glasgow, 1977), p. 13.

52. Thomas, *The Manawaka World of Margaret Laurence*, p. 134.

53. Sherrill Grace, "A Portrait of the Artist as Laurence Hero," *Journal of Canadian Studies* 13, no. 3 (Fall, 1978), 66.

54. David Blewett, "The Unity of the Manawaka Cycle," *Journal of Canadian Studies* 13, no. 3 (Fall, 1978), 35.

55. Ibid., p. 32. See also Patricia Morley, *The Mystery of Unity. Theme and Technique in the Novels of Patrick White* (Montreal, 1972), "God's Fool," pp. 85–95.

56. Correspondence with Clara Thomas, Oct. 27, 1977, in Thomas, "The Chariot of Ossian: Myth and Manitoba in *The Diviners*," *Journal of Canadian Studies* 13, no. 3 (Fall, 1978), 63. The next two paragraphs in the text are indebted to this article.

57. See John Ayre, "Bell, Book and Scandal," *Weekend Magazine* 26, no. 35 (August 28, 1976), 9–12, for a detailed account of the 1976 controversy in the Peterborough area.

58. See William French, "The Good Book versus good books," *Globe and Mail* (June 15, 1978); and Ayre, "Bell, Book and Scandal," p. 12. John Scopes was a Tennessee high school teacher who dared to teach the theory of evolution in 1925, defying local fundamentalists.

59. Toba Korenblum, "Once more out of the closet," *MacLean's* 91, no. 28 (November 20, 1978), 56, emphasis added. See also Edward Shorter, "The Private Life of the Ruling Class," *Saturday Night* 93, no. 8 (October, 1978), 21–28.

60. Ayre, "Bell, Book and Scandal," p. 12.

61. Engel, "Steps to the Mythic," p. 74.

62. Ayre, "Bell, Book and Scandal," p. 10. Hogan spoke of the novel's themes of self-awareness, self-acceptance, tolerance, filial responsibility, and the sanctity of honest relationships. See also Timothy Findley, "Better Dead than Read? An Opposing View," *Books in Canada* 7, no. 10 (December, 1978), 3, where Findley reports that local residents of Huron County, Ontario, were contacted by an evangelical association called Renaissance International, which was established with a budget of $100,000. Findley describes the

evangelical campaign against books such as *The Diviners* as "a truly evil manipulation of people's genuine fear and uncertainty about the world we live in."

63. Thomas, "The Chariot of Ossian," p. 59.

64. See Joseph Kinsey Howard, *Strange Empire*, Swan Edition (New York, 1965), p. 39. This incident is reputed to have sparked the Seven Oaks skirmish, 1816.

65. Michael Peterman, "Margaret Laurence," *Journal of Canadian Studies* 13, no. 3 (Fall, 1978), 103–104. Admittedly, an editorial of this type does not provide a forum for detailed analysis.

66. Thomas, *The Manawaka World of Margaret Laurence*, p. 131.

67. Denyse Forman and Uma Parameswaran, "Echoes and Re-frains in the Canadian Novels of Margaret Laurence," *Margaret Laurence*, William New, ed. (Toronto, 1977), p. 88.

68. "A Conversation About Literature: An Interview with Margaret Laurence and Irving Layton," taped by Clara Thomas, *Journal of Canadian Fiction* I, no. 1 (Winter, 1972), 67.

69. The use of the gatling gun by Canadians in their suppression of the Métis uprising in 1885 corroborates Laurence's claim. The The first successful machine gun ever devised, an American invention, was operated in Saskatchewan by Lieut. Arthur Howard of New Haven, Connecticut, who used the Métis uprising as a test-ground for his weapon: see Joseph Kinsey Howard, *The Strange Empire of Louis Riel*, Swan Edition (New York, 1965), pp. 380–81.

70. Joe Sawchuk, *The Métis of Manitoba. Reformulation of an Ethnic Identity* (Toronto, 1978), pp. 19–21.

71. W.L. Morton, *Manitoba: A History* (Toronto, 1957), p. 92.

72. Howard, *Strange Empire*, p. 22. Cf. Morton, *Manitoba*, pp. 492–94.

73. Howard, *Strange Empire*, p. 21.

74. Donald Creighton, *John A. Macdonald. The Young Politician* (Toronto, 1952), p. 309.

75. George Woodcock, *Faces from History. Canadian Profiles and Portraits* (Edmonton, 1978), p. 104. See also Adele Wiseman, *Testimonial Dinner* (1978), where Wiseman graphically depicts the enduring relation between Riel and Macdonald by having Macdonald support Riel on his back throughout the play.

76. George Woodcock, *Gabriel Dumont. The Métis Chief and His Lost World* (Edmonton, 1975), p. 243.

77. Ibid., p. 249.

78. Ibid., pp. 36, 44–46. See also Morton, *Manitoba*, p. viii, where Morton speaks of the "simple, sturdy virtues of hard work, thrift"

which have been "cherished and transmitted" in his province. Laurence's Manawaka portrays pride and intolerance as the other face of these virtues.

79. See Thomas Flanagan, *Louis 'David' Riel* (Toronto, 1979), Chapter 8, concerning Riel's belief that the Métis were the new Chosen People.

80. Sawchuk, *The Métis of Manitoba*, pp. 12, 70.

81. Ibid., pp. 45, 83.

82. Cf. the symbolic union of English and French Canada suggested by the marriage in Hugh MacLennan's *Two Solitudes*.

83. *The Other Side of Hugh MacLennan. Selected Essays Old and New*, Elspeth Cameron, ed. (Toronto, 1978), p. 270.

84. Edward Sapir, "The Status of Linguistics as a Science," *Culture, Language and Personality. Selected Essays*, David G. Mandelbaum, ed. (Berkeley, 1964), p. 69.

85. Robin Mathews, *Canadian Literature. Surrender or Revolution* (Toronto, 1978), p. 134.

86. Margaret Laurence, "Ivory Tower or Grassroots? The Novelist as Socio-Political Being," *A Political Art. Essays and Images in Honour of George Woodcock*, ed. William H. New (Vancouver, 1978), pp. 18–19.

87. Sinclair Ross, *The Lamp at Noon and Other Stories*, Introduction by Margaret Laurence, NCL 62 (Toronto, 1968), p. 7.

88. Ibid., p. 12.

89. See Henry Kreisel, "The Prairie: A State of Mind," *Canadian Anthology*, 3rd ed., Carl F. Klinck, ed. (Toronto, 1974), p. 621; and Donald G. Stephens, ed., *Writers of the Prairies*, Canadian Literature Series (Vancouver, 1973), p. 1.

90. Ibid., p. 4.

91. Kreisel, "The Prairie: A State of Mind," pp. 625–26.

92. *Stories from Western Canada*, selected and introduced by Rudy Wiebe (Toronto, 1972), p. xii.

93. See Adele Wiseman, *Testimonial Dinner* (Toronto, 1978), Introduction: ".... the past influences the present ... is alive and functioning in the present...."

94. Dick Harrison, "Cultural Insanity and Prairie Fiction," *Figures in a Ground. Canadian Essays on Modern Literature Collected in Honour of Sheila Watson*, Diane Bessai and David Jackel, eds. (Saskatoon, 1978), p. 286.

95. *The Other Side of Hugh MacLennan*, Cameron, ed., p. 270. Cf. Mathews, *Canadian Literature*, p. 136: "All art is propaganda, though all propaganda is not art."

96. Laurence, "Ivory Tower or Grassroots?" pp. 24–25.
97. Ibid., p. 25.
98. Georg Lukács, "The Intellectual Physiognomy of Literary Characters," *Radical Perspective in the Arts*, Lee Baxandall, ed. (Middlesex, England, 1972), p. 91.
99. Ibid., pp. 99-103.
100. David Blewett, "The Unity of the Manawaka Cycle," *Journal of Canadian Studies* 13, no. 3 (Fall, 1978), 31.
101. Ibid., p. 32.
102. See ibid. passim; cf. George Woodcock, *The Human Element*, David Helwig, ed., pp. 153–60.
103. See William New, ed., *Margaret Laurence* (Toronto, 1977), p. 2; and Clara Thomas, *The Manawaka World of Margaret Laurence* (Toronto, 1975), p. 189. See also the film, *Margaret Laurence. First Lady of Manawaka* (1979), Director Robert Duncan, Producer William Weintraub, Distributor National Film Board of Canada, typescript pp. 5–6, where Laurence states: "Well after having not gone to church for years, about two years ago I suddenly felt I would like to return to the church of my ancestry, and yet I do, I go to the United Church." Timothy Findley finds "concern for people and compassion for the human condition" in Laurence's work: "Better Dead than Read?" *Books in Canada* 7, no. 10 (December, 1978), 3.
104. See *The Other Side of Hugh MacLennan*, Cameron, ed., pp. 283–84.

## Epilogue

1. Margaret Laurence, "The Shack," *HS*, pp. 187–88.
2. Laurence, "Living Dangerously ... by Mail," *HS*, pp. 179–80.
3. Helen Lucas, interview with Patricia Morley, King City, Ontario, May 29, 1988.
4. Laurence, "My Final Hour," in *Margaret Laurence: An Appreciation*, Christl Verduyn, ed. (Peterborough, 1988), p. 251.
5. Ibid., p. 261.
6. Lucas to Morley, May 29, 1988.
7. Enid Delgatty Rutland, ed., *The Collected Plays of Gwen Pharis Ringwood* (Ottawa, 1982), p. xiv.
8. Hugh MacLennan, "Margaret Laurence Memorial Address," *Canadian Woman Studies/les cahiers de la femme* 8, no. 3 (Fall, 1987), 25.

9. Timothy Findley, interview with Patricia Morley, Cannington, Ontario, August 11, 1987.

10. June Callwood, "Clear Sight Is as a Precious Gift," *Canadian Woman Studies/les cahiers de la femme* 8, no. 3 (Fall, 1987), 56.

11. Alice Olsen Williams, "In Her Memory and in the Spirit of Our Ancestors," *Canadian Woman Studies/les cahiers de la femme* 8, no. 3 (Fall, 1987), 12.

12. Margaret Laurence Memorial Service, Toronto, January 9, 1987.

13. Lois Wilson and Margaret Laurence in dialogue, "Why Pick on Margaret Laurence?" *The Observer* (February, 1980), pp. 10–12.

14. Lois Wilson, letter to Patricia Morley, 7/5/88: sculpture by Almuth Lutkenhaus.

15. To Marian Engel Margaret wrote (4/1/84) that she had had five typewriters and had given all but one names. Her most recent manual, a trouble-maker, had not been christened. One machine was "Pearl Cavewoman," a version of her own name (*Margaret*, a pearl; *Weymss*, a cavedweller). Whether it was true or not, Margaret chose to believe that her family had descended from the Picts, the ancient people of Scotland.

16. Laurence, "A Constant Hope: Women in the Now and Future High Tech Age," *Canadian Woman Studies/les cahiers de la femme* (1985), 14.

17. Lucas to Morley, May 29, 1988.

18. Joan Johnston, interview with Patricia Morley, Lakefield, Ontario, May 30, 1988.

19. Laurence, "A Constant Hope."

20. Johnston to Morley, May 30, 1988.

21. Findley to Morley, August 11, 1987.

22. Laurence, "Books That Mattered to me," [1981], *Margaret Laurence*, Christl Verduyn, ed., p. 239.

23. Lucas to Morley, May 30, 1988.

24. Ibid.

25. Findley to Morley, August 11, 1987.

26. See *Canadian Woman Studies/les cahiers de la femme* 8, no. 3 (Fall, 1987), photograph, p. 73, and Joan Johnston, "Remembering Margaret," pp. 8–9.

27. Ibid., p. 9.

28. Johnston to Morley, May 30, 1988.

29. Wilson to Morley, 8/5/88.

30. Wilson and Laurence in Dialogue, "Why Pick on Margaret Laurence?"

31. Findley to Morley, August 11, 1987.

32. Lucas to Morley, May 29, 1988.

33. See Dan Lett, "Neepawa Forgives Its Most Famous Citizen," *Sunday Star*, October 18, 1987, D5. By July, 1988, the house where Laurence was born at 321 First Avenue had been declared a provincial historic site. Her body is buried in the Neepawa Cemetery.

34. Johnston to Morley, May 30, 1988.

35. Findley to Morley, August 11, 1987.

# Selected Bibliography

PRIMARY SOURCES

*A Tree for Poverty: Somali Poetry and Prose.* Published for British Protectorate of Somaliland. Nairobi: Eagle Press, 1954. Rpt. Dublin: Irish University Press, 1970; Hamilton: McMaster University, 1970.

*This Side Jordan.* Toronto: McClelland and Stewart; London; Macmillan; New York: St. Martin's Press, 1960. Introduction by G.D. Killam, NCL, Toronto: McClelland and Steward, 1976.

*The Tomorrow-Tamer.* Toronto: McClelland and Stewart; London: MacMillan, 1963; New York: Knopf, 1964.

*The Tomorrow-Tamer and Other Stories.* Introduction by Clara Thomas, NCL, Toronto: McClelland and Stewart, 1970.

*The Prophet's Camel Bell.* Toronto: McClelland and Stewart; London: Macmillan, 1963. Under the title *New Wind in a Dry Land*, New York: Knopf, 1964. Toronto: McClelland and Stewart, 1977.

*The Stone Angel.* Toronto: McClelland and Stewart; London: Macmillan; New York: Knopf, 1964. Introduction by William H. New, NCL, Toronto: McClelland and Stewart, 1968.

*A Jest of God.* Toronto: McClelland and Stewart; London: Macmillan; New York: Knopf, 1966. Introduction by G.D. Killam, NCL, Toronto: McClelland and Stewart, 1974.

*Long Drums and Cannons: Nigerian Dramatists and Novelists 1952–1966.* London: Macmillan, 1968. New York: Praeger, 1969.

*The Fire-Dwellers.* Toronto: McClelland and Stewart; London: Macmillan; New York: Knopf, 1969. St. Albans, Herts.: Panther Books, 1973. Introduction by Allan Bevan, NCL, Toronto: McClelland and Stewart, 1973.

*A Bird in the House.* Toronto: McClelland and Stewart; New York: Knopf; London: Macmillan, 1970. Introduction by Robert Gibbs, NCL, Toronto: McClelland and Stewart, 1974.

*Jason's Quest.* Illustrated by Staffan Torell. Toronto: McClelland and Stewart; New York: Knopf; London: Macmillan, 1970.

*The Diviners.* Toronto: McClelland and Stewart; New York: Knopf; London: Macmillan, 1974. New York: Bantam, 1975. Introduc-

tion by David Staines, NCL, Toronto: McClelland and Stewart, 1978.
*Heart of a Stranger.* Toronto: McClelland and Stewart, 1976.
*The Olden Days Coat.* Toronto: McClelland and Stewart, 1979.
*Six Darn Cows.* Toronto: James Lorimer, 1979.
*The Christmas Birthday Story.* Pictures by Helen Lucas. Toronto: McClelland and Stewart, 1980.
*Dance on the Earth. A Memoir.* Edited by Jocelyn Laurence. Toronto: McClelland and Stewart, 1989.
"Ivory Tower or Grassroots? The Novelist as Socio-Political Being." In *A Political Art: Essays and Images in Honour of George Woodcock*, ed. William H. New, pp. 15–25. Vancouver: University of British Columbia, 1978.
"My Final Hour." *Canadian Literature* 100 (Spring, 1984), 187–97.
See also essays and stories by Laurence in the following anthologies or special editions: *A Place to Stand On*, ed. George Woodcock; *Journal of Canadian Fiction* 27, (Summer, 1980); *Margaret Laurence. The Writer and Her critics*, ed. William New; and *Margaret Laurence. An Appreciation*, ed. Christl Verduyn.

SECONDARY SOURCES

BAILEY, NANCY. "Margaret Laurence, Carl Jung and the Manawaka Women." *Studies in Canadian Literature* 2, no. 2 (Summer, 1977), 306–21. A provocative examination of Laurence's feminism, and of her fiction in Jungian terms. Bailey acknowledges that Laurence's male characters are unsatisfying, but defends this situation in terms of Laurence's fidelity to "the female process of self-discovery."
BUSS, HELEN. *Mother and Daughter Relationships in the Manawaka Novels of Margaret Laurence.* Victoria: University of Victoria Press, 1985. A careful and perceptive study.
CAMERON, DONALD. *Conversation with Canadian Novelists*, Part One. Toronto: Macmillan, 1973, pp. 96–115. A sensitive interview, in which Laurence speaks of her recurring themes, her Presbyterian background, her religious attitudes, and her concept of time.
– "The Many Lives of Margaret Laurence." *Weekend Magazine* 24, no. 29 (July 20, 1974), 3–5. One of the best of the many informal articles which followed publication of *The Diviners.*
DUNCAN, ROBERT, film director. *Margaret Laurence, First Lady of Manawaka.* Produced by William Weintraub, distributed by the National Film Board of Canada, 1978. A fifty-minute documen-

tary filmed in Penn, Buckinghamshire, in Lakefield, Ontario, and in Neepawa, Manitoba. Includes statements by Laurence, readings from the Manawaka novels, and comments by critics and friends.

GIBSON, GRAEME. *Eleven Canadian Novelists*. Toronto: Anansi, 1973, pp. 185–208. Gibson follows a set pattern of questions which focus on form in fiction. Laurence acknowledges the influence on her work of Sinclair Ross, and comments on the Manawaka novels.

GRACE, SHERRILL. "Crossing Jordan: Time and memory in the Fiction of Margaret Laurence." *World Literature Written in English* 16, no. 2 (November, 1977), 328–39. Building on Laurence's article, "Time and the Narrative Voice," Grace compares her view of time, memory, and human perception with the theories of Bergson and Coleridge.

GUNNARS, KRISTJANA, ed. *Crossing the River. Essays in Honour of Margaret Laurence*. Winnipeg: Turnstone Press, 1988. Twelve previously unpublished essays celebrate Laurence's life and work in the year following her death by cancer. Contributors include Diana Bryden, Helen Buss, Keith Louise Fulton, Hans Hauge, Paul Hjartarson, Constance Rooke, Per Seyersted, Walter Swayze, Craig Tapping, Aritha van Herk, David Williams, and Herbert Zirker.

HEHNER, BARBARA. "River of Now and Then. Margaret Laurence's Narratives." *Canadian Literature* 74 (Autumn, 1977), 40–57. A comparison of the narrative technique in *The Diviners* with that of the earlier Manawaka works leads to the conclusion that the former novel is "a noble work with obvious flaws."

HIND-SMITH, JOAN. *Three Voices. The Lives of Margaret Laurence, Gabrielle Roy, Frederick Philip Grove*. Canadian Portrait Series. Toronto: Clarke, Irwin, 1975, pp. 1–60. The series is designed for students and the general reader. Biographical comments blend with narrative summaries.

MCCOURT, EDWARD A. *The Canadian West in Fiction*. Toronto: Ryerson, rev. 1970, pp. 108–18. Sets Laurence's work in the context of Canadian prairie fiction, but sees her greatest gift, after compassion, as "a way with words."

MINER, VALERIE. "The Matriarch of Manawaka." *Saturday Night* 89, no. 5 (May, 1974), 17–20. From an interview in Lakefield and at Trent University shortly after publication of *The Diviners*. Focuses on Laurence's attitudes towards women and society. Informal and informative.

MORLEY, PATRICIA. "The long Trek Home: Margaret Laurence's Stories." *Journal of Canadian Studies* 11, no. 4 (November, 1976),
19–26. Examines the thematic unity of Laurence's two collec-
tions of short stories, set in Africa and Canada, in terms of the
search for inner freedom and the difficulties inherent in that
search.

– Review of *Heart of a Stranger* in *Quill and Quire* 42, no. 15
(November, 1976), 30. Calls attention to the significance of
Laurence's collection of essays which (unlike her other books)
has been published *only* in Canada.

– "No Mean Feat." *Canadian Newsletter of Research on Women* 7,
no. 2 (July, 1978), 25. Comments on Laurence's importance in
the field of Women's Studies through her female protagonists
and her own increasingly political vision.

– "Margaret Laurence's Early Writing: 'a world in which others have
to be respected.'" *Journal of Canadian Studies* 13, no. 3 (Fall,
1978), 13–18. Demonstrates the continuity of Laurence's African
writing and her Canadian-based fiction, and the theoretical influence of the French ethnographer O. Mannoni. The issue, edited
by Michael Peterman, is devoted entirely to Laurence's work.
It includes "A Laurence Log" by Susan J. Warwick (biographical
data in the form of a chronological list), and significant articles
by George Woodcock, John Watt Lennox, David Blewett, Clara
Thomas, Marian Engel, Sherrill Grace, Kenneth J. Hughes, and
William H. New.

– "Canada, Africa, Canada: Laurence's Unbroken Journey," *Journal
of Canadian Fiction* 27 (Summer, 1980), 81–91. Examines the
place of Africa in Laurence's experience, its impact on her
literary vision, self-knowledge, and developing maturity.

– "Margaret Laurence: Feminist, Nationalist and Matriarch of Canadian Letters." *Laurentian University Review* 14, no. 2 (February, 1982), 24–33. Laurence's fiction is feminist "because it
affords a woman's-eye view of the world, an awareness of what
it means to be a woman in a particular society at a particular
time." Morley, like Woodcock, compares Laurence's power to
interpret the collective life with that of Tolstoi.

– Introduction to *Two Stories by Margaret Laurence*, vol. 1, edited,
with notes, by Yoshimi Matsuda. Kyoto: Apollon-sha, 1988. "To
Set Our House in Order" and "The Loons," from *A Bird in the
House*, introduce Japanese students and general readers to Laurence's work in English, with the aid of copious notes in Japanese
on the idioms found in the stories.

 - *Margaret Laurence.* Twayne's World Authors Series, no. 591. Boston: Twayne/G.K. Hall, 1981. The first edition of the present work, it lacks the epilogue (1990) and has a shorter Selected Bibliography. This critical and biographical treatment of Laurence's life writing is the second book on her (after Clara Thomas's study). Morley's comprehensive analysis emphasizes the importance of Laurence's African writings in relation to her Manawaka fictions, and the centrality of her feminist vision.

NEW, WILLIAM, ed. *Margaret Laurence. The Writer and her Critics.* Critical Views on Canadian Writers Series. Toronto: McGraw-Hill Ryerson, 1977. This anthology of criticism and interviews includes three key essays by Laurence. A valuable resource book.

 - "Every Now and Then: Voice and Language in Laurence's *The Stone Angel.*" *Canadian Literature* 93 (Summer, 1982), 79–96.

ROOKE, CONSTANCE. "A Feminist Reading of *The Stone Angel.*" *Canadian Literature* 93 (Summer, 1982), 26–41.

SORFLEET, JOHN R, ed. "The Work of Margaret Laurence," *Journal of Canadian Fiction* 27 (1980), passim. This special Laurence issue contains eight critical essays and four stories by Laurence as well as her previously unpublished 1969 paper "Gadgetry or Growing? Form and Voice in the Novel."

STEPHENS, DONALD G., ed. *Writers of the Prairies.* Canadian Literature Series. Vancouver: University of British Columbia Press, 1973, pp. 132–74. Like Edward McCourt's study, this anthology of articles reprinted from *Canadian Literature* allows the student to see Laurence's work in the context of the Canadian literary tradition. Three of the essays by and about Laurence are reprinted in the anthology edited by William New. A key article by George Bowering defends *A Jest of God* against charges by early reviewers that the novel lacks distance.

THOMAS, CLARA. "The Novels of Margaret Laurence." *Studies in the Novel* 4, no. 2 (Summer, 1972), 154–64. Examines *The Stone Angel, A Jest of God,* and *The Fire-Dwellers* as studies of "women in our times."

 - transcriber. "A Conversation about Literature: An Interview with Margaret Laurence and Irving Layton." *Journal of Canadian Fiction* 1, no. 1 (Winter, 1972), 65–68. Laurence talks about her roots, her ancestors ("These people are our myths. This is our history"), and her central theme of inner freedom.

 - *Margaret Laurence.* Canadian Writers Series 3. Toronto: McClelland and Stewart, 1969. This sixty-four page paperback provides an excellent introduction to Laurence's work, with the exception of *The Diviners* and *Heart of a Stranger.*

– *The Manawaka World of Margaret Laurence.* Toronto: McClelland and Stewart, 1975. Expands and updates the 1969 study. Includes a long chapter on *The Diviners* and a sixteen-paged checklist of criticism compiled by Margaret Pappert. Thomas sees Laurence as a religious humanist whose vision has been formed by the prairie town where she grew up.

– guest editor. *Canadian Woman Studies* 8, no. 3 (Fall, 1987), *passim.* This special issue of the feminist journal, entitled "Margaret Laurence: A Celebration," published in the year of Laurence's death, constitues an enthusiastic biographical and critical tribute by close friends and some of Canada's best known writers. Coloured illustrations include art by Helen Lucas and a loon-patterned quilt by Alice Williams. A collector's item.

– "Towards Freedom: The Work of Margaret Laurence and Northrop Frye," *Essays on Canadian Writing* 30 (Winter, 1984–85), 81–95. A comparative analysis full of insights, the culmination of nearly two decades of work on Laurence's fiction.

VERDUYN, CHRISTL, ed. *Margaret Laurence. An Appreciation.* Peterborough, Ontario: *Journal of Canadian Studies*/Broadview Press, 1988. Essays span a twelve year period (1976–88) and witness to changing patterns in criticism on Laurence's work. Many were first published in the *JCS.* Contributors include Verduyn, Woodcock, Morley, New, Thomas, Engel, Michael Peterman, Evelyn Hinz, Kenneth Hughes, Sherrill Grace, David Blewett, John Lennox, Robert Chambers, Susan Warwick, and Laurence herself.

WARWICK, SUSAN J. *Margaret Laurence: An Annotated Bibliography.* Downsview, Ontario: ECW Press, 1979. An invaluable resource, limited by its date of publication. Annotations are substantial and accurate. Warwick's "A Laurence Log," in *Margaret Laurence: An Appreciation*, ed. Christl Verduyn, updates the bibliography found here.

WOODCOCK, GEORGE. *Gabriel Dumont: The Métis Chief and His Lost World.* Edmonton: Hurtig, 1975. This biography of Riel's military commander, and of the Métis in the latter nineteenth century, provides a background to Laurence's concern for the Métis as expressed in the Manawaka cycle (especially *The Diviners*) and in several key essays in *Heart of a Stranger.*

– "Many Solitudes. The Travel Writings of Margaret Laurence." *Journal of Canadian Studies* 13, no. 3 (Fall, 1978), 3–12. Deals with *The Prophet's Camel Bell* and *Heart of a Stranger*, calling the former "one of the finest and most provocative travel books ever written by a Canadian."

– "The Human Elements: Margaret Laurence's Fiction." In *The Human Elements. Critical Essays*, ed. David Helwig, pp. 134–61. Ottawa: Oberon Press, 1978. A valuable analysis of Laurence's panoramic sense of space and history, and of the unity of the Manawaka cycle.

– ed. *A Place to Stand On. Essays by and about Margaret Laurence.* Western Canadian Literary Documents, no. 4. Edmonton: NeWest Press, 1983. A significant anthology containing five essays by Laurence, an interview with her conducted by Michel Fabre, and essays by Thomas, New, Engel, Henry Kreisel, *et al*.

See also the introductory essays to individual works in the NCL (New Canadian Library) editions to Laurence's works listed in Primary Sources.

# Index